Magic as Metaphor
in Anime

ALSO BY DANI CAVALLARO
AND FROM MCFARLAND

---

*Anime and the Visual Novel: Narrative Structure,
Design and Play at the Crossroads of Animation
and Computer Games* (2010)

*Anime and Memory: Aesthetic, Cultural and
Thematic Perspectives* (2009)

*The Art of Studio Gainax: Experimentation, Style and
Innovation at the Leading Edge of Anime* (2009)

*Anime Intersections: Tradition and Innovation in
Theme and Technique* (2007)

The Animé Art of Hayao Miyazaki (2006)

*The Cinema of Mamoru Oshii: Fantasy,
Technology and Politics* (2006)

Magic as Metaphor in Anime

A Critical Study

Dani Cavallaro

McFarland & Company, Inc., Publishers
Jefferson, North Carolina, and London

Library of Congress Cataloguing-in-Publication Data

Cavallaro, Dani.
    Magic as metaphor in Anime : a critical study / Dani Cavallaro.
      p.   cm.
    Includes bibliographical references and index.

    ISBN 978-0-7864-4744-2
    softcover : 50# alkaline paper ∞

    1. Magic in motion pictures.   2. Metaphor in motion pictures.
  3. Animated films.   I. Title.
  NC1766.5.M34C38   2010
  791.43'34 — dc22   2009049614

British Library cataloguing data are available

©2010 Dani Cavallaro. All rights reserved

*No part of this book may be reproduced or transmitted in any form
or by any means, electronic or mechanical, including photocopying
or recording, or by any information storage and retrieval system,
without permission in writing from the publisher.*

Cover art ©2010 ATOMix/Shutterstock

Manufactured in the United States of America

*McFarland & Company, Inc., Publishers
  Box 611, Jefferson, North Carolina 28640
    www.mcfarlandpub.com*

To Paddy,
with love and gratitude

Contents

*Myth is often contrasted with reality. Myths flourish in the
absence of precise knowledge. Thus in the past Western man
believed in the existence of the Isles of the Blest, the Northwest Passage,
and Terra Australis. Now he no longer does. Myths are not, however,
a thing of the past, for human understanding remains limited.
Political myths today are as common as weeds.... The knowledge we
have as individuals and as members of a particular society
remains very limited, selective, and biased by
the passions of living.* — Yi-Fu Tuan, 2008

Preface

*Try and penetrate with our limited means the secrets of nature
and you will find that, behind all the discernible concatenations, there
remains something subtle, intangible and inexplicable.* — Albert Einstein

The world is its own magic. — Shunryu Suzuki

Anime has engaged assiduously with themes, symbols and narrative strategies drawn from the realm of magic since its inception as an art form. Some shows have deployed magic to chronicle out-of-this-world occurrences that preclude explanation by the laws of nature, science or logic. Others have resorted to magic as the backbone of mythical domains (sometimes based on documented legends) and the quests unfolding therein. Others still have focused on the imbrication of magic with mysteries and secrets in order to weave yarns centered on patterns of investigation and resolution akin to detective stories. Characters endowed with special powers and *mana* have featured recurrently in all of these typologies. Many of the elements found in such productions are still in evidence in contemporary anime but in recent years, the medium has increasingly turned to magic specifically as a metaphor for the exploration of a range of cultural, philosophical and psychological concerns. Some earlier anime harbored metaphorical potentialities insofar as they did not tackle magic merely as an end in itself—i.e., a repertoire of motifs designed to yield spectacle and entertainment per se — but rather as a vehicle through which they could engage with wide-ranging preoccupations. For example, *Sailor Moon* (1992–1997) used magic largely to foster the advancement of inveterately Japanese ethical values, such as the paramount importance of perseverance and hard work, while *Fushigi Yuugi* (a.k.a. *Mysterious Play*, 1995–1996) employed it as a lens through which the here-and-now could be assessed by ironic contrast with alternate realities, and *Cardcaptor Sakura* (1998–2000), relatedly, harnessed it to the portrayal of the tension between playfully innocent fantasy domains and real-world imperatives.

However, recent titles signal a substantial intensification of the metaphorical proclivity, in consonance with anime's increasing tendency to articulate subtly nuanced psychological dramas, pilgrimages of self-discovery and, fundamentally, mature speculations about the nature of humanness and the meaning of living as humans. These preferences are not only notable in anime that are overtly imparted with serious connotations but also in shows that veer towards the jocular or even the carnivalesque, which invests the field under scrutiny with refreshing diversity and a tantalizing dose of unexpectedness. While assessing the role played by magic in a selection of recent anime, this study takes the shift towards the metaphorical as its pivotal point of reference.

Chapter 1 addresses magical thinking as an overarching concept uniting the titles under scrutiny despite their substantial generic and tonal diversity. It then examines a range of Eastern and Western approaches to magic (focusing on their affinities and their divergences), reflects on the relationship between Japan's magic traditions and aesthetic proclivities, and finally addresses the specific significance acquired by the notion of magical thought vis-à-vis the medium of animation. Chapters 2 through 6 concentrate on instances of anime that employ magic-related elements as metaphorical correlatives for particular issues of concurrently narrative and existential relevance. In each chapter, the collusion of anime and magic is examined with reference to a specific topos. Both Eastern and Western perspectives on magic discussed in the context of the opening chapter are brought to bear on the analysis. Close study of the cardinal titles is complemented by allusions to ancillary productions in order to situate the medium's fascination with magic within an appropriately broad historical context.

The five themes in light of which the analysis-based chapters are constellated concatenate as follows. The discourse of magic is not a vaporous fantasy apparatus with no anchor in reality but a web of interpersonal duties and objectives that bind individuals to reciprocal obligations akin to contracts based on formal decrees. These, in turn, are part of a chain of missions seeking to establish new identities or else to retrieve occluded histories, both private and communal. Such exploits draw their undertakers into the wide world of nature — in its manifest and its ineffable forms — while also taking them on inner journeys of self-exploration and maturation comparable to bildungsromans. All of these enterprises coalesce to shape the destinies of singular individuals and whole cultures alike.

Chapter 1

The Frame of Reference

What is essential is invisible to the eye.—Antoine de Saint-Exupéry

Superstition is the poetry of life.—Johann Wolfgang von Goethe

The collusion of contemporary anime and magic gives rise to a comprehensive structure of metaphoricity. This revolves around a commodious grasp of magical thinking as virtually any kind of nonscientific reasoning that includes an acceptance of the mind's ability to influence the phenomenal realm; a profound respect for the power of symbols (and related imagery); and a refined sensitivity to situations that seem random and chaotic or otherwise signal a suspension of the law of probability as the guarantee for the recurrence of familiar patterns. Such situations are typically valued by magical thinking so as to give space and a chance to develop to events which science might dismiss as contingencies or coincidences. Principles of necessity or ineluctability still obtain within the purview of magical thinking but are seen to lie with inscrutable rhythms rather than empirically observable facts and data. The character of Yuuko, the "Dimensional Witch" immortalized by the CLAMP manga *Tsubasa: RESERVoir CHRoNiCLE* and *xxxHolic* (and their respective anime adaptations) neatly encapsulates this proposition: "There's no such thing as coincidence," she maintains. "There is only inevitability." In his discussion of ancient magical systems, Kurt Seligmann analogously observes: "To the magus, there exists no accidental happening" (Seligmann, p. 28). The faith in inevitability is comparably prominent in the tradition associated with a favorite source of magical imagery in anime that has also often been deployed in the production of spin-offs and ancillary merchandise—i.e., the Tarot. "No calculation or scientific observation is necessary for the Tarot game," argues Seligmann. "Its entire magic theory rests upon the belief that in nature there is no accident.... The most insignificant event is subject to this fundamental rule: cards mixed at random do not yield haphazard results but a suit of figures bound magically to the diviner and to the inquirer" (p. 409). No less crucially, magical thinking also finds a direct correlative in the ethos of playful freedom (*jijuu*) promulgated by Zen Buddhism, whereby cold rationalism is irreverently debunked in favor of a child-like perception of the world in all its forms.

Furthermore, the fascination with phenomena that transcend or bypass empirical verification by striving instead towards the ungraspable and the unnamable draws the discourse of magic into close collusion with some foundational tenets of Japanese art and aesthetics. These indeed evince a marked preference for approximation, adumbration, inconclusiveness and incompleteness, allied to a deep attraction to the impenetrable component of the creative experience. Nancy G. Hume vividly illustrates this idea as follows: "When looking at autumn mountains through mist, the view may be indistinct yet have great depth. Although few autumn leaves may be visible through the mist, the view is alluring. The limitless vista created in imagination far surpasses anything one can see more clearly" (Hume, pp. 253–254). In cultivating an ethos of understatement, Japanese art concurrently defies the principles of classic realism (with its mimetic or representational imperatives) in the service of an aesthetic of presentation that does not demur from a frank exposure of artificiality. In the process, figure and pattern, abstraction and embodiment, stylization and naturalism meet in variable constellations marked by a preference for fluid lines, bold colors, airiness and an adventurous take on both composition and perspective.

As Charles Dawson observes, even though Japanese visual culture at large defies mimetic accuracy, it still pursues its own distinctive brand of realism. It does not utilize techniques, such as "Modelling and chiaroscuro," intended to help the artist "pretend that the paper he works on is anything else but flat." In fact, the artist typically "takes no trouble to deceive the eye with contours." Nevertheless, "while he never imitates, he is a wonderful realist. With marvellous energy and power he seizes the very essence of what he wishes to portray, grips it intensely and allows nothing of its vivid and lifelike qualities to escape him" (Dawson, p. 96). Natalie Avella corroborates this point: "Japanese design ... does not present the viewer with an accurate representation of form or object; colors are exaggerated or eliminated; an object is reduced to its barest elements; any superfluous element is discounted." At the same time, the preference for subtle suggestion rather than explicit statement is attested to by "a tendency to work in similes and vague nuances" (Avella, p. 15). In this regard, Japan's visual arts resemble the magical arts insofar as they engage with latent essential realities that evade rational scrutiny and representation, striving to articulate them by recourse to tastefully measured hints and supple tropes.

At the same time, Japanese art is never staunchly committed — in the way Western art has characteristically been since at least the enthroning of mimetic realism in the Renaissance — to the effacement or elision of the perceptible markers of productivity, such as the vestiges of corrections or modifications undergone by a work in the course of its creation. In fact, as Joan Stanley-Baker explains, "the human qualities of imperfection" are intimately "built into the artwork" (Stanley-Baker, p. 11), and even unpolished aspects of the creative act which much Western art endeavors to conceal in the name of perfection are honestly revealed — e.g., "rough edges, fingerprints or chisel marks" (p. 13). The completed — and, by implication, immutable — artifact is not Japanese art's ultimate goal. The idea that things are always *in medias res* is, in fact, culturally widespread. This stance coalesces with magical thinking as an ongoing process analogously devoted to the exploration of forever unfinished aspects of human experience wherein chance and contingency often play far more conspicuous a role than rationalistic plans or fantasies of plenitude.

Above all, magical thinking urges us to ponder the richness of the human imagination as a far more multifaceted power than one might be inclined to acknowledge. Echoing Colin McGinn's philosophical enterprise, it thus demonstrates that "imagination is a faculty that runs through the most diverse mental phenomena; it is the theme on which there are variations. We need imagination to have mental images, to dream, to believe, to represent possibilities, and to mean" (McGinn, p. 5). By maximizing the imagination's speculative and creative potentialities to an arguably unmatched degree, magical thinking signals a desire to look at the world from fresh perspectives and in accordance with novel modes of cognition. It thereby weaves a poetry of invisibility predicated upon the premise that the number of untapped possibilities coursing beneath the surface of the visible always exceeds by far that of explored and verified hypotheses. Rainer Marie Rilke beautifully encapsulates this idea: "We are bees of the invisible. We madly gather the honey of the visible to store it in the great golden hive of the invisible" (Rilke, p. 48). To approximate knowledge of the world, we must be prepared to acknowledge the inextricability of visible presence from deep wells of ghostly absence, haunting agencies we cannot access and yet can never conclusively dodge precisely because we are powerless to access them. As Maurice Blanchot remarks, "What haunts us is something inaccessible from which we cannot extricate ourselves. It is that which cannot be found and therefore cannot be avoided" (Blanchot, p. 11). Magic could be therefore described, by recourse to a paradox, as a form of obscure illumination: the revelation, by cryptic means, of powerful but often unheeded forces swirling at the core of existence. Just as sound is produced by musicians to enfold silence and buildings are erected by architects and builders to capture empty space, so magical thinking is articulated to envelop many aspects of life that appear to defy thought. In all of these instances, presence is predicated upon absence, plenitude upon lack.

Junichirou Tanizaki advocates a germane world view in his captivating essay *In Praise of Shadows* by suggesting that light cannot be understood without darkness — that light, somewhat ironically, does not dissipate darkness but is actually illuminated by it. This is borne out, in the context of Japanese art, by the handling of materials whose essence and beauty can only be properly appreciated with the benefit of darkness. "Lacquerware decorated in gold," for example, "should be left in the dark," only partially touched by "a faint light." It is by unobtrusively lurking in the shadows that the substance abets the genesis of "the dream world built by that strange light of candle and lamp, that wavering light bearing the pulse of the night" and indeed laying "a pattern on the surface of the night itself" (Tanizaki, p. 24). It is in the architectural realm that the power of shadows as an immensely varied source of beauty declares itself, and that invisible forces of spectral distinction yield their magic. The cultural preparedness to regard spaces that generously accommodate "lack of clarity" as an appealing attribute ushers in a world of "magic" imbued with "a quality of mystery and depth superior to that of any wall painting or ornament" (p. 33).

It is in the indigenous ideation of "ghosts" that the "propensity to seek beauty in darkness" is emphatically demonstrated: "Japanese ghosts," Tanizaki points out, "have traditionally had no feet; Western ghosts have feet, but are transparent. As even this trifle suggests, pitch darkness has always occupied our fantasies, while in the West even ghosts are as clear as glass" (p. 47). Self-immersion in a dusky ambience is a spontaneous tendency in the culture depicted by Tanizaki, in much the same way as the incidence of otherworldly occurrences on the here-and-now is perceived as a fairly natural phenomenon and not as a dangerous violation of sanctified boundaries. The distinctively Japanese take on the collusion of tenebrousness and spectrality is lyrically reinforced by the writer's description of old edifices wherein the very "color" of darkness could be sensed in the "suspension of ashen particles" pervading the rooms. "It must have been simple," Tanizaki avers, "for specters to appear in a 'visible darkness,' where always something seemed to be flickering and shimmering, a darkness that on occasion held greater terrors than darkness out-of-doors. This was the darkness in which ghosts and monsters were active" (p. 53).

Despite the Western attitude to spectrality described by Tanizaki, the aesthetic importance of shadows has not gone unrecognized in the West. In Pliny the Elder's *Natural History* (written circa A.D. 77), for example, the origins of painting and clay modeling are associated with the anecdote of the

Corinthian maid Dibutade, said to have outlined her departing lover's shadow on the wall to preserve his image during his absence. The girl's father, a potter, subsequently filled the shadow-based outline of the youth with clay and fired it alongside his artifacts for her benefit. It is also noteworthy that shadows constitute a liminal realm between light and darkness and therefore mark a locus of undecidability suitable for the emergence of powers that elude clear-cut explanations. Hazy, ambivalent and indeterminate spaces in general provide magical thought and agency with appropriate homes, since they emblematize the boundary over which life might assume enigmatically unexpected forms. As Marina Warner notes, another paradigmatic instance of such a territory is supplied by clouds as "a magical passkey to the labyrinth of unknowable mysteries, outer and inner; they convey the condition of ineffability that the unknown and the divine inhabit" (Warner 2006, p. 83). In this same matter, the German philosopher G. E. Lessing has intriguingly remarked: "the cloud is an arbitrary and unnatural sign with the painters ... they use it as frequently to make the visible invisible as they do the reverse" (Lessing, p. 50). It may not be by sheer coincidence that shadows and clouds alike are places in which the eye sometimes perceives imaginary shapes holding equally formidable measures of eeriness and charm.

In assessing magical thinking as a world picture, it is vital to realize that even though some of its facets may carry transhistorical and cross-cultural value, we must at all times be prepared to recognize and uphold a significant degree of local diversity. In other words, magical thinking should not be simplistically adopted as a blanket term, designed to catch as many societies, epochs and traditions into its net, but rather respected as the repository of varied, multifarious and heterogeneous ideas and practices. It is for this reason, as argued below, that this study invites appreciation of both the affinities and the divergences evinced by distinct aspects of Eastern and Western thought.

A poignant definition of magic that tersely captures the take on that discourse uniting the key titles here studied is supplied by the philosopher and art and communication theorist Vilém Flusser: "The universe of traditional images, as yet unclouded by texts, is a world of magical circumstances; a world of eternal recurrence in which everything lends meaning to everything else and everything signifies everything else: a world full of meanings, full of 'gods'" (Flusser 1992). This definition is especially pertinent to this book because it straddles Eastern and Western approaches to magic. Indeed, the idea of eternal recurrence is quintessentially Oriental in provenance, whereas the concept of spiritual ubiquity is equally pivotal to Japanese tradition — and above all Shinto — and to Western developments in the history and theory of magic that can be traced back to some of the most ancient recorded civilizations. A few key ideas defining each of these two areas are here worthy of consideration.

While in the Judaeo-Christian creed, the divinity is thought of as external to both time and space, in Shinto, spiritual forces (*kami*) are believed to fill the entire cosmos — mountains and trees, rivers and waterfalls, rocks and stones, as well as human beings and other animals. The Judaeo-Christian tradition also teaches that a more peaceful and balanced world could only be accomplished by a transcendental god, whereas in Shinto, the notion that the spiritual principle is omnipresent entails that any creature, in theory, holds the potential to affect reality. Heavenly and earthly entities alike comprise three attributes: body, spirit and soul. As Percival Lowell explains, the spirit progressively "clarifies" until "it approaches soul and finally becomes it" (Lowell, p. 27). Commenting on the thaumaturgic activities specifically associated with Shinto shamans, the *kannushi* (male practitioners) and the *miko* (their female counterparts), "The Shinto Tradition" explains that "Shinto magic originates in the relationship between the practitioner and the *kami*" and "primarily concerns itself with ensuring that the practitioner acts in harmony with the *kami* spirits, with magic being a natural extension of this harmony."[1]

A major challenge for the practitioner is posed by the sheer diversity and abundance of *kami* throughout the universe. Indeed, *kami* "come in all varieties, from elemental spirits to the ghosts of ancestors to strange and wonderful animals. They are so numerous that they are commonly referred to as the 'Eight Million Kami.' Some are kindly and helpful, while others are mischievous or selfish. Shinto *kannushi* use many ritual tools in their magic, including *haraigushi*, a wand covered in paper streamers used to purify an area, and *ofuda*, paper prayer strips used for good luck or to deal with malicious spirits" ("The Shinto Tradition," p. 41). In the logic of Shinto, magic emanates from the *kami* and the land itself. This makes it, at least hypothetically, attainable by all who seek it. Other forms of indigenous magic regard the practitioner as more of a specialist. For example, sorcery rooted in the teachings of the Tao, originating from China, depends on sternly trained magicians devoted to the understanding and spiritual control of the five elements: earth, water, air, fire and the void. Confucian mages, for their part, specialize in the interpretation of the *I Ching* (the most ancient of China's classic texts) for divinatory purposes.

Not only do good and evil *kami* coexist in mutual suffusion throughout the universe: *kami* also host discordant forces within their very being. As Michael Ashkenazi notes, each spiritual entity is held to accommodate "three *mitama* (souls or natures): *aramitama* (rough and wild), *nigimitama* (gentle and life-supporting), and *sakimitama* (nurturing). ... one or another of these natures might predominate in any particular myth" (Ashkenazi, p. 31). The notions of diversity and multifacetedness ascribed to all *kami* parallel a fundamental tenet of Japanese art inspired by both Shinto and Buddhism: namely, the belief in the inseparability of serenity and turmoil, peace and discord. The portrayal of movement typically benefits from the application of this lesson to artistic endeavor, often resulting in the truly magical evocation of a sense of calm and harmony (*wa*) through asymmetry, tension or even turbulence. The latent animateness of even seemingly inert forms is thereby thrown into relief. At the same time, the dynamic properties of space are vibrantly communicated, as the artifact allows the eye to travel beyond the frame of a picture or the physical boundaries of a sculpture. This reflects the Japanese aversion to stark distinctions between the inside and the outside, most memorably conveyed by native architecture and its tendency to establish an ongoing dialogue between a building and its surroundings (e.g., through the use of ethereal space dividers such as *shouji*, paper-covered sliding doors/windows, and *fusuma*, interior sliding partitions). Manmade edifices and the natural world are hence posited as fluidly interdependent and this generates an unparalleled sense of airiness and openness.

Japanese art's aversion to dualism is further confirmed by its persistent synthesis of tradition and innovation, indigenous and global influences, Eastern and Western styles — and, most vitally in this context, pragmatic and visionary tendencies. As John Reeve points out, "Compared with most countries, traditional culture is still remarkably intact and respected in 21st-century Japan — its craft skills, theatre and music, temples and rituals. One reason for its survival is the Japanese ability to fuse the new and the old, the innate and the imported" (Reeve, p. 8). No less distinctive a trait of Japanese culture, according to Reeve, is a profound respect for nature in all its manifestations. In the domain of art, this has incrementally contributed to the genesis of a wide "symbolic vocabulary from nature" that makes itself felt in indigenous art — for example, in the representation of animals and plants held to either carry mystical connotations or embody demonic agents in disguise. "For the artist," the critic comments, "the challenge is to convey the essence of the seasons or the creature" (pp. 38–39).

Shinto's reverence toward each and every facet of the natural realm as the receptacle of spiritual powers is mirrored by Japanese art's emphasis on the material properties of its objects rather than abstract philosophical values. This celebration of the corporeality of art is sustained by the deferential attitude toward their materials typically demonstrated by Japanese craftsmen and artists for time immemorial, and is fostered by the appreciation of the concrete dimension of life and of the coalescence of intellectual and sensuous pleasures that is rooted in the teachings of Zen Buddhism. A corollary of this approach is the extension of the concept of art beyond the realms of the fine and performing arts to encompass all manner of practical activities (e.g., martial, culinary, calligraphic, horticultural and sartorial exploits, as well as paper-folding, paper-processing and packaging crafts). All hands-on, embodied activities ultimately qualify as "art." Across these various pursuits, the partnership of the small and the beautiful is assiduously promulgated. According to Sarah Lonsdale, the "reverence of materials" is typically exhibited by Japanese fashion in the "selection, treatment and manipulation of fabric" seeking to harmonize "functionality with beauty" and ensuring that "textiles ... are highly tactile in nature" and are therefore capable of proving "just as exquisite to the touch as they are to the eye" (Lonsdale, p. 36). Disparate magical practices confirm this idea by showing that the sensory properties of particular fabrics deployed in the course of their performance play concurrently symbolic and pragmatic roles. No less crucially for the purpose of the topic here explored, Japanese art seeks to bring out the sensory qualities of diverse forms of iconography. This is evinced by its handling of patterns and emblems, allied to a delight in tasteful decoration (*kazari*) that finds a close correlative in the very nature of the indigenous written language. In the representation of magical iconography, such as the pentacle, the magician's circle or the *yin-yang* symbol, the titles here examined imaginatively mirror this aesthetic trend.

In the West, the Shinto world view finds a parallel in countless mythologies likewise founded on a belief in the ubiquity of spiritual forces and on the cognate belief in the coexistence of malign and benevolent demons at all times. Within those systems, dangerous powers are held to dwell within humans themselves. Magic, in this regard, is deemed capable of directing people toward good or evil. As Seligmann observes, a potent illustrative instance is offered by the legends and rituals of Mesopotamia, where "beneficent powers dwell in the dark abyss" and "spiteful forces," by contrast, may "live side by side with charitable ones. In these beliefs, man would have been the prey of chaos had he not employed magical arts to protect himself against evil influences. Through magic, he established his society; it coordinated his daily life. The arts flourished, merchants attended to their business, troops maneuvered in the plain, from the temples rose the smoke of sacrifices, hunters roamed the northern mountains, and in the king's palace the wise assembled to discuss affairs of state" (Seligmann, p. 25). Magic has the potential to "free the soul from fear and stimulate man's imagination. It was for magical purposes that images were carved, poems written, music played, and public monuments erected" (p. 26). An ongoing fascination with the eerie and the undisciplined retained its hold for centuries even in the apparently most enlightened of cultures — e.g., Golden-Age Greece.

Indeed, as Simon During notes, although the Greeks disparaged magic on preeminently Orientalist grounds, deeming its "exoticism" incompatible with the rationalist principles they sought to champion, neither they nor the Romans after them ever presumed to eradicate it conclusively (During, p. 5). For one thing, "Magic was ... rooted in the Greek and Roman time concept, which differed from the linear time of later rationality insofar as past, present, and future were seen as interacting with one another outside of contingency or causality" (p. 6). In the realm of magical thinking, chronological linearity is routinely subordinated to the appreciation of time as a multidimensional constellation of discrete poignant moments and attendant affects regardless of their specific temporal situation. Those moments may or may not coincide with momentous occurrences: what truly matters is that they can be treasured by the individuals that experience them as unique. This perspective ushers in an understanding of life itself not as a teleologically oriented sequence but rather as a medley of interlinked yet relatively independent stages, without prefigured outcomes predicated on the law of causality.

This idea is especially relevant to the present argument due to the prominence of cognate approaches to temporality in Eastern thought. It should also be stressed that the philosophical tenets fostered by Classical Greece and Rome were not univocally associable with rationalism any more than their religious systems were wholly coterminous with the Olympian pantheon. In fact, esoteric practices and rites steeped in older traditions shaped by Eastern influences maintained their appeal, though often in the interstices of official culture. This is borne out by the enduring hold of Dionysiac cults and Mithraic mysteries. These examples suggest that even though progress may dismiss the belief in supernatural forces as puerile, many people go on trusting their existence, albeit subliminally or secretly. Relatedly, pagan elements have infiltrated, and still infuse today, both ceremonies and lore central to Christianity. Writing in 1768, John Wesley opined that "Giving up witchcraft is in effect giving up the Bible" (cited in Seligmann, p. 255). These ideas will be revisited at a later point in the present discussion.

As Lowell emphasizes, Shinto's belief in the pervasiveness of spiritual agencies throughout the entire fabric of the cosmos entails not only that "Everything, from gods to granite, has its god-spirit" but also, no less tantalizingly, that "Spirit never dies, it only circulates. When a man or animal or plant dies its body duly decays, but its spirit either lives on alone or returns to those two great reservoirs of spirit, the gods *Takami-musubi-no-kami* and *Kami-musubi-no-kami*. From them a continual circulation of spirit is kept up through the universe" (Lowell, p. 28). The primary aim of esoteric Shinto is to compel spirit to circulate. Self-purification is especially important since it allows one's body to be possessed by the spirit of a different body and thus enables the original self to be, at least temporarily, expelled or subjugated. "This shift in spirit," Lowell advocates, "may take place between any two bodies in nature." While supernatural possessions of "things" are typically designated as "miracles," possessions of "people" go by the name of "incarnations" (p. 30). Incarnations, often conceived of as possessions by ghostlike visitants from the spirit-world, are privileged as "practical mediums of exchange between the human spirit and the divine" (p. 98). Additionally, as Ashkenazi emphasizes, many of Shinto's rituals consist essentially of "propitiation and divination"— namely, magic-imbued practices par excellence. Also significant, in the context of a study devoted to a form of popular recreation such as this, is Shinto's accommodation within its ceremonial repertoire of "elaborate rituals" that entail "some form of entertainment, whether dance, a magical play, or some music" (Ashkenazi, p. 31).

Japanese art and aesthetics closely mirror Shinto's perception of the universe at large as a scenario of relentless transformation by approaching reality as a process of continual flux, as impermanence (*mujou*), and hence partaking at all times of everlasting cycles of birth, death and rebirth. The evanescence of the seasons is often invoked in classic Japanese poetry as a favorite topos precisely in order to capture the spirit of *mujou*. This proposition is typically illustrated by this snippet from the seventeenth-century poet Matsuo Bashou's oeuvre: "Spring soon ends —/ Birds will weep while in / The eyes of fish are tears" (Bashou, p. 348). The five mainstays of Japanese aesthetics bolster this philosophy of transience by drawing attention, with variable degrees of explicitness, to the impermanence inherent in all facets of human experience. Thus, the principle of *mono no aware* acts as a constant reminder of the ephemerality of pleasure, beauty and life itself; *sabi* draws attention to imperfection and fragmentation, while the germane notion of *wabi* upholds the spiritual richness of the aged and the flawed; *kire* captures the Zen teaching according to which to look at the world with eyes unclouded by contingencies, the self must consciously embrace a state of rootlessness; *yugen*, finally, valorizes the timeless and unfathomable facets of the universe defying empirical perception.

According to Andrew Juniper, when an artistic practice is specifically informed by Zen, and hence reflects the lifestyle of its monks, *wabi sabi* is especially vital. Its primary objective is "to try and express, in a physical form, their love of life balanced against the sense of serene sadness that is life's inevitable passing." In so doing, it communicates "the precepts of simplicity, humility, restraint, naturalness, joy, and melancholy as well as the defining element of impermanence" and thus prompts us to "rediscover the intimate beauty to be found in the smallest details of nature's artistry" (Juniper, p. ix). Turning to nature as the ultimate source of inspiration, Japanese art captures the concept of *mujou* most vividly in its efforts to experiment with deftly balanced orchestrations of the elements. As Donald Richie emphasizes, the principal lesson derived from the natural realm concerns the paramount value of "simplicity"—a value tersely communicated by the fact that "There is nothing merely ornate about nature: every branch, twig, or leaf counts" (Richie, p. 19). In myriad expressions of magical thinking, likewise, the seemingly least notable minutiae of nature's treasurehouse acquire unique worth and are accordingly treated with due respect.

Shinto's miracles, incarnations, propitiations and divinations bear witness to a striving toward not only self-perfection but also possibilities of endless transformation: magic's most deep-rooted concern. This appetite for tropes of mutation, transfiguration, inversion, shape-shifting and self-displacement finds an apposite Western correlative in the tradition of witchcraft and its closest narrative relation, the fairy tale. Continual change is indeed pivotal to the very institution of witchcraft as an adventurous exploration of nature's riddles that would by and by give birth to the natural sciences. The passion for change is likewise axial to fairy tales, where metamorphosis functions as fantasy's primary means of communication. The time-honored belief system enshrined in witchcraft and the fairy-tale tradition celebrates the principle of ongoing transformation as an implied rebellion against the myth of stability imposed on Western thought by the contemporaneous establishment of the nation state, monotheism, capitalism and anthropocentric humanism. In anime, the witch is subject to numerous adaptations but its depiction almost invariably points to that figure's implication with a long and venerable heritage. As Michelle Rogers observes, in anime, the witch frequently embodies "the instinctual, inner Self," "the archetypal aspect of the Great Mother," or "a kind of guide" helping humans to negotiate "'the other' or 'the other world.' Deal with her correctly and the rules of this world correctly, and the hero or heroine comes through it the stronger or more aware (in Jungian terms, the individual will come into consciousness through it)" (Rogers). A further connection between Western tradition and Shinto lies with the art and philosophy of alchemy, whose practitioners maintained that no aspect of the cosmos amounted merely to inorganic matter for the reason that all matter is infused, at least potentially, with life.

Despite their local diversity, the titles under scrutiny are brought together by a shared desire to engage with events, situations and phenomena wherein magic spills into ordinary life. At times, they express this yearning through the dramatization of realms situated beyond or outside everyday existence. At others, they focus on individuals endowed — either by chance or by design — with the power to internalize alternate domains and experience them as integral parts of their very being. At practically all times, the boundary between this world and the other world is destabilized with variable levels of gravity or pathos. Interactions between the ordinary world and the magical domain, therefore, can be ideated according to diverse modalities. Across all of these, however, the logical categories of time, space and causality crumble and the barrier between the material and the spiritual is concurrently rendered nebulous or even irrelevant. These unsettling interventions are crucial expressions of magical thought at large, and it is therefore critical to recognize their importance. Yet, it is no less vital to respect the magical domain's irreducible alterity and resist the temptation to domesticate it by enforcing its full-blown integration into the everyday world: far from constituting a commodious acceptance of magic (which it might at first appear to connote), such an attitude would inevitably amount to a colonialist normalization of magic which deprives it of its essential core of thought-provoking inscrutability.

Returning now to Flusser, a few more concepts central to the philosopher's opus pertinent to the topic here examined deserve attention. One of these is Flusser's definition of "creativity" along lines akin to those traced by magical thought as described earlier — namely, "the production of previously non-existent information" by means of inventive efforts to "restructure ... preceding items." This is precisely what magic seeks to achieve by reconfiguring the phenomenal realm through the creative manipulation of its images and materials. Another related concept addressed by Flusser is "imagination" as a faculty based on the experimental ideation and interpretation of symbols: that is to say, "the ability to make images of (external or 'internal') circumstances, and the converse ability to recognize these circumstances in the images. In other words: the ability to encode phenomena in ... symbols and to read these symbols." "Reality" itself, in this scenario, is not a given but a mutable "threshold value." Finally, it is in his formulation of the concept of "existence" that Flusser encapsulates most memorably a world view of immense relevance to magical thinking and many of the practices it bolsters: "'Existence' is an attitude ... the attitude of negation. We have the ability to withdraw from our condition (to 'ex-ist') because we can take a negative attitude towards it. Such a withdrawal from the living world creates an imagined world, and makes the withdrawn existence into a subject of imaginings" (Flusser 1992). While deeply apposite to the realm of magic, Flusser's definition of existence is also linked to specifically Eastern philosophies by its emphasis on negativity — a key concept in Buddhism and other related systems. It is also noteworthy that Flusser's approach to magic locates this phenomenon within a nexus of ideas regarding specifically the nature and impact of the visual image. This renders it additionally relevant to the present context. For Flusser the very "significance of images" is "magical" insofar as they do not capture events as crystallized sets of data but rather replace events by states of things and translate them into scenes" (Flusser 2000, p. 9). One has to "allow one's gaze to wander over the surface" of the visuals, "feeling the way as one goes" in order to experience and heighten the magical significance of images (p. 8).

Magical thinking acquires a very distinctive meaning when it joins forces with the medium of animation — a medium that is proverbially renowned for its affiliation with magic in concurrently metaphorical and technological terms. As Ellen Besen pithily maintains, "This is the medium where, at the outset, anything can happen and it's through this property that we achieve magic. Other media can refer to metaphor but animation makes it real" (Besen). Animation could thus be said to fulfill an aspiration underpinning earlier arts devoted to the simulation of life through a symbolic defiance of death, such as the production of waxworks aiming to emulate meticulously the real bodies on which they were fashioned and thus appear to enflesh the inanimate.

The imbrication of magic and technology underpinning the art of animation — and, to a considerable extent, the world of fantasy-oriented videogaming — is, according to Eddo Stern, a phenomenon with a drawn-out and complex history: "ever since the Middle Ages, the discourse of magic emanating primarily from the pagan remnants of the Roman Empire and that of the new scientific reason have battled for sovereignty over the human soul's epistemological allegiance. The science and magic of farming calendars, home remedies, astronomical maps and alchemical concoctions are only a few examples of preoccupations that originated in the context of magical belief systems and were gradually transitioned to fall under a scientific rubric during the Middle Ages" (Stern, p. 259). Nowadays, the critic contends, "technology operates to realize what was previously in the hypothetical realm of magic. There is definitely some connection in the way both magic and technology create a sense of wonder as they seem to expand upon the notions of what is or has been feasible in the realm or the real." Appropriately, Stern cites A. C. Clarke's famous dictum — "any sufficiently advanced technology is indistinguishable from magic" — to corroborate his thesis (p. 260).

Warner pursues a cognate line of argument in proposing that "modernity did not by any means put an end to the quest for spirit and the desire to explain its mystery" (Warner 2006, p. 10). Developments in the technological realm validate this hypothesis: "As the vast army of modern inventions began to change our experience of the world — from the telescope and the microscope onwards — their advent interacted with imagery from antiquity and theology which had dominated thought about the stuff of the spirit." The "patterns of data and thought" imprinted on the human mind are pervaded by "the figures of the inner world, unavailable to the senses" (p. 12). During fully concurs with this hypothesis: "The enlightened critique of superstition did not immediately erase magic from natural philosophy; in the early modern period, science and magic were much more entangled than enlightened thinkers were willing to admit. Indeed, the scientific revolution developed as much out of so-called natural magic as against it" (During, p. 17). Natural magic, in this context, designates a cluster of practices deemed capable of advancing the cause of science by studying closely the secrets of nature, the intrinsic properties of its elements, and its ongoing rhythms of generation and decay. Strictly speaking, natural magic so understood is not supposed to concern itself with spiritual or prodigious phenomena. Yet, as During emphasizes, it "still situated the objects of its attention across a spectrum which included marvels at one end and intimations of supernatural intervention at the other" (p. 18). This indicates that magic preserved a potent hold on the world views and procedures promoted by the exponents of progress. As Romanticism progressively punctured the promises of the Enlightenment, magic came increasingly to be associated with the imagination and the creative drive. The German poet and philosopher Friedrich Schlegel explicitly advocated this position, maintaining that "Poetry is the finest branch of magic" insofar as it constitutes an "invisible spirit" (Schlegel, p. 80). The kinship of magic and the domain of the invisible is here foregrounded again in the pithiest of terms.

According to During, moreover, "Since about 1850 the human sciences have also, reflexively, found magic in enlightened modernity.... The archive of human science history is crammed with examples.... For Marx, capitalism's drive to increase consumption provoked magical thinking that conjures away the labor required for commodity production, so that commodities seem magically to speak for themselves." At roughly the same time, Freud "argued that, far from being dead, magical thinking is the bedrock upon which rational processes are based" (p. 25). More recently, as Raymond Williams contends, the advertising industry itself has come to operate as a "magic system" that capitalizes (quite literally) on the human thirst for fantasies able to supply people with imaginary identities and role models (Williams, Raymond, p.

335). John Berger advocates an analogous position, arguing that through that industry, "All hopes are gathered together, made homogeneous, simplified, so that they become the intense yet vague, magical yet repeatable promise offered in every purchase" (Berger, p. 153).

The anime here examined indubitably benefit, from a stylistic point of view, from the infusion of their narratives with numinous archetypes, time-honored symbolism and esoteric tropes. What ultimately makes them valuable, however, is their caliber as vehicles for the communication, in metaphorical guise, of some pressingly honest messages about the human condition. It is in this respect that the titles under scrutiny assert most memorably the confluence of animation and magic. After all, the bond between the two arts is historically borne out by animation's roots in magic acts begot by the enchanting universe of optical projection: the Magic Lantern, the Camera Obscura, the Magic Mirror and the Shadow Show. The magical quality of these devices is reinforced by their choice of content. Indeed, as Warner emphasizes, the "first proto-cinematic spectacles" which they spawned were especially eager to "conjure ghosts and spectres, fantasies and nightmares" (Warner 2006, p. 15). Similarly, the type of show launched by Etienne-Gaspard Robertson in the late 1790s, the *phantasmagoria* (the Greek word for "assembly of ghosts"), deployed the new technologies to conjure up worlds pullulating with "devils, ghosts, witches, succubi, skeletons, mad women in white, bleeding nuns, and what he termed 'ambulant phantoms'" in a morbidly kaleidoscopic interpretation of Gothic horror (p. 149). Like the art of magic, animation fosters a performative philosophy informed by a desire to guide the viewer's eye so that no trick or coup de théâtre might be wasted or superfluous. The selected titles are hence capable at once of absorbing their audiences into spellbinding fantasy realms and of promoting attentive reflection and this, ultimately, is where their true magic lies.

Chapter 2

Magic Contracts

*A man's maturity consists in having found again the seriousness
one had as a child, at play.* — Friedrich Wilhelm Nietzsche

*Vision without action is a daydream. Action without
vision is a nightmare.* — Japanese Proverb

Anime's treatment of the topos of magic contracts exhibits remarkable narrative suppleness. Even though certain basic ingredients tend to recur across a number of titles issuing from disparate studios and directors, individual yarns yield kaleidoscopic diversity. The anime examined in this chapter corroborate this proposition by showing that a magically binding pact may be governed by solemn vows enshrined in lore (*Hell Girl*'s three seasons); be underwritten by business-driven commitments and familial responsibilities (*Rental Magica*); involve whole communities of rival psychics equipped with paranormal faculties (*Darker than Black*); or even stem from sheer accident (*Ghost Hunt*). At all levels, however, the shows intimate the endurance of magical thinking in modern quotidian institutions. Kenneth Burke's theories on magic are especially pertinent, in this respect, as an eloquent testament to the ineradicability of magic from social organization. According to Burke, magic contributes vitally to the genesis and perpetuation of the very structure of human language: "the magical decree," he states, "is implicit in all language; for the mere act of naming an object or situation decrees that it is to be singled out as such rather than something other. ... an attempt to eliminate magic, in this sense, would involve us in the elimination of vocabulary itself as a way of sizing up reality" (cited in Covino, p. 91).

The terms "contract" and "decree" are intimately related, in the present context. Indeed, a decree — as a decision or order carrying the weight of a law — constitutes a sternly binding arrangement akin to the type of enforceable agreement established by a magic contract. As particular contracts are fulfilled, with variable degrees of flair or conviction, by the anime actors bounden unto them, magic powers are often psychologized on the basis of their connection with personal mental dispositions. Thus, the deployment of those faculties is ideated not only in terms of ritualistic performance but also as an expression of an individual's imagination and creativity. Magic, in this scenario, comes to represent an art identifiable both performatively — i.e., at the level of its public manifestations — and psychologically — i.e., at the level of its inward operations.

All of the animated tales discussed in this chapter render magic events and characters both arresting and unsettling by their knack of couching out-of-this-world adventures in a matter-of-fact style that enables them to emplace themselves as pictures of everyday existence in spite of their extraordinariness. The shows thus erode the barrier between the magical and non-magical realms with irreverent gusto by grounding magic in familiar terrain. At the same time, however, the anime refuse to allow their enchanted kingdoms to be so firmly incorporated in reality as to become normalized or anodyne. In fact, they preserve the intrinsic otherness of those worlds as a sine qua non of their uncanny charm. They thus enjoin us to address the ethical implications of the phenomenal world's involvement with an ineffable dimension that ultimately precludes conclusive integration by the factual domain. Consequently, the anime foreground the fluidity of magical discourse by situating it at once within and beyond the real, and hence throwing into relief both its bizarre tendency to infiltrate daily life almost unobtrusively — and with great adaptability to its rhythms — and its staunch resistance to ideological colonization.

The concept of the magic contract operates as an effective mechanism for bridging the magical and the non-magical worlds while also allowing magic to retain its necessary alterity. Indeed, the term "contract" locates the supernatural element in a pragmatic reality. Yet, by teaming with forces that clearly bypass normal legalistic considerations, it compels us to appreciate the distinctive workings of agreements founded on otherworldly obligations and rules as phenomena irreducible to the dictates of known and nameable human milieux. *TV Tropes* amusingly elucidates this idea, arguing that in the domain of fantasy, ordinary contracts rarely (if ever) obtain, largely as it is "pretty vague what kind of government most fantasy cultures use.... Not to mention the fact that we have contracts in Real Life, and they're usually pretty boring.... Sometimes it is implied that the magic punishment for breaking a clause is somehow contingent on the permission being given by the one who signed the contract. Really, the easier explanation most of the time is that A Wizard Did It" ("Magically Binding Contract").

As argued earlier, the anime here explored draw palpable solace from the interweaving of magical and non-magical levels of existence, while also highlighting that bringing magic into everyday life should not result in its taming but should actually endeavor to honor its essential alterity. This is intriguingly communicated by the anime's approach to space. Their magical places indeed propose novel versions of the myth of the *terra incognita* as a fantasy of discovery, ultimate knowledge, penetration and domestication that is also, equivocally, a tale about mystery and the irreducibility of otherness. Even in an exhaustively explored and mapped out world, where frontiers have been pushed to the limits of outer space and to the tiniest particles of matter and energy, space still retains obscurities and secrets. Discovery does not yield final knowledge but rather the desire, forever renewed and forever deferred, for further knowledge. As J. K. Wright observes: "if there is no *terra incognita* today in the absolute sense, so also no *terra* is absolutely *cognita*," since "the unknown stimulates the imagination to conjure up mental images of what to look for within it, and the more there is found, the more the imagination suggests for further search" (Wright, p. 4).

Furthermore, as Aldous Huxley emphasizes, the beguiling myth of unexplored territory survives unscathed today insofar as "our mind still has its darkest Africas, its unmapped Borneos and Amazonian basins.... A man consists of ... an Old World of personal consciousness and, beyond a dividing sea, a series of New Worlds — the not too distant Virginias and Carolinas of the personal subconscious ... the Far West of the collective unconscious, with its flora of symbols, its tribes of aboriginal archetypes; and, across another, vaster ocean, at the antipodes of everyday consciousness, the world of Visionary Experience.... Some people never consciously discover their antipodes. Others make an occasional landing" (Huxley, pp. 69–70). Along analogous lines, and with forceful resonance for the discourse of magic, David Lowenthal argues that "every image and idea about the world is compounded of personal experience, learning, imagination, and memory. The places that we live in, those we visit and travel through, the worlds we read about and see in works of art, and the realms of imagination and fantasy each contribute to our images of nature and man" (Lowenthal, p. 260).

In sustaining the establishment and fulfillment of diverse types of contract, magic enables the chosen anime to forge intriguing metaphors for the genesis of social cohesion. Time and again, the magic contract indeed supplies the figurative basis for adventures whose objective — either voiced or implied — is the facilitation of cooperativeness and solidarity among disparate, even initially adversarial, parties. It might seem ironical that so pragmatic an aim should not be advanced through the rule of reason but by recourse to frankly irrational means. Yet, it is often the case that the human mind reaches answers, albeit purely provisional ones, through routes that have precious little to do with ratiocination and hard-nosed sequential inference. Harlan Coben vividly conveys this idea: "Logic is never linear. It dashes to and fro and bounces off walls and makes hairpin turns and gets lost during detours. Anything can be a catalyst, usually something unrelated to the task at hand, ricocheting your thoughts into an unexpected direction — a direction that inevitably leads to a solution linear thinking could never have approached" (Coben, p. 301).

As anticipated, *Ghost Hunt* (TV series; dir. Rei Mano, 2006–2007) enters the magical domain as a result of a purely accidental occurrence. In the show's opening segment, first-year high-school student Mai Taniyama, whose only involvement with the supernatural up to this point has consisted of a passion for ghost stories, unwittingly interferes with the investigative activities of Kazuya Shibuya, the manager of "Shibuya Psychic Research," and his right-hand man Lin, causing the latter's injury and temporary incapacitation. When Kazuya requests that she stand in for Lin as his pro tem assistant, Mai has no choice but to comply. The transition, in the show's opening frames, from Mai's exchange of spooky tales with two of her schoolmates in the evocative setting of a gloomy classroom to her absorption in the *real* supernatural "industry" is so smoothly dramatized and elegantly edited as to operate as a powerful metaphor for the flimsiness of the boundary between fiction and reality in the realm of magical thinking.

Although the heroine's appointment is initially provisional, and hence intended to come to an end once Lin has recovered from his mishap, she ends up obtaining permanent part-time employment with the organization. This unexpected development gets Mai involved in some actual ghost stories in the company of Kazuya himself—whom she nicknames "Naru" in reference to his narcissistic self-esteem and snooty demeanor and soon begins to regard as an object of romantic interest — as well as the saturnine Lin (also a proficient and eclectic magic practitioner) and an assortment of experts drawn from various fields of psychic practice to lend their services. *Ghost Hunt* provides a splendid example of magic syncretism in the handling of this composite cast, as the psychic protagonist and his assistants, in their efforts to identify the causes of diverse inexplicable occurrences, cooperate with a motley crew comprising the "self-styled" Shinto priestess (*miko*) Ayako, the Buddhist monk (*hakkaisou* or *bouzu*) and rock bassist Housho (a.k.a. "Bou," short for *bouzu*), the Australian Catholic exorcist John Brown and the kimono-clad indigenous medium Masako (among other spiritualistic types making cameo appearances in individual installments).

It must also be noted, in this respect, that the anime's eclectic approach to spiritualism often entails a playful, even irreverent repudiation of realism. For example, in real life, it is unlikely that Catholic priests, Buddhist monks and Shinto shamans would happily cooperate and even perform their cleansing rites in unison. Relatedly, the exorcisms of each tradition are deliberately simplified and, occasionally, fictionalized for dramatic effect. This should not be read as grossly inadvertent lack of accuracy on the director's part. In fact, it constitutes a deliberate move intended to underscore, in a tastefully understated fashion, the idea that the magic of animation, in the context of the show, ultimately carries greater authority than the magic embedded in ratified religions or creeds. *Ghost Hunt*'s cast, on the whole, is flawlessly balanced in the attribution to each of its members of specific psychological traits, somatic features, types of behavior and assorted quirks. The Mai-Naru pairing epitomizes the cumulative character equilibrium by juxtaposing the girl's lively, adventurous and intuitive disposition with the male lead's penchant for deductive reasoning, businesslike pragmatism and impenetrable composure. While Mai's extrovertness and inquisitive spirit make her amiable without degenerating into formulaic *shoujo* naivety, Naru's cold professionalism is tempered by undercurrents of vulnerability that poignantly remind us of his fundamental humanity despite the crowning revelation that he possesses unparalleled psychic abilities.

Ghost Hunt elliptically invokes several aspects of indigenous lore that are here worthy of some consideration. Japanese legends and entertainment-driven tales teem with ghosts (*yuurei*). These fall into various categories. The *gaki*, or hungry ghosts, normally harbor the souls of deceased members of a household whose descendants have failed to honor their memory through appropriate worship and offerings. Mythology also features prominently the ghosts of fallen warriors revisiting the circumstances of their departure at symbolically laden moments. The figure of the "ghost mother" continuing to look after her offspring beyond the grave is no less popular, and often placed at the center of exceptionally touching stories of truly timeless emotional poignance. In the culture of Japan's aboriginal people, the Ainu, ghosts generally typify the evil side of the departed (dubbed *tukap*) and are wont to appear in dreams to convey important messages from the *kamui* (the Ainu version of the *kami*) and enjoin the sleeper's soul (*ramat*) to undertake a quest as a result of which the person may come to sudden death. When malevolent ghosts are not simply keen on exacting revenge but also pursue ulterior nefarious ends, such as the perpetuation of their own existence by violently destroying living creatures, they cease to be regarded just as spectral apparitions and are placed instead in the categories of the *oni* (demon) or the *bakemono* (monster).

Despite these implicit connections with facets of Japanese mythology, however, the series leaves its ghosts very much to the viewer's imagination, and it is here that one of its greatest dramatic strengths indubitably lies. The famous theorization of the fantastic as a genre formulated by the structuralist critic Tzvetan Todorov supplies insights of great relevance to Mano's treatment of supernatural phenomena and to the distinctive mood this serves to generate. Todorov describes the fantastic as a liminal state poised between the "uncanny," where seemingly supernatural events can ultimately be traced back to natural causes, and the "marvelous," where genuinely supernatural explanations obtain. A truly fantastic text does not fully subscribe to either of these polarities but actually handles the supernatural so subtly as to leave the reader or viewer with a sense of uncertainty regarding its causes: "*hesitation* is therefore the first condition of the fantastic" (Todorov, p. 160). The fantastic's persistent suspension of clear answers impacts on three interrelated aspects of the narrative: "First, the text must oblige the reader to consider the world of the characters as a world of living persons and to hesitate between a natural or supernatural explanation of the events described. Second, this hesitation may also be experienced by a character; thus the reader's role is so to speak entrusted to a character, and at the same time the hesitation is represented, it becomes one of the themes of the work — in the case of naive reading, the actual reader identifies himself with the character. Third, the reader must adopt a certain attitude with regard to the text: he will reject allegorical as well as 'poetic' interpretations" (p. 33).

It would be arduous to conceive of more apposite an account of the *Ghost Hunt*'s overall tenor and timbre. In the first half of the series, *Ghost Hunt* asserts itself primarily as a supernatural mystery anime laced with myriad variations of magic thought and magic performance. While numerous scenes exude menacing intensity, the adventure seldom ventures into truly dark territory. With the transition to the second half, more macabre complications incrementally come to dominate the action and the tone accordingly veers towards nerve-cracking suspense and a creepy sense of the lurking unknown that invests the show with more overt horror traits. At the same time, the exploration of the esoteric facets of several types of mystical magic gains an increasingly prominent role and this also serves to augment the mounting sense of gravity.

Bolstered throughout by high production values and an intelligent script averse to clichés, *Ghost Hunt*'s style and ambience emit a subtle balance of suspenseful drama and touches of humor. Animation techniques and cinematography of the stature seen in *Ghost Hunt* eloquently confirm the reputation enjoyed by its producers, J. C. Staff, as one of the most esteemed anime studios currently on the scene. The underlying artwork is largely responsible for the success of the moving images populating the screen, insofar as it harmoniously integrates appealing character designs, rife with varied wardrobes and accessories and sporadically enlivened by the inclusion of drawings in the *chibi* ("child-body") mode, punctiliously detailed backgrounds, well-modulated color schemes, and an inspired use of black-and-white, sepia, and solarized frames as well as chromatic overlays for flashbacks and moments of heightened pathos. On the cinematographical plane, these assets are felicitously complemented by sharp camerawork, polished cuts, arresting character entries and exits and impeccable overall execution, with occasional homages to the documentary style through simulations of shaky hand-filmed footage. The consistent deployment of this elaborate technical formula often results in rapid-fire filmic concatenations capable of inducing the viewer to look forward to the next sequence with almost visceral keenness even when the issues at hand carry grave metaphysical implications. In this regard, the art of animation again works as a metaphor for the léger de main proverbially associated with stage magic and the wizardly arts at large while these, in turn, operate as metaphors for the web of contractual duties binding the key characters indissolubly together.

Technically, one of the anime's most unusual facets lies with its handling of the opening and closing sequences. Some reviewers and commentators have criticized these sequences for their seeming cheapness — an impression arguably resulting from the deliberate avoidance of complex montages and special effects of the kind one often encounters in contemporary anime series. However, attentive evaluation of the openings and endings utilized by Mano will reveal that they actually exude a unique cinematic magic of their own by eschewing flashy spectacle and conspicuous cuts precisely to reinforce with refreshing economy the story's more elusive or downright inscrutable themes. Explicitly dazzling visuals would feasibly have detracted from *Ghost Hunt*'s dedication to the unobtrusive capture of — or, at any rate, allusion to — the dimension of invisibility which, as argued in some depth in Chapter 1, constitutes one of magic's most salient and inveterate attributes. Moreover, the mood built up by those sequences through their images is gorgeously enriched by orchestral music of remarkable caliber, distinguished by an elegant handling of both tempo and dynamics — allegro played from mezzo piano to fortissimo for the opening, and largo ranging from mezzo forte to piano for the ending.

The series comprises eight investigative cases, taking the protagonists from an allegedly haunted school building under demolition, through a patrician household in thrall to a sinister doll, a school beset by incidents related to an ancient curse, a park where dating couples have water poured over them from thin air, a church possessed by the ghost of a little boy, a school obsessed with a spirit-summoning game, a labyrinthine mansion afflicted by recurring disappearances (and some baleful hints at vampirism), to a family tormented by a whole army of malevolent spirits and zombies. Thanks to meticulous plotting, each of the cases is carefully individuated, and hence capable of delivering its own distinctive take on the supernatural. Furthermore, each instance contains well-paced diegetic complications associated with the requests of an appropriately diversified clientele, that enjoin viewers to navigate the story's twists and turns with an open mind, and gradually arrive at the roots of a crisis by separating its red herrings from its reliable clues, its random repercussions from its essence. At times, the truth is so thoroughly obfuscated until the point of resolution that guessing the identity of the culprit is virtually impossible even for the most Sherlockian of spectators. At others, it may be possible to identify the party responsible for particular occurrences at a relatively early stage in the adventure, yet his or her motives remain unfathomable prior to the dénouement.

As the investigations unfold, numerous concepts, theories and practices are invoked as the team engages with each successive case "file." These include recurrent exorcisms; Shinto protective charms; the *Kuji-in*, the Shinto-Buddhist "Nine-Syllable Seal" used as an incantation to ward off evil spirits; poltergeists; voodoo and the cognate practice of *Enmi* (a cursing method employing evil spirits and doll-like effigies); the *ouija* board and its Japanese correlative, *Kokkuri-san*; *Kodoku*, a powerful Chinese curse; *Shoukon*, a method of summoning spirits through the Chinese *Fukodou*, an ancient conjuration in the dark arts; vampirism and the associated characters of Vlad Tepes, his father Vlad Drakul, Bram Stoker's Dracula and the Countess Erzsébet Báthory; ESP; psychokinesis (including PK LT, the control of living organisms; PK ST, the power to influence still objects as seen in spoon-bending; and PK MT, the ability to affect moving entities); the talismanic powers of *Ebisu*, objects drifting ashore from the immortal land beyond the sea; the perception of demon fire (a.k.a. will-o'-the-wisp); the *Kamaitachi*, a Japanese monster taking the form of a slashing whirlwind; psychometry; *onmyoujou*, an indigenous system of divination and magic here discussed in some detail in Chapter 4; and spatial manipulation. While magical thinking plays an important part in the characters' procedures, the anime is also eager to emphasize the collusion of magic and technology — particularly by recourse to detailed depictions of the protagonists' specter-detection equipment — and the often psychological and affective triggers of seemingly supernatural disturbances with implicit reference to intelligently handled psychoanalytical theories (e.g., in the case involving a female adolescent with psychic powers whose pathological yearning for recognition fortuitously triggers commotions that mimic the conduct of a poltergeist). Prophetic and revelatory dreams also play a key role as Mai, initially presumed to host no spiritualist talent whatsoever, proves increasingly capable of experiencing oneiric visions that either foreshadow future outcomes or shed light on past events responsible for triggering the disturbances which Kazuya's firm is appointed to investigate and resolve.

At several junctures, *Ghost Hunt* further enhances its frame of magical reference by recourse to the figure of the doll as the quintessential incarnation of uncanniness: an emblematic status grounded in the doll's traditional function as a trap for human souls. (Dolls also play an important role in *Hell Girl*, examined later in this same chapter, in *Mai-Hime* [Chapter 3] and, most memorably, in *Rozen Maiden* [Chapter 6].) It should also be noted, on this point, that dolls play a significant role in Japanese culture at large. Known as *"ningyou,"* i.e., "human figures," they have been traditionally molded in a wide variety of shapes: fairy-tale characters and innocent children, protective deities and fierce warriors, heroes and demons, and still feature as pivotal to popular festivities such as *Hina Matsuri* ("Doll Festival" or "Girls' Day") and *Kodomo no Hi* ("Boys' Day" or "Children's Day"). In the Heian Period (794–1185), dolls served primarily ritualistic purposes and were deemed capable of absorbing a person's sins. In the Edo Period (1603–1867), dolls exhibiting exceptional artistic merit in the manipulation of their materials and in the execution of both their costumes and their mechanical properties became axial to a vibrant market of collectible merchandise and were avidly treasured by the swelling ranks of wealthy businessmen. Dolls are still produced today in many regions of Japan as a distinctive indigenous craft and prodigally purchased by shrine pilgrims and international tourists alike. The ceremonial costume worn by Ayako when she performs her exorcisms vividly recalls the attire of classic *hina* types in its colors, accessories and approximately pyramidal effect. Traditional doll-centered imagery is used to analogous dramatic effect, and with frequently splendid cinematic results, in the magic-saturated TV series *Touka Gettan* (dir. Yuji Yamaguchi, 2007).

If the magic contract central to *Ghost Hunt* is essentially the offshoot of an utterly unforeseen accident, a fortuitous mishap is no less instrumental in paving the way to the supernatural pact imposed on Yuri Shibuya in *Kyo Kara Maho!* (TV series; dir. Junji Nishimura, 2006). The character leads a perfectly ordinary student life until he is dunked into a toilet after trying to rescue a classmate from a gang of bullies. What should have amounted to nothing more than a rowdy goliardic flourish suddenly turns into the trigger for a metaphysical journey, as Yuri is sucked into an alternate world redolent of medieval Europe. He is here informed that he is destined to become the next "Maoh," the king of the "Mazoku" — namely, a race inimical to humanity with scarce consideration for notions of kindness and justice. Yuri, who is naturally magnanimous, peaceful and considerate to his subjects' utter dismay, finds himself bound to a peculiar contract that requires him to fulfill his duties as monarch of an unknown land, while also preserving his instinctive concern toward humans and negotiating a whole set of customs, values and codes that are quite alien to his origins and habits.

What abides in memory most tenaciously about *Ghost Hunt* is the sheer exuberance with which it conveys, arc after arc, the human proclivity — childish, yet atavistic — to feel drawn to what scares us, to savor the pleasures of the inscrutable, the forbidden and the uncanny despite, or perhaps *because of*, their lurking menace. According to Julia Briggs, what magnetizes humans toward the dark terrain of spectrality and terror is a peculiar amalgam of juvenile cheekiness and analytical inquisitiveness. In her investigation of ghost tales, specifically, the critic observes: "there is nearly always a distinct moment when the hero commits some error, perhaps a form of hubris, by taking a wrong decision, or by choosing against advice to prosecute some scheme.... There is no apparent folly in such undertakings and the act of hubris then lies in not heeding warnings or signs. But perhaps the emotion that most frequently lures the unwitting hero on is curiosity ... the innocent curiosity of Bluebeard's wife ... Faust's hunger for forbidden knowledge" (cited in Bloom, p. 114). In *Ghost Hunt*, the protagonists' often foolhardy forays into haunted territory can also be seen to stem from a flamboyantly perverse desire to transgress the counsel of both sanity and safety. In this regard, they bring to mind Edgar Allen Poe's daunting words: "We stand upon the brink of a precipice. We peer into the abyss — we grow sick and dizzy. Our first impulse is to shrink from the danger. Unaccountably we remain.... Examine these and similar actions as we will, we shall find them resulting solely from the spirit of the Perverse. We perpetrate them merely because we feel that we should *not*" (cited in Bloom, pp. 26–27).

If *Ghost Hunt*'s articulation of the coalescence of magic and accident finds a parallel in *Kyo Kara Maho!*, its recurrent use of the figures of the Undead and the Walking Dead is mirrored by the TV series *Zombie Loan* (dir. Akira Nishimori, 2007). Replete with allusions to indigenous lore — or, at any rate, a fictitious interpretation thereof— the anime revolves around Michiru Kita, a schoolgirl endowed with "Shinigami Eyes": namely, the ability to perceive a dark mark around a person's neck that signifies that person's imminent death. Gray at first, the mark turns black when the subject actually dies. The theme of the magic contract comes into play as Michiru discovers that two of her classmates sporting black rings, Chika Akatsuki and Shito Tachibana, are not in fact dead and that the force that keeps them alive issues from a supernatural agreement with the "Zombie Loan" secret agency. Chika and Shito can preserve their human existence as long as they fulfill a contract requiring them to hunt zombies on the agency's behalf. As Michiru gets involved with the two boys, the scope for lively incursions into the magical unknown progressively grows.

Like *Ghost Hunt*, the TV series *Rental Magica* (dir. Itsuro Kawasaki, 2007–2008) yields a variegated ensemble of magic-imbued tales held together by contractual commitments. Following the mysterious disappearance of his legendary father Tsukasa (the last of the "Fairy Doctors"), young Itsuki Iba is obliged to take over the family business: a magician dispatch service dubbed "Astral" that employs numerous magicians and supernatural creatures to provide its clients with professional magical assistance. Regrettably, though kind and well-meaning, Itsuki appears to lack any of the credentials one would expect to find in the prospective director of a challenging venture. In fact, he repeatedly comes across as cowardly, inexperienced and unsociable, which makes him ill-equipped to interact adequately with his staff on the basis of either managerial skills or team spirit. No less alarmingly, Itsuki's shaky personality is initially compounded by an ostensible lack of magical ability. As it turns out, Itsuki is not altogether inept as a mage for he actually hosts "Glam Sight" ("Fairy Eye") in his right eye. When deployed, this faculty noticeably augments Itsuki's confidence and strength, allowing him to perceive magic and its flaws, to affect the flow of spell waves and even peek into the memories of the practitioners that seek to oppose him. However, this skill comes at a steep price insofar as it is exceedingly painful for him to deploy it. As a result of Itsuki's lack of formal training in the field, it is also hazardous to his vigor and health. Indeed, the youth's use of Glam Sight often causes him to suffer spell-wave poisoning, the magical equivalent of radioactive contamination. Moreover, Itsuki's Glam Sight was supposedly tainted by a childhood encounter with a magical baby dragon in a haunted house, though his memories of this incident have been occluded.

The anime chronicles Astral's magical adventures, focusing on the many spirits and phenomena which these deliver with unflinching gusto, humorously underscoring throughout the protagonist's laborious efforts to learn how to deal with his own employees, on the one hand, and the rival companies, rogue members and taboos threatening the family business, on the other — while also struggling to pay the bills and successfully completing enough tasks to avoid abolition. While positing the idea of the magic contract as pivotal to its entire diegesis, the series also constructs a meticulously detailed and hierarchical universe in which chance and contingency are recognized as crucial facets of magical thought, yet also partially contained within well-defined structures of power. An especially important role is played by the "Association," an organization held to preside over more than a hundred magical bodies and punish those who break taboos — i.e., acts which no respectable magician should ever wish to perform — in order to prevent the spread of magical pollution that inevitably occurs whenever a taboo is violated. One of the most opprobrious taboos, associated with the practices of the Dark Mages Society, Ophium, consists of a magician's attempt to become one with a certain form of magic by incorporating the relevant demonic forces.

Rental Magica's most striking attribute, where the dramatic treatment of magic themes and imagery is concerned, lies with the sheer exuberance with which it brings together — sometimes in defiance not only of historical consistency but even of reason itself— an astounding variety of esoteric traditions. It is important to note, in this respect, that in the logic of the series, "magic" encompasses all sorts of paranormal abilities and uses of so-called "spell power" (*juryoku*). Each of the traditions invoked by *Rental Magica*, moreover, is associated with at least one character whose defining abilities, personality, physical appearance, accessories and professional tools lends it distinctive narrative weight. Shinto rituals, for example, are brought into play through the character of Mikan Katsuragi, a contract employee for Astral that has joined Itsuki's firm after fleeing the parental home, determined to prove her autonomous worth in the face of an ancient and globally esteemed dynasty of Shinto practitioners. The character of Honami Takase Ambler, Itsuki's childhood friend and unofficial secretary and tutor, is an expert in Witchcraft, fortunetelling and Celtic magic, having channeled her formidable talent and sheer determination into the revival of the lost art of the Druids and managed to accomplish this feat in merely two years, while also having benefited from advanced training in England. Celtic magic reputedly draws upon the natural energies embedded in forests and rocks — with mistletoe and stone circles as recurrent motifs of its symbolic repertoire — and makes use of sacred chants passed down from generation to generation exclusively by means of oral instruction. Honami's style departs radically from orthodox Druidic practice in resolutely shunning sacrificial ceremonies and preferring instead to magnetize lunar power through sorcery. (Notably, the girl's powers temporarily diminish with a crescent moon.)

With Ren Nekoyashiki, Astral's executive director, *Rental Magica* brings into play the syncretic magic of *onmyoudou* — an art already touched upon in relation to *Ghost Hunt* and here discussed in depth, as noted, in the context of Chapter 4. A cat lover (his family name means literally "cat mansion"), Ren relies on four feline familiars (*shikigami* or *shikineko*) to perform his magic. (Please note that preternatural cats are also important presences in *Aria*, examined in Chapter 4, while the concept of the familiar is axial to *The Familiar of Zero*, where it is rendered with the word *tsukaima*— an anime assessed in Chapter 5.) *Onmyoudou*'s association with the natural environment is hinted at by the *shikineko*'s names, all of which make explicit reference to the four cardinal points — that is, Seiryu (Azure Dragon of the East), Byakko (White Tiger of the West), Suzaku (Vermillion Bird of the South) and Genbu (Black Tortoise of the North). With Manami Kuroha, Astral's only ghost employee, *Rental Magica* introduces the practices of poltergeist and apport (*kengen genshou*), while also capitalizing on magic's intimate connection with the topos of metamorphosis by highlighting the girl's ability to transform parts of her ethereal constitution into other forms of matter. Alchemy, another esoteric art here addressed in detail in Chapter 4, simultaneously features in Kawasaki's anime with a certain prominence, as does Buddhist magic with its ritual objects and mantra. Astral's most valiant competitor is the "Magicians' Society Goetia" (from the Greek *goeteia*, i.e., "sorcery"). The organization is so named after an ancient practice pivoting on the ritualized evocation of demons, described in detail in the seventeenth-century grimoire titled *The Lesser Key of Solomon* and edited by Aleister Crowley in 1904. Its head, Adelicia Lenn Mathers, has followed in her ancestors' footsteps and specialized in King Solomon's magic — of which, as the *Wikipedia* entry for the show elucidates, "there are two types: summoning magic conducting and evoking seventy-two demons, and amulet magic using seven planets' power which affect the seventy-two demons.... Even if the users have first-class magic talent, they can usually summon only one kind of demon in their entire lives" (*Wikipedia, the free encyclopedia* — *Rental Magica*). Adelicia's family is, at least to date, the sole known exception to that rule.

The anime also alludes to the intriguing tradition associated with Rune magic. As Jennifer Smith explains in *The Runic Journey*, this draws much of its energy from textual performance since "the very act of writing something in runes is a spell in itself, bringing the statement into concrete reality." Additionally, runes corresponding to diverse mystical and natural forces can be arranged in rows meant to advance specific spells: for instance, a rune row intended to augment one's "psychic abilities" would feasibly include "laguz/ water (relating to the subconscious and mysteries), perth/dice-cup (for divination and magic), ansuz/Odin (the God of the runes), and kenaz/torch (for inspiration)." Runic inscriptions may also be inscribed on "a talisman — a permanent, physical manifestation of the magic of the runes" or else employed to achieve more contingent results, in which case the practitioner could carve the runes into a piece of wood and then burn it or into a candle and then allow it slowly to extinguish itself (Smith).

As observed in Chapter 1, in the domain of magical thought, chronological linearity is repeatedly flouted in favor of a perception of time as a mobile galaxy of single significant instants. Whether or not these instants correspond to important events is immaterial. In fact, the degree of their importance depends not so much on their objective content as on the extent to which they can be cherished as special by the people that live through them. Human life as a whole, in this world view, is not conceived of as a logical chain governed by teleological imperatives but rather as an assortment of interconnected but somewhat discrete phases unfettered by the ethos of cause and effect. Certain stages may have accommodated accomplishments of durable import. Others may have gone by almost unnoticed and yet still carry an unpretentious bequest of their own. *Rental Magica* encapsulates this perspective by presenting its episodes out of chronological order. In defying the logic of causality, *Rental Magica* creates a world in which everything appears interlaced with everything else in both temporal and spatial terms. In so doing, the anime weaves a tapestry of subtle connections and correspondences, linking together seemingly disparate events and fusing fragments of the past with glimmers of the future by means of densely layered images.

In the TV series *Hell Girl* (dir. Takahiro Ohmori, 2005–2006) and its sequels *Hell Girl Second Cage* (dir. Ohmori, 2006–2007) and *Hell Girl: Cauldron of the Three* (dir. Kenichi Kanemaki, 2008), magic provides the leading thread for several interrelated tales of haunting, pursuit and revenge — namely, themes that have positively saturated Japanese art and culture for time immemorial. The story's premise is that people seeking to wreak vengeance on their tormentors may place a post at the exact stroke of midnight on a website named "*Jigoku Tsushin*," "Hotline to Hell" or "Hell Correspondence" (depending on the translator). It is then up to Ai Enma (the titular heroine) to decide whether or not to assist the supplicants, and hence appease their thirst for retribution, by ferrying the villains to eternal perdition. Ai carries out her onerous duty with imperturbable resignation, never appearing to derive any personal satisfaction or even gratification from the stipulated agreement. Her measures are consistently effective in alleviating the summoners' afflictions. Yet, her contractual parameters involve a fearful symmetry (to borrow William Blake's perturbingly evocative phrase), since the people they support are ultimately no less doomed to certain damnation than their casualties are. The contracts fulfilled by Ai only benefit her clients on a provisional basis. In order to situate Ohmori's anime in an appropriate frame of reference, it is important to appreciate that the revenge topos has pervaded Japanese lore and entertainment industries for time immemorial, bringing together areas of cultural production and consumption as diverse as traditional theater, the indigenous art of woodblock printing (*ukiyo-e*), the recounting of ghost stories in domestic and small-community milieux, manga and anime, videogaming and live-action cinema. In this last context, a major instance is provided by the film *Ringu* (dir. Hideo Nakata, 1998), adapted by Hollywood four years later as *The Ring* (dir. Gore Verbinski).

If in *Ghost Hunt* dolls are unquestionably accorded great dramatic and symbolic vigor, in *Hell Girl*, they rise to the level of diegetic pivots. Indeed, they constitute the very currency, metaphorically speaking, in which the transactions entailed by Ai's contracts are conducted. At one point, the anime also makes overt reference to an indigenous practice in the dark arts, known as *ushi no kouku mairi*, based on a curse performed by nailing a straw effigy to the trunk of a tree situated in the hallowed grounds of a Shinto shrine. Most importantly, when Ai decides to respond to the people that seek her assistance, she first presents them with a straw doll with a piece of red string tied round its neck and tells them in unequivocal terms that if they truly wish to eliminate their antagonists, they must untie the string, at which point they will "officially enter into a contract" with Ai and her three (metamorphic) associates. The wrongdoers they seek revenge upon will thenceforth be taken to Hell without further delay. It is at this stage in the negotiations that Ai also tells her supplicants that were she to deliver their vengeance, they must make restitution to her — in other words, they must realize and accept that "when one person is cursed, two graves are dug" and that when they themselves eventually die, therefore, they will also be dragged "into the pit of Hell." Their spirits will roam sempiternally the dismal land in "pain and suffering," forbidden ever to behold paradise. The moment the string leaves the straw doll (at which point the doll itself evaporates leaving only the baleful string in the client's possession), the "Seal" of the "Covenant" appears on the chest of each of Ai's clients in the form of a tattoo representing an arcane crest-shaped emblem of concurrently Eastern and Celtic resonance.

Hell Girl's affiliation with the supernatural is sustained throughout by the deployment of recurrent allusions to indigenous traditions, as well as emblems more or less overtly linked to the spirit world. The anime's settings ooze with references to Japan's time-honored arts, particularly in the depiction of Ai's home at both the architectonic macrolevel and the decorative microlevel. The sartorial vogues typically associated with the heroine and her enigmatic grandmother are also informed by ancestral native fashion down to the minutest details — e.g., repeated references to the *nagajuban* (underwear typically donned with a kimono) which awaits Ai at the end of her ritualistic bathing in a gorgeous open-air hot spring. *Hell Girl*'s devotion to traditional imagery is also recurrently encapsulated by the use of the image of the river leading the damned to their appointed otherworldly destination. Rivers indeed play crucial symbolic and iconographic roles in both Buddhism and Shinto. Buddhist mythology features, as one of the most conspicuous aspects of its Hell, both an actual river, Shozukawa, which the souls of the departed cross after being divested of their earthly belongings, and a dry riverbed shrouded in fog where the souls of the innocent, powerless to move on to more desirable locations, are stranded. Shinto's heaven, for its part, is traversed by a riverbed dammed upstream so as to provide an appropriately ample meeting venue for its countless *kami*.

One of the anime's most significant symbols is the image of the *higanbana* ("spider lily"), a myth-encrusted emblem for the Buddhist concept of repetition. The *higanbana* blossoms every year during the autumn equinox and withers during the vernal equinox, to disappear altogether again until the following autumn. Since the equinoctial points are traditionally considered felicitous moments for communicating with the world of spirits and demons, the flower has come to be associated with the supernatural domain and indeed gained popular designations such as "spirit flower" or "Hell flower." The plant's possession of highly poisonous bulbs has no doubt fuelled its awe-inspiring credentials. The anime's traditional underpinnings are bolstered by its implicit evocation of the principle of Eternal Recurrence. In portraying its various predators and victims with punctilious attention to individual character traits and dramatic ramifications, thus avoiding the danger of repetitiveness inherent in eminently episodic adventures of this kind, *Hell Girl* nonetheless revisits with haunting consistency the same basic narrative pattern. From one episode to the next, the protagonist metes out poetically appropriate punishments to the evildoers and alerts her supplicants to the tribulations that await them with the same peremptory insistence. In addition, Ai always gives her clients the opportunity to have the doll removed from their presence and to leave their crucial decisions to a later point, which allows for the possibility of their opting not to take full advantage of the pact. Yet, the string is ineluctably untied sooner or later. Similarly, Hell Girl and her team do give the culprits one last chance of acknowledging their sins before inflicting their punishment but their pleas invariably fall on deaf ears.

Given the pervasiveness of cruelty, abuse and despair blighting the human world, it comes as no surprise to see Ai at the receiving end of all manner of appeals from the victims of violations and crimes deemed dire enough to warrant their perpetrators' fall into the nethermost depths of Hell. Accordingly, the ghostly procession of villains, each of whom Ai ceremonially addresses as "pitiful shadow clouded in darkness" and then proceeds to ferry to eternal damnation, never loses either size or momentum. The sources of the postulants' afflictions, clearly delineated in all of the first season's self-contained arcs as each drama is clinically observed from inception to climax, are extremely varied. This diversity contributes vitally to impart the anime with a tantalizing element of unpredictability which the generally iterative structural orchestration might at first appear to foreclose. Thus, the contexts within which the individual stories are placed alter significantly from one installment to the next.

At times, the tale unfolds in a predominantly academic milieu — e.g., in the case of the schoolgirl subject to ruthless blackmail and bullying and almost driven to prostitution by a spiteful classmate and her lackeys, or the one focused on a student unjustly accused of the murder of one of his friends who has actually been bludgeoned to death by a vain baseball prodigy. At others, the setting is emphatically domestic, as in the case of the girl seeking Ai's support out of a desperate desire to extricate her mother from the machinations of a perverse neighbor whose adulterous liaison the woman has unintentionally witnessed. At others still, although the focus is still on the plight of tormented individuals, the adventure reverberates with sinister echoes of widespread societal malaise. This typology is illustrated by the episode in which a brilliant technowizard is roped into corporational sleaze by a power-hungry entrepreneur who will stop at nothing to consolidate her financial empire. Another paradigmatic example is the story centered on the young girl who tragically loses the dog that has constituted her entire family from an early age as a result of the unscrupulous conduct of a self-seeking vet blinded by his own greed and conceit. Further instances of the same basic modality are the installment devoted to a stalked girl whose victimizer is none other than the senior policeman appointed to investigate the case, and the one where the culprit is a murderous mayor backed by the mafia. As these illustrative cases show, what Ai and her assistants often take on is not merely an isolated offender but a manifestation of pervasive cultural iniquity.

A subtle variation on the established pattern is the story of the aspiring actress unable to untie the string that would consign to perdition her callous adoptive mother since a victim of her own cruelty, a brutally persecuted rival actress, has also obtained Ai's support and managed to use the same straw doll first. Another interesting twist is supplied by the episode in which the central antagonists' enmity is resolved before the fateful string has been undone, and the glimmer of a happy ending is thereby allowed, yet an accidental dramatic inversion results once more in a fate of irrevocable torment. A no less disturbing variant is supplied by the tale of a nurse who, though considered a paragon of virtue by patients and colleagues, becomes the victim of the utterly unmotivated hatred of a drug addict she has never even met. A bleakly amusing adaptation of the leading theme comes with the episode centered on the character of the arrogant psychic who claims to have once dodged Hell and its punishments, only to have his hubris repaid by Ai with a true taste of the terrors of damnation.

There are also occasions in which *Hell Girl* surprises us by ushering in disquietingly peculiar locations, such as an old-fashioned, eerily grotesque circus, and an abandoned sanatorium shrouded in impenetrable fog whose sole resident is a vengeful doll harboring the memories of her long departed owner. Doll-related imagery is also brought into play in the case of the "doll bride," a girl seeking revenge on her mother-in-law — an obsessive doll-maker Hell-bent (literally, as things turn out) on turning her daughter into a living *ningyou*. The strict training to which the girl is routinely subjected in order to sap any latent trace of vitality from her body and soul is in itself dramatically compelling in its meticulous rendition of stylized postures and expressions, alongside weirdly robotic movements of the kind one would readily associate with the highly sophisticated mechanical dolls of the Edo Period (*karakuri*). No less memorable, in purely dramatic terms, is the climactic sequence in which Ai's assistants attempt to force the tyrannical hag to acknowledge her sins, where the dolls she has been tirelessly constructing as a surrogate humanity over which she might exert godlike authority come to life, and the woman's own body gradually morphs into that of a jointed puppet. Sadly, once the old woman has been dutifully ferried to Hell by Ai, the tale's protagonist discovers that her husband is no less eager to have her behave like a soulless doll than his obnoxious parent ever was. It would seem that the unfortunate girl will have to taste infernal anguish even before death consigns her to her appointed destination.

Although variations and unusual twists of the kind described above serve an important dramatic role in unobtrusively alluding to novel aspects and ramifications of the show's dominant premise, it is vital to remember that the insistent repetition of certain elemental motifs is integral to the anime's communication of its world view and related aesthetic goal. This ultimately amounts to a dispassionate, anatomically itemized exposure of the least palatable facets of human nature and interaction. Such a message is unfailingly conveyed by images that transude silent menace and harrowing beauty and find an ideal match in both oppressive lighting and a musical score combining eerie vocals, echoing chimes and some truly forbidding guitar strains. Additionally, marginal departures from the established pattern help the anime transcend the limitations of a purely repetitive diegesis and elevate repetitiveness itself to the status of a guarantee of narrative coherence. *Hell Girl*'s structure also benefits, for the purpose of continuity, from the employment of the supporting characters of Hajime Shibata and his seven-year-old daughter

Tsugumi. A reporter eager to discover the truth about Hotline to Hell out of what initially appears to be simple curiosity, Hajime gradually develops a veritable obsession with the website and its purpose as he realizes that it amounts to much more than merely an urban legend. Hajime's concern escalates as Tsugumi increasingly reveals an ability to communicate telepathically with Ai and hence experience visions that provide clear insights into Hell Girl's successive contracts and clients. (The child's uncanny insight into the supernatural will be further corroborated in both of the sequels.) Afflicted by the regret he feels regarding his deceased ex-wife, Hajime is convinced that one must live with anything life yields, no matter how painful, and that revenge can only deliver heart-rending results.

Tsugumi, conversely, for a while believes that Ai's dark mission is morally sound since the people Hell Girl prods down the path to damnation are inherently evil. Tsugumi has a change of heart when the innocent nurse is unreasonably thrown into Hell, and has further reason to question her alter ego's modus operandi when she nearly dies in a traffic accident and, acknowledging that the man who could have unwittingly caused her death is a good person, understands how reprehensible it would have been for Hajime to want him punished out of his thirst for vengeance. In exploring Tsugumi's rocky emotional evolution, the anime provides a highly convincing portrayal of a child whose personality struggles to reconcile the adult demeanor required by her unconventional single-parent upbringing and an underlying element of infantile naivety congruous with her actual age. Tsugumi's ethics receive a fierce blow when Ai resolves to play her trump card by revealing the circumstances surrounding Tsugumi's mother's death and Hajime's indirect responsibility for it, insistently tempting the little girl to seek revenge on her father. At one point, Ai even conjures palpably credible images of Tsugumi's mother in immense physical and emotive distress to confuse the little girl and contaminate her normally mature power of judgment. For the first time in the series, Hell Girl actually takes the initiative of presenting her potential client with one of her portentous straw dolls without even having been properly summoned.

Ai's past remains cloaked in mystery until half way through the first season, where Tsugumi has a vision of the preternatural girl in the context of an old bookshop packed with rare tomes. Hajime locates the venue and interviews both the toadish owner and his stunningly loquacious parakeet to obtain information about Hotline to Hell. In the process, he discovers a book containing references to a character dubbed "Purgatory Girl" and the related concept of a "Hotline to Purgatory" in a story penned and illustrated by a man named Fukumoto some fifty years earlier, which bears uncanny similarities to Ai's procedures. Following this at first tenuous lead, Hajime finds that the depiction of Purgatory Girl originally drawn by the artist — and subsequently replaced by the publishers with a more sensual image to attract buyers — was a portrait of Ai herself. It is also revealed, in a magisterially suspenseful fashion, that the old tale's protagonist was an illustrator with a very beautiful wife and that the latter, violated by her husband's best friend, took her own life. Having managed to locate the now dying artist in a decrepit apartment on the city's outskirts, Hajime discovers that the story's plot closely mirrors Fukumoto's personal experience, his spouse having likewise been the victim of his closest friend's illicit attentions and committed suicide in her shame. The artist confirms the existence of Hotline to Hell, admitting to have relied on its services to eliminate his wife's seducer and to have then spent his entire life desperately trying to forget about the baleful mark on his chest by immersing himself wholeheartedly in all sorts of activities and pursuits — his art, strict religious observance, gambling, voluntary work — but never succeeded in anesthetizing for more than the briefest of instants his knowledge of the impending fate.

In Fukumoto's days, we are told, the means of contacting Hell Girl was a newspaper announcement: her address would appear, were she willing to proffer her assistance, in a blank space in the announcement. The evolution of the communication channels entailed by Hotline to Hell from the printing press to the internet (and later to a mobile site accessible by cell phone) attests to magic's imbrication with technology — an aspect of the discourse to be examined in some detail in the next chapter and encapsulated in *Ghost Hunt*'s presentation of sophisticated equipment as a means of tracking supernatural phenomena. When Hajime explicitly asks Fukumoto who Hell Girl is, the artist provides the first truly important clue to the heroine's identity, at first riposting that she is "something inhuman," and then opining that it might be more correct to assume that she was human at some unspecified point in the remote past. This hypothesis is corroborated by Fukumoto's revelation that descriptions of Hell Girl can be traced back to magic-related traditions of ancient epochs. One of the most intensely beautiful moments in the entire series comes in the climax of this pathos-laden installment, as Fukumoto places the final touches on a large portrait of Ai he has been executing (and knows full well is destined to be his last work), and tears first well up and then roll down the magical being's cheeks, bearing witness to her underlying humanity and long personal history of torment and rancor.

Crucial revelations regarding Hell Girl's tragic history come thick and fast in the course of the first season's climactic installments. We thereby learn about an ancient custom, the "Seven Sendings," on the basis of which every seven years, a seven-year-old girl would be sacrificed to the mountains to secure "immunity from ailments and a good harvest." Ai, it slowly transpires, was once designated as one such victim. In this context, *Hell Girl* explicitly invokes the magic of *yin* and *yang* (here discussed in detail in Chapter 4), seven being the number that symbolizes the principle of *yang* and being therefore held to bring good fortune. Hajime and Tsugumi obtain some precious clues not only to Ai's past but also to their latent connection with her plight when they visit a holy edifice known as the "Temple of the Seven Children," built in the remote past to appease the "wandering spirits" of the little girls immolated to the mountain *kami*. The builder of the temple, intriguingly, had borne the name Sentarou Shibata. A connection between Hajime and Ai is thus alluded to. The meaning of the patron's given name, for its part, emerges as we discover that a boy called Sentarou was Ai's cousin and sole childhood friend in ancient times, and often bravely confronted other kids that regarded the girl's magical powers as clear indications that she was a "monster" (*mononoke*). The same sinister moniker is applied to the eponymous heroine of Hayao Miyazaki's film *Princess Mononoke* (1997) due to her intimate connection with the natural world and its *kami*: forces which the profit-oriented classes seeking to eliminate the forest to make room for mercantile ventures and foundries do not regard as objects of worship but as a mere inconveniences.

Ai's selection as an appropriate sacrificial offering was rooted in the superstitious belief that her village would benefit from her disappearance. With Sentarou's loving support, Ai managed to elude capture for six years but upon her eventual discovery in the depths of the mountains, the irate villagers did not for one moment hesitate not only to capture and bind her but also to force Sentarou to bury her alive as a means of gaining forgiveness from the angered *kami*. Ai has been silently carrying her hatred in her heart for the four centuries separating those dismal events from the present, meanwhile fulfilling her cosmic role with stoical resignation. The realization that Hajime and Tsugumi, who are supposedly Sentarou's descendants, are after her reawakens the heroine's own first for revenge to stupendous extremes. It is at this point that she first attempts to destroy them by means of brute force and then resorts to cunning in order to corrupt Tsugumi into blaming Hajime for her mother's death and consigning him to Hell. While Ai's actions are unremittingly disturbing, in chronicling the character's performance as the contract-bound enforcer of magical laws, they do not come across as gratuitously nefarious so much as amoral. There are even recurrent hints at Hell Girl's aversion to her task when various appeals reach her monitor. However, once her dormant hatred has been rekindled and her human affects have accordingly resurfaced, Ai grows into a full-fledged monster and the show's tenor leaves the level of restrained spookiness to approach the acme of undiluted terror.

It was in order to wreak vengeance on the villagers that had callously sentenced her to a sacrificial death that Ai first embarked on her career as Hell Girl. Having been allowed to rise from the dead and endowed with immortal life by the God of Hell, a character that features regularly throughout the series in the shape of an iridescent three-eyed Spider speaking in a cold male voice, Ai proceeded to burn down the entire village and destroy each and every one of her erstwhile tormentors. Her appointment as Hell Girl was the punishment she was forced to endure to atone for her own brutal actions, and it is not known whether she will ever be freed of it. In addition, Ai is fated to remain stranded in the Twilight Realm located on the shores of Hell, forbidden ever to enter the infernal domain itself. Were Ai to rebel and break the contract stipulated by the formidable Spider, her parents — whose souls the God of Hell holds as hostages — would be condemned to wander in darkness for eternity. Through these incremental revelations, it becomes evident that the contracts binding Ai and her human clients are only one facet of a contract-ruled history of cosmic immensity. When the heroine attacks Hajime and Tsugumi, the Spider decides to ferry her to Hell after all but she is too strong for even the god to restrain her and hold her captive without her consent. (Please note that the Spider's true identity as the infernal ruler is not disclosed until the closing installment of the anime's second season.)

Alongside Ai, the Spider, Hajime and Tsugumi, other recurrent characters worthy of examination are the heroine's grandmother and her three assistants. The old lady is never actually seen in *Hell Girl* as anything other than as a dim silhouette shadowed by a paper screen. She appears to be constantly engaged in operating an old-fashioned spinning wheel, which alludes to her metaphorical connection with the Spider, as well as with mythical figures held responsible for spinning the threads of people's destinies. The Wheel is also assigned an important place in Eastern philosophy as a symbol of recurrence, and is deemed by numerous mythologies all over the world to emblematize wisdom. Ai's assistants are themselves magical beings that feel deeply indebted to their employer having been personally released by her from the torments of Hell. They are also, in both dramatic and narrative terms, some of the most painstakingly portrayed personae in the anime as a whole (which is no mean feat when one takes into account the huge cast entailed by a series as protracted and as reliant on multiple narratives as *Hell Girl* indubitably is). The three characters exhibit fresh levels of complexity as the action progresses, having to negotiate their personal moral standards when Ai becomes determined to punish Hajime and Tsugumi at the end of the first anime against both reason and logic. Wanyuudou is a proficient shapeshifter, often seen in the form of an elderly man garbed in a traditional *yukata* (cotton kimono), a long-sleeved *haori* (lightweight silk jacket) and a conspicuous red scarf. This morphs into the baleful red string when Wanyuudou himself assumes the shape of a black straw doll to be handed by his employer to a client. It eventually transpires that the creature was once a royal carriage that fell off a cliff and caught fire, killing all of its passengers in the process, and thereafter became a *youkai*: a demon in the guise of a flaming wheel endowed with the face of a man.

Bearing the appearance of a handsome (and occasionally vain) young man, Ren Ichimoku contributes most vitally to Ai's mission by projecting a giant eye into even the most impervious of buildings and thus observing closely her clients and victims. Ren, who can morph into a blue straw doll, is revealed to be a *tsukumogami*, a supernatural spirit originating in an artifact — in his case, a traditional Japanese sword (*katana*) left on a rock by its vanquished owner. Endowed with the form of a charismatic woman garbed in a formal kimono when she inhabits Ai's realm but in casual and sometimes alluring modern clothing when she enters human society, Hone Onna repeatedly displays impressive skills as both a knife-thrower and a contortionist and sometimes turns into a red straw doll. Her mythological predecessor is a creature of the same name, which translates literally as "Bone Woman": Ai's assistant confirms her connection with the legendary ancestor by often exposing the bones in her body to terrify her employer's victims.

The appetite for diversity seen to characterize *Hell Girl*'s choice of contexts and character types continues unabated in *Hell Girl Second Cage*, often evincing a preference for provocative social commentary allied to psychological reflection. As in the case of the episode revolving around the doll bride and her pernicious mother-in-law from the first season, so in some of the second season's tales, the ending suggests that Ai's fulfillment of her petitioners' desire for revenge does not automatically grant them any solace even in this world. This is borne out by the story of the schoolgirl that successfully gets rid of a bullying tutor courtesy of Hell Girl, only to discover that a classmate pretending to be her friend has also been secretly persecuting her. In another installment, a man who has agreed to commit a murder in cold blood and subsequently obtained Ai's support to eliminate his enemy in order to gain money for the sake of his ailing wife is eventually rewarded, through a cruel twist of dramatic irony, with his beloved spouse's amnesia and attendant inability to even recognize his face. An especially intriguing tale from the second season is the one centered on the restless soul of a victim of abduction, rape and murder that seeks to access Ai's site via her sister's spirit (and computer). The episode is most remarkable as an inspired variation not only on the revenge theme assiduously dramatized throughout Ohmori's anime but also on the possession topos so central to Japanese mythology and Shinto's shamanic magic.

The show's flair for original plotting is also confirmed by the story based on the creation and circulation of a fake Hotline to Hell within a school, with shifting attributions of responsibility for the deed serving to complicate the affair at each turn of the action. It is in the handling of familial affairs that the second season offers some of the most remarkable examples of scriptwriter Kenichi Kanemaki's unique sensitivity to the subtlest psychological nuances. This is borne out, for instance, by the installment in which a girl afflicted by her mother's total lack of concern for her well-being in the aftermath of her brother's tragic death eventually resolves to send the woman to Hell in order to free both herself and the desperate parent from their joint plight. Also notable is the tale centered on a young man harboring an obsessive love for his sister that repeatedly induces him to dress up as a girl and steal her boyfriends from her, thereby finally incurring her revenge through Ai's service. More or less direct references to political corruption, corporate greed and a plethora of foolish crimes resulting from widespread anomie consistently enrich the anime's topical framework.

The second season introduces another important character, that of the mysterious girl from Hell named Kikuri who is able to migrate at will between the mortal domain and Ai's Twilight Realm. Childlike, yet prone to maliciously destructive acts such as cutting off Ai's precious *higanbana* out of sheer spite, Kikuri displays astonishing magical powers unsettlingly incongruous with her size and demeanor. Occasionally, she appears to derive perverse satisfaction from interfering with Ai's companions' tasks and even to indulge in mindlessly mischievous ruses such as dragging a human to the Twilight Realm just for fun. Keen on damaging anything Ai holds dear, Kikuri nonetheless respects her senior's authority and only seems prepared to take orders from her. However, Kikuri is not truly acting of her own free will since her body, we discover, is possessed by the God of Hell unbeknownst to the girl herself.

At a later point in the sequel, the anime focuses on the character of Takuma Kurebayashi, a quiet boy putatively hosting magic abilities that is blamed for causing the chain of inexplicable disappearances plaguing the ironically named conurbation of "Lovely Hills." These, in fact, are caused by the townsfolk's reckless use of Hotline to Hell. In *Second Cage*, Ai comes across as a more emotional, communicative and essentially human creature than she ever did in the original series, which often results in her freer interaction with both victims and clients. At times, Ai's newly rediscovered humanity is conveyed in a light-hearted, semi-humorous manner — for instance, in the episode where she can be seen perusing a fashion magazine while her companions observe their client. At others, it is attested to by the concern she exhibits toward hapless humans such as the mother who takes her own life to spare her daughter the dire consequences she would face if she were to send her to Hell, and toward Takuma, whose ruthless persecution smartingly reminds her of her own wrongful treatment in the ancient past.

Following a series of tragic events threatening to tear his family apart, Takuma is suspected of having murdered his mother and seriously injured his father. Although lack of conclusive evidence has prevented his apprehension, he is still branded by most of the townspeople as the "devil's child." The detective in charge with investigating the multiple disappearances — and Takuma's possible part in them — begins to unravel the case when he comes across a book about Hell Girl written by Hajime. (At this point, we also discover that following the events chronicled in the first season's climax, the reporter resolved to pen Ai's biography and then vanished without a trace having grown tired of trying to stop people from being sent to Hell.) Having ascertained that Takuma's body does not bear the Seal of the Covenant, and being therefore convinced that the boy is innocent, the detective is brutally attacked by one of Takuma's neighbors, who has made use of Ai's service and does not wish to see the truth regarding Hotline to Hell publicly exposed. Ai gradually becomes so intimately involved in Takuma's predicament as to defy the God of Hell and the terms imposed by his magic contract. Hence, she agrees to take the boy back to the human world just as he is being ferried to Hell due to his sister's appeal, resumes her original human identity, and ultimately sacrifices herself to rescue Takuma from his foes.

The Buddhist notion of recurrence, as argued, plays a vital role in *Hell Girl* as a structural mainstay. The related concept of reincarnation, no less axial to both Buddhist philosophy and magical principles inspired by its lessons, is firmly enthroned as the third season's underpinning. *Cauldron of the Three* takes place in the aftermath of Ai's death and dissolution into an ethereal trail of *sakura* petals. The series dramatizes Kikuri's reappearance to announce Ai's return and recruit Hell Girl's former assistants, who have been leading human lives in the absence of their employer in what they regard as their own version of Hell. Alongside the original trio, Ai now also benefits from the services of the formidable *youkai* Yamawaro, a creature based on a mythical mountain-dwelling specter with a magical proclivity to morph into a moving heap of mushrooms. Ai's revival coincides with her possession of the body of a seemingly ordinary human schoolgirl named Yuzuki Mikage, who actually turns out to have perished in childhood in the sole company of a large teddy bear following her mother's demise but somehow managed to linger in the human world. Although Yuzuki is appointed as Ai's successor in the capacity of Hell Girl and is meant to retain this position indefinitely, Ai eventually resumes her original role to spare Yuzuki from damnation when the Spider consigns her to Hell as punishment for allowing her personal feelings to interfere with her supernatural duties. With her innocent voice and bright blue eyes, Yuzuki at first infuses a breath of fresh air into the anime's generally sombre and sometimes oppressive atmosphere. In a way, she brings to mind a younger version of Ai, seemingly less disillusioned and innerly scarred than the original Hell Girl. However, as the exact nature of Yuzuki's connection with Ai is incrementally exposed, alongside her desire to cease to function as Ai's passive vessel and the pain she experiences whenever she sees what Ai sees, the dark mood that characterized the first and second seasons reasserts itself once more as the third anime's dominant trait.

Cauldron of the Three incurs a drawback which has arguably less to do with its intrinsic aesthetic and dramatic quality than with its standing as the third building block in a cumulatively sizeable anime edifice (amounting to seventy-eight episodes to date): it occasionally conveys the impression that its narrative ramifications are becoming somewhat predictable and that its action's rhythm, relatedly, is marginally stagnating. What prevents this potential blemish from escalating into a major fault is the third season's ability to capitalize once more on the principle of diversity. In this specific instance, this is signalled by a significant departure from the previous series in the representation of the nature of the various revenges on which the plot revolves. The first two seasons deliberately refrained from drawing a neat line between good and evil, yet the majority of Ai's petitioners invited an element of sympathy as victims that deserved support or advice. This moral stance evaporates in the third series, where most of Hotline to Hell's clients come across as utterly imprudent and deluded failures seeking revenge on people that do not even seem to have done anything particularly wrong. The effect of this ruse is twofold. On the one hand, it causes some of the contracts to look quite pointless, if not downright ludicrous. On the other hand, it offers plenty of scope for an unsentimental exposure of the abusive structures of power endemic to *Hell Girl*'s society — and, by implication, its real-life correlatives all over the globe. Indeed, it is often to protect the nefarious interests of corrupt politicians and law-enforcers that some grotesquely unmotivated revenge schemes are concocted and carried out. Moreover, the third season ushers in a feel-good factor despite its entanglement with dismal subject matter by portraying all of its recurrent characters as appealing and ultimately likeable regardless of their often dubious ethics. The overwhelming beauty of the visuals, allied to heightened animation standards and subtle mood shifts, also contributes significantly to the show's overall success.

The principle of multiplicity, as indicated, constitutes one of the most salient traits of *Hell Girl*'s treatment of magic contracts — not only because each successive adventure pivots on a distinct contract binding a client to Ai but also because the various agreements thereby established are interwoven with the heroine's own contractual obligations to the God of Hell. Multiple magic contracts are also dramatized in the TV series *Fate/stay Night* (dir. Yuji Yamaguchi, 2006), where seven powerful magicians known as "Masters" periodically engage in epic wars with the objective of attaining the "Holy Grail," a legendary relic held capable of fulfilling any imaginable desire, with the assistance of reincarnations of mythical spirits named "Servants" and their magical weapons, the "Noble Phantasms." Masters and Servants are contractually bound to one another, as Masters are able to control Servants by means of "Command Seals" imprinted on their bodies in the guise of stigmata by the will of the Holy Grail itself, while Servants alone are ultimately entitled to touch the prize in virtue of their intrinsically spiritual constitution. The rules governing the contracts are very strict and stipulate that whenever a Master issues an order that contradicts the Servant's personal preferences, he or she must relinquish one of the Command Seals. Were all of the Seals to be lost, a Servant would be free to break the contract and even turn against the Master. Alternately, were a Master to die, the Servant would be at liberty to enter a fresh contract.

Multiplicity is also crucial to Hayao Miyazaki's handling of the topos of magic contracts in his movie *Howl's Moving Castle* (2004). Two main contracts are here at stake. One of these involves the heroine, Sophie, a young girl transformed into a withered old woman by the Witch of the Waste and cursed to be powerless to tell anybody about it, and the fire demon Calcifer, who is bound to the titular castle's hearth with no inkling to the cause of his entrapment. The other contract involves Calcifer himself and the wizard Howl, and strikes its roots in the latter's surrender of his heart by magical means in order to save the dying star whence the fire demon has originated. The contract binding Sophie and Calcifer decrees that each will endeavor to ascertain the reason for the other's plight and bring it to an end. As for the Faustian pact in which Howl and Calcifer are locked, it is ultimately up to Sophie to unveil its source, thereby releasing the demon from his prison and the wizard himself from the malefic sorcery to which the loss of his heart has enslaved him. Another effervescently staged double contract, in this case rife with supernatural manifestations, possessions and shamanistic rituals, courses through the TV series *Moribito — Guardian of the Spirit* (dir. Kenji Kamiyama, 2007). This anime revolves around the spearwoman Balsa, a roving warrior committed to the task of saving lives to atone for a past sin. The contract here entailed binds Balsa to the supernatural forces held capable of granting her absolution. At the same time, the valiant fighter is bound to a prince whose life she has saved and whom she has been thereafter enjoined to protect in the capacity of a bodyguard. All manner of complications ensue as it is revealed that the emperor, the prince's father, wants him dead.

One of the most onerous magic contracts ever dramatized in anime form lies at the core of the two-season series *Tsubasa: RESERVoir CHRoNiCLE* (dir. Koichi Mashimo, 2005–2006). This is triggered by the sinister spell causing the soul of Princess Sakura of Clow, a girl endowed with latent supernatural powers, to shatter and her memories to disperse across multiple worlds in the guise of delicate feathers. These fragments also host magical powers, which may be deployed to benevolent or malign effects depending on the motives of the individuals that fall in their possession. Since, deprived of her soul and memories, Sakura is doomed to die, her childhood friend Syaoran bravely resolves to retrieve as many of the scattered feathers as humanly feasible by entering with Sakura the alternate dimensions into which they have accidentally drifted. To do so, he has no choice but to strike a bargain with the "Dimensional Witch" Yuuko, who has the means of enabling both him and his protégée to world-hop an indefinite number of times. However, Syaoran must also accept that in exchange for this portentous ability, he has to surrender to Yuuko the thing he holds dearest — since, the sorceress claims, cosmic equilibrium can only be maintained if any one gain is counterbalanced by a loss of analogous magnitude. Therefore, the boy may only help Sakura if he agrees to give up the special place he occupies in her heart, and resign himself to the fact that she will never be capable of remembering — regardless of how many feathers might be recaptured — either his identity or the depth of her and Syaoran's mutual love. The kaleidoscopic adventures that unfold on the basis of this premise never allow us to forget or ignore the sheer sense of pain inherent in Yuuko's irrevocable conditions. (Please note that *Tsubasa* shares the character of the Dimensional Witch with the anime *xxxHolic*, here explored in depth in Chapter 5.) [1]

Darker than Black (TV series; dir. Tensai Okamura, 2007) proceeds from the premise that ten years prior to the beginning of the story chronicled in the anime, an inexplicable and catastrophic concatenation of energies caused the emergence of an abnormal field within the Tokyo area, dubbed "Hell's Gate," that has inflicted severe damage to both the earthly environment and the sky. Most spectacularly, in this regard, the stars vanished to be replaced by fake simulacra of the original galaxies. The centrality of the topos of the contract to Okamura's series is pithily borne out by the denomination used for its principal actors: namely, individuals equipped with unusual abilities (such as "gravitational powers" and "teleportation via matter substitution"). Emotionless, unscrupulous, and glacially logical, "Contractors" are routinely appointed as assassins, thieves and spies by a plethora of both officially recognized and secret organizations vying with one another for the possession of top-secret data. Each Contractor corresponds to one of the artificial stars in Tokyo's overhanging sky and is accordingly identified by that celestial body's number in the *Messier Catalog.* (This text, compiled by the French astronomer Charles Messier [1730–1817], designates all the galaxies, nebulae and star clusters by means of code numbers.) The stars typically pulsate when the Contractors with whom they are connected are in the process of deploying their special powers and disappear altogether when the Contractors die. "The reason Contractors are so named," Okamura's elegantly refined script informs us, "is that they're psychotically compelled to complete a certain act, their obeisance, after using their powers, as though cursed to do so." Although the actions compulsively performed by Contractors as obeisance are taxing to their sensorium (either physically or psychologically), the creatures' maintenance of affective equilibrium depends vitally on their completion for they regard them as the only rightful form of payment or remuneration they could conceivably expect to receive when carrying out a mission.

On the basis of this somewhat cursory description, Contractors might not strike the reader as hugely original anime presences. After all, the medium abounds with merciless killers and this is attested to by shows of both science fictional and epic-historical orientation. Nevertheless, there is something quite unique, even rare, about Contractors that singles them out as notable specimens — something disarmingly simple and effective by virtue of its very simplicity: they do not aim to annihilate either humanity or the Earth, as comparable anime villains are lamentably wont to do, but are just committed to carrying out their tasks to the best of their abilities. This makes the contractual bonds tying individuals to their jobs, while negotiating both their private intuitions and pressures from their bosses and their foes alike, a central preoccupation of the series as a whole. Such a concern lends *Darker than Black* a gritty realism and down-to-earthness one would not readily associate with post-apocalyptic or otherwise dystopian yarns. Furthermore, the coldly calculating rationality with which Contractors handle their assignments, deploying their particular powers flexibly in accordance with contingent strategic priorities rather than purely in the service of raw instinct, contributes significantly to the show's standing as an intellectually stimulating anime across its multiple arcs. Like other arc-based series here explored (e.g., *Ghost Hunt, Hell Girl, Natsume Yuujinchou*), *Darker than Black* inevitably evinces a certain degree of fluctuation where entertainment value is concerned. Yet, one senses throughout a steady commitment on Okamura's part to the portrayal of a multilayered world pullulating with hidden agendas and opportunities for unexpected dramatic convolutions. As a result, the show delivers a chain of tightly packed stories pervaded by a healthy appetite for the methodical disclosure of many interwoven riddles.

At first sight, *Darker than Black*'s imagery might seem dominated by fundamentally technological imperatives and its contracts, accordingly, to have precious little in common with the realm of witches and wizards, shamans and soothsayers. However, is soon transpires that the show's repertoire is veritably saturated — at both the lexical and the visual levels — with magical concepts and metaphors. These include possessions, hauntings, enchantments, spells, charms, body swaps, curses, mediums, spirit observers and specters. In addition, both the cat and the crow, animals replete with magical connotations all over the globe, feature at important junctures in the action. Dolls have again a part to play in this anime but in this instance, they do not represent basically inert, though magic-imbued, effigies as they did in *Ghost Hunt* and *Hell Girl.* In fact, Okamura's "Dolls" are emotionless mediums created to imitate the human form. These entities serve a variety of purposes, often operating as observer spirits through particular channels — such as a natural element. The magic of animation as a medium is also consistently thrown into relief, primarily by means of impeccably timed transitions from hyperkinetic and even horrific action sequences to moments of suburban tranquility and meditative stillness. The sequence in which the protagonist uses his powers to bring to life a deserted fair ground at nighttime succinctly epitomizes the magical potential held by the art of animation to instill vibrant dynamism into the most inert — or indeed nonexistent — of forms. *Darker than Black* thus confirms the proposition, advocated in Chapter 1, that magic is intimately related to technology and, concomitantly, that animation itself communicates the collusion of magic and technology with arguably unmatched poignance. As anticipated, this topic will be revisited at some length in Chapter 3, insofar as it acquires special prominence in the anime discussed therein.

The protagonist, ostensibly an affable and unassuming exchange student from China named Li Shengshun, is the ruthless Contractor Hei (a.k.a. "The Black Reaper") — a member of his species apparently exempt from the burden of obeisance that is capable of generating and bending formidable amounts of electricity. While Li/Hei might seem totally callous when it comes to carrying a contract through to fruition without ever pausing to reflect on its moral implications, he is gradually revealed to harbor very human emotions, including compassion and grief. The protagonist's human dimension is most potently thrown into relief by the scenes in which he struggles to obtain information about the whereabouts of his lost sister Pai. On a more mundane level, Li comes across as palpably human as a result of his gargantuan appetite.

The show's pivotal Contractor is not alone in demonstrating his breed's possession of genuine — indeed intense — affects. The Contractor known as Alma likewise comes across as a deeply emotional creature in her desperate struggle to establish her private religion with the intention of providing a symbolic sanctuary for her despised colleagues. Alma is also the first character to elucidate what the Contractors really are and to spell out how they differ from regular human beings. Shihoko Kishida also evinces a rich emotional substratum: her contract, which allows her to shatter an individual's internal organs quite effortlessly, entails that whenever she deploys her powers, she is also bound to regain temporarily a human sensibility. Especially touching is the scene in which Shihoko notes that her recollections of moments spent with Huang (i.e., the protagonist's field supervisor) enable her to experience a rare feeling of warmth.

Organizations of variable size, caliber and level of nefariousness are axial to the show's diegesis, often exceeding in terms of dramatic significance the value of the individuals which they employ or oppose. The protagonist (alongside the characters of Huang, Yin and Mao) works for an organization known as the "Syndicate," which is initially presented as just one of many mysterious groupings with no obvious goals but gradually turns out to be a cover for a global organization mendaciously claiming to aim to stabilize the Earth, eliminate Hell's Gate and engineer the genocidal massacre of the Contractors. The Syndicate, most crucially, controls "Pandora," a scientific base established by the UN for the purpose of researching the reasons for the appearance of Hell's Gate in Tokyo. Due to the Syndicate's despotic power over the organization, Pandora frequently seems to operate as a façade for unpalatable secrets rather than a true force of scientific enlightenment. Another notable body is the Tokyo Metropolitan Police Department, and particularly the Public Security Bureau of Foreign Affairs, Section 4, employing the indomitable Misaki Kirihara as its Chief and committed to the investigation of all manner of cases involving Contractors. In its activities, the Bureau consistently relies on the assistance of the National Astronomical Observatory of Japan, which monitors the motions of the fake stars corresponding to living Contractors and can thus supply information (or at least clues) regarding a particular Contractor's location and level of martial engagement. Some real-world organizations also come into play, most notably the CIA, the British Secret Intelligence Service (MI6) and the Federal Security Service of the Russian Federation (FSB). "Evening Primrose," headed by the Contractor Amber, is an establishment seeking to reveal the existence of Contractors to the public, expose their personal ordeals, and thus promote equal rights for their race.

At first, nothing appears to stand between Contractors and their appointed goals. "We never questioned why we spied, why we killed," the Contractor Amber remarks in the anime's climactic installment. "We just followed our orders, never wondering why." Little by little, however, things "started to change. No single one of us began it. The process was slow and steady. Before we knew it, we were fighting for the same cause and gathering a great deal of information." The "cause" referred to by Amber consists, unsurprisingly, of opposing the Syndicate's genocidal plans. Ultimately, it is up to the protagonist, who is revealed to have always been "human" despite his apparently unquestioning acceptance of his dire contractual obligations, to decide "which side to support" in the final confrontation between humans and Contractors. One of the several attributes of the contracts dramatized in *Darker than Black* that renders them particularly intriguing is their positioning within a time span so protracted as to be potentially limitless. The contracts themselves, as a result, acquire the aura of magical pacts capable of defying the strictures of temporality itself. "The contracts we've made," Amber declares, "are naught but the beginning, the start of events that may only conclude one hundred, one thousand, or even one hundred thousand years from now."

Darker than Black repeatedly exposes the ambivalent character of the notions of darkness and blackness as metaphors for evil — a figurative proclivity endemic in many cultures — by suggesting that the forces of light are not, by definition, benevolent. For example, the aforementioned Pandora organization associated with ongoing research into the mysteries of Hell's Gate could be expected to be coterminous with an enlightening agency committed to the revelation of the truth and hence capable of advancing an honest cause but its imbrication with the sinister Syndicate shows that it is actually embroiled in a web of secretiveness and obfuscation. Darkness has time and again been associated with the baser instincts, primordial chaos, fear, sorrow and the absurd, as the condition suffered by a puny humanity in the face of a meaningless cosmos. Christianity has damned it by portraying the Devil, the Prince of Darkness, as the enemy of God's Logos. In Hindu mythology, darkness emblematizes Time the Destroyer; in Iranian mythology, it is the power embodied by Ahriman, Lord of Lies; in Islam, it symbolizes indiscretion.

Yet, light is not universally perceived as coterminous with goodness. After all, many popular ghosts are made fearful by their very luminescence, paleness, transparence or pearly-white translucence. The "Jack-o'-lantern" (a.k.a. "will-o'-the-whisp," "fairy light," "demon fire," or "fox fire") is a potentially beautiful light but is also associated with witches, vengeful souls and ill omens. Light is also the hallmark of bewitching mirages such as the ones summoned by the mermaid-like Breton "Morganes" and the Italian "Fate Morgane," all descendants of the inauspicious apparitions contrived by the Arthurian figure of Morgan le Fay. Study of folklore have even indicated that the most intimidating of all imaginable chromatic effects is, as Marina Warner points out, the "absence of colour: the whiteness of negation, found in night-flyers such as barn owls and certain moths.... The owl that hunts and screeches, gleaming ghostly in the shadows ... has a paralyzing effect on its prey" (Warner 2000, pp. 180–181). Moreover, the association of darkness with the inchoate does not automatically render it malevolent, for the state of seemingly amorphous undifferentiation is the precondition of form and of the light that grows out of it: germination takes place in the dark earth, while embryos develop in the darkness of the womb. Finally, it must also be taken into account that darkness has been often connected with rites of passage and notions of spiritual initiation, as evinced by the trope of the "Dark Night of the Soul" advocated by St. John of the Cross. Defamatory evaluations of darkness have traditionally gone hand in hand with a tendency to conceive of it as black in accordance with colonial and patriarchal prejudices intent on demonizing it as the province of the feral and the impenetrably hostile. Like all myths, those discriminatory positions are context-bound and hence open to interrogation. For instance, while in the West it has been common, as Warner notes, to "scare the young into obedience" by recourse to people such as "Gypsies, Jews, Turks, blacks" (p. 161)—as borne out by the Italian appellation of the bogeyman as "l'Omo nero" (literally, the black man)—a "lullaby from the plantations of Gran Canaria" describes the monster keen on devouring children as "the white devil" (pp. 162–163). It is salutary to remember, therefore, that images of whiteness are no more unequivocally propitious than figures of light are.

Darker than Black foregrounds the philosophical preoccupations outlined above by intimating that the forces of light do not automatically militate in favor of probity and peace. This is eloquently corroborated by the arc revolving around Kouzou Tahara, a Japanese researcher previously employed by a nefarious organization dubbed Meyer and Hilton that "used Contractors as experimental weapons for the U.K. during the war with Argentina.... They inbred Contractors, hoping to mass-produce them, attempted to mix different powers though hybridization and eugenics, and even experimented with forcibly entering normal people into contracts via brain surgery." Dr. Tahara was the sole survivor of the first catastrophic expedition into Hell's Gate, in the course of which he was able to retrieve a plant whose seeds, he surmised at the time, could prevent a Contractor's powers from awakening when implanted into his or her body. Upon discovering that his own daughter, Mai Kashiwagi, harbored latent Contractor powers, the scientist resolved to use the girl as a "guinea pig": he thus placed a seed into Mai's wrist, meant to prevent her from developing full-fledged Contractor abilities, that bore the semblance of a tiny star and Mai would thereafter poetically allude to as a "magic charm." Regrettably, the scientist's efforts prove futile and Mai eventually degenerates not even into one of the standard Contractors but into one of the worst imaginable "brain-dead monstrosities" to be found within their ranks: a "Moratorium." This term designates a Contractor "temporarily relieved" of the need to perform the act of obeisance. "Unlike the standard Contractors," moreover "Moratoria cannot control their powers." In Mai's case, this leads to a chain of bloodcurdling acts, including her annihilation by fire of one of her school friends and her dad. Although Dr. Tahara endeavored to discover a means of preventing the eruption of violence and crime, his experiments ultimately led to the very opposite outcome and inadvertently facilitated the surfacing of dark forces even more abominable than those he sought to eradicate. The light of science, in this instance, is paradoxically shown to usher in the most tenebrous of evils.

Another apposite example is provided by the arc focusing on the "Regressor" Havoc, a Contractor once renowned for her unparalleled ruthless that has lost both her powers and her memories. Defective as Havoc's faculties might be, she is nonetheless well aware of the dangers of enlightenment. Specifically, she knows that although proximity with Hell's Gate could restore her memory and hence reveal important but suppressed truths about the past, it is also most likely to reactivate her lethal skills and turn her again into a cold-blooded mass-murderer. Thus, the forces of light (as revelation, disclosure, illumination) are ultimately bound to unleash the most unspeakable horrors. The theme of memory, incidentally, is pivotal to the anime's entire narrative and not merely to the Havoc-centered arc, since "the nations of the world" methodically deploy "ME, a new technology developed through Gate research, to erase the memories of those who come into contact" with Contractors and associated superhuman forces.

In one of its arcs, the anime also adopts a semi-humorous approach to the theme of darkness through ironical distortion of the codes and conventions of film noir, exploiting many of the standard settings, set pieces and character typologies associated with hard-boiled detective fiction (including the smoky office, privacy-guarding roller blinds, creepy maid and ravishing widow). The segment's protagonist, the private investigator Gai (Guy) Kurasawa even poses as a Marlowe-like disenchanted loner — even though he vitally depends on the support of the sassy child assistant Kiko, especially as he is cowardly, unpractical and blighted by an especially acute case of ailurophobia. Dark irony is also used, with graver overtones, in the arc focusing on Chiaki Shinoda, a former Pandora researcher who knows some of the organization's least savory secrets. Chiaki feels "a sort of connection" with Contractors insofar as she saw her parents being assassinated by a creature of that ilk when she was still in school and never managed to repress that memory. Her story is rendered especially touching by Okamura's use of irony, as Chiaki's fascination with Contractors turns, unbeknownst to her, into a sort of literal identification with them. This occurs as her memories are implanted into a Doll and the creature is then utilized to lure Li out by his opponents while he seeks to obtain a package containing top-secret information which Chiaki is supposed to be holding.

These unsentimental exposures of light's ineluctable complicity with darkness echoes Dennis Lester McKiernan's proposition that "It is always dark. Light only hides the darkness" (McKiernan, p. 548). Light, within the world view promulgated by *Darker than Black*, is no unequivocal savior. On this point, the anime brings to mind Ramsey Campbell's reflections on the relationship between shapes rendered spooky by darkness and their equivalents in daylight: "Some of it may look like a big city at night, but is it only litter we see scuttling away from the streetlamps? Why is that bin liner grinning as it swoops towards us on the wind? You might hope daylight would drive such presences away, but here light only makes the shadows darker and shows us things that would have done better to stay in the dark" (Campbell, R.).

Chapter 3

Magic Missions

I sometimes think that people's hearts are like deep wells. Nobody knows what's at the bottom. All you can do is imagine by what comes floating to the surface every once in a while. — Haruki Murakami

'Tis enough to say that in all ages and religions the greatest part of mankind have believed the power of magic, and that there are spirits or spectres which have appeared. This, I say, is foundation enough for poetry. — John Dryden

The fusion of performative and psychological factors effected by magic contracts crosses over into the domain of magic missions as the contractually bound parties embark on quests of variable magnitude and complexity in order to fulfill their obligations. The high level of diversity demonstrated by the anime in the handling of magic contracts can again be observed in the treatment of magic missions. In *Mai-HiME* and its alternate-world semi-sequel *Mai-Otome*, the tasks undertaken by a heterogeneous crew of school-girls and young women endowed with supernatural powers form the crux of the shows' narrative edifice, and assiduously impart the performance-oriented dimension with ebullient dynamism. At the same time, however, psycholog-ical states and conflicts are brought to the fore by the two anime's sensitive exploration of their protagonists' inner struggles to come to terms with their abilities and figure out their place in a scheme of veritably cosmic propor-tions while also attempting to function as regular people. *Ghost Hound*, in dramatizing three junior-high-school boys' quests to mediate between the parallel realities of the apparent and the unseen worlds, offers quite a differ-ent perspective on the topos of the magic mission. Yet, it also operates on both the performative and the psychological planes simultaneously by inti-mating that the protagonists' exploits do not only constitute pretexts for the dramatization of spectacular kinetic phenomena but also inward voyages of self-discovery haunted by a traumatic childhood legacy. In *Sola*, the male lead's efforts to unlock the mysteries surrounding a strange girl with magical affiliations provides the core of a momentous mission comparable to the one embraced by *Ghost Hound*'s protagonists. However, the anime proclaims its distinctiveness in the interweaving of this action-driven strand with an affective component focusing on the principal character's quest as a passionate attempt at artistic self-expression through the medium of photography. A radically different type of mission is dramatized in *Magikano*, whose protagonist is unwittingly burdened with preternatural duties of intergalactic enormity as an offshoot of complications that at first come across as trivial or even semi-farcical. In *Kagihime*, the pivotal mission unfolds amid a dreamlike interplay of the ordinary world inhabited by its protagonist and his little sister, on the one hand, and the fantastic domain issuing from a cryptically reconfigured version of Lewis Carroll's *Alice* stories, on the other hand. The anime series *Natsume Yuujinchou* and its sequel *Zoku Natsume Yuujinchou* similarly interweave the everyday and the supernatural on the basis of a text imbued with esoteric significance.

The role of the imagination as a concomitantly personal and collective power is comprehensively addressed by this cluster of anime. Most crucially, the shows under examination emphasize that magic is not so much concerned with the mental act of seeing as with the speculative process of visualizing: of seeing, as it were, through the mind's eye. The images it thus creates do not appear to occupy corporeally perceived space but rather to be suspended in a spatial limbo of their own. Magic, in other words, possesses a figurative space sui generis. As Ludwig Wittgenstein phrases it, "What is imagined is not in the same space as what is seen" (Wittgenstein, sec. 622). This realization invites us to ponder the specifically spatial attributes of imaginary magical situations. In the anime here studied, magic missions typically unfold in places that posit the world at large as a matter of partial, relative and localized geographies, largely based on instinctual, intuitive and unconscious experiences. To this extent, the anime could be read as an implicit attack against the heavy baggage of prejudices, hampering much traditional geography, predicated on the existence of a singular correct perception and representation of space. As David Lowenthal maintains, although people's spatial abilities vary enormously, "the most fundamental attributes of our shared view of the world" tend to be "confined ... to sane, hale, sentient adults" (Lowenthal, p. 244). Idiots, psychotics and children are excluded from the spatial consensus which shapes dominant conceptions of space. "Geography," argues Steve Pile, "has left behind its more primitive, childlike, feminized world-views" (Pile, p. 12). Magical space metaphorically rehabilitates these marginalized perspectives by intimating that though personal geographies are supposed to lack the objectivity of publicly shared configurations of space, this does not obliterate their power. If anything, the partiality and contingency of private geographies serve to remind us that even the most rigorously rationalized world is traversed by dreams and fantasies, both conscious and unconscious.

Magic-centered anime that aim to maximize the theatrical aspect of the action frequently play with the idea that magic has the power not only to visualize objects but also to bring them literally, tangibly and even sensationally into being within the ordinary empirical domain. Shows characterized by more symbolic or reflective proclivities, conversely, do not dwell on the overt materialization of imagined objects within the here-and-now with quite the same degree of prominence. In fact, they prioritize the ideation of parallel spaces of their own over conjuring tricks and prestidigitatory flourishes. In ideal dramatic circumstances, a subtle balance between exuberant stage magic and philosophical reflection is achieved, thereby regaling the eye with both tantalizing spectacle and meditative poise. No less importantly, the process of creative visualization fostered by magic — alongside the pictures thereby summoned — boldly quizzes the authority of the actual in order to migrate imaginatively into a prismatic universe of virtually inexhaustible modality. As a means of classifying disparate hypotheses on the basis of whether they profess to be necessary, possible or impossible, modality may generally aspire at definitive categorization. Magic frustrates this domesticating ambition by conjuring up worlds in which one and the same proposition may be deemed necessary, possible or impossible at the same time, thus releasing a whole galaxy of alternative and potentially coexistent scenarios.

The collusion of magic and the mission topos engenders multifaceted opportunities for a metaphorical interrogation of the boundaries which virtually all human cultures erect in order to promulgate their official versions of the real and, by extension, the truth. The arbitrariness of those demarcators is thus assiduously exposed, and the ideological strategies deployed to police them are accordingly mocked. It is only when a society feels vulnerable, it is suggested, that it needs to proclaim its inviolability and impregnability in the most sonorous of voices. Therefore, magic missions give figurative expression to cultural vicissitudes of global and topical resonance.

The TV series *Mai-HiME* (2004–2005) and *Mai-Otome* (2005–2006), both of which were directed by Masakazu Obara, are two of the most popular anime series of this century. Having rapidly acquired a substantial fan base on domestic soil, both have then proceeded to establish themselves as favorite instances of magic-adventure anime in the West. *Mai-HiME* offers a paradigmatic illustration of the vicissitudes undergone by the character type of the ostensibly ordinary but actually superpowered adolescent enjoined by fate to embark on a mission of cosmic proportions. The topos is so frequent in anime as to frustrate any logical attempt to itemize even only the most renowned titles. In this instance, the teenager in question is first-year high-school student Mai Tokiha. Traveling in the company of her sickly younger brother Takumi to their new school, the prestigious Fuka Academy, Mai is caught in the midst of a grim battle deploying equal measures of magic and *mecha* power. It is at this critical juncture that the girl discovers her hidden abilities and possession of a magical nature she cannot either suppress or evade — that of a "HiME" (short for "Highly-advanced Materializing Equipment"). It is precisely because she is a creature of this ilk that Mai has been admitted to Fuka Academy, whose mistress is busy assembling HiMEs to combat the "Orphans," preternatural monsters that have recently begun to infiltrate the Earth.

While *Mai-HiME* may not stand out as a hugely innovative piece of anime, it does deserve praise as a title distinguished by an exceptionally well-paced and balanced diegesis. Most commendable, in this respect, is the elegant rhythm with which the series alternates between introducing and then developing its actors and settings, interspersing the moments of serious reflection with mild comedy and a sprinkling of fan service, and doling out generous portions of high-octane action sequences able to combine fluid transitions and flashy acrobatics, without ever pushing any of these components to extremes. Where action sequences are concerned, the anime's magic emanates principally from the so-called "Children," the *mecha* cast in the roles of guardians or familiars tied to the HiMEs that are capable of summoning them. These take a spellbinding variety of shapes, including that of a towering dragon, a wolf-like automaton with side-mounted guns and a sentient sword. The Children are unquestionably mechanical, and their manufactured status is highlighted in variable degrees by their specific designs, but this does not impair the essentially magical quality of the capacities that the HiMEs bring to bear on the creatures' materialization and activation.

On a more mundane level, the show gains memorable individuality from its portrayal of the central character, who is very possibly one of the most amiable and endearing anime heroines of recent decades. A deliberate restraint from exaggeration in the depiction of Mai's facial features, allied to a touching blend of maternal instincts and budding eroticism in the character's psychological delineation, makes her far more convincing than many other heroines cast in similar roles. At the same time, the adventure is nourished by an intrepidly variegated ensemble of supporting characters. These include, for example, the feral kid Mikoto Minagi, the apparently supercilious but deeply sensitive Natsuki Kuga, the frank, loyal and sometimes absurdly coura-geous Yuuichi Tate, the pathologically possessive Shiho Munakata, the princely but power-hungry Reito Kanzaki, the robotically glacial Miyu Greer and the angelic yet paradoxically ominous Alyssa Searrs.

While the Orphan breed might at first seem to constitute the HiMEs' sole opponent, it gradually transpires that no less formidable an enemy lies with the "Searrs Foundation," an ancient organization that has been promoting its nefarious schemes from the shadows for time immemorial and seeks to appropriate the HiMEs' powers with the aid of cutting-edge technology. Miyu and Alyssa turn out to be synthetic beings created by the shady corporation to advance their ends, which at least partly explains their forbiddingly inhuman aura. No less formidable an enemy is the character of the "Obsidian Prince," a figure whose authentic significance does not become fully clear until late in the series, that is also eager to exploit the powers of the HiMEs to recreate the world according to his personal desires and possesses Reito's body to achieve this aim. These complications (periodically compounded with romantic entanglements and excursions into several actors' buried pasts) engender plenty of scope for quasi-magical sleights of hand in the orchestration of the narrative and in the gradual disclosure of its secrets. It is in the show's finale that *Mai-HiME*'s anime magic comes most gloriously to the fore, offering a magnificent battle royale in which all of the HiMEs engage in unison. Even more remarkable than the martial sequences themselves, however, is the daring reversal of outcomes whereby the various characters are given a second chance and hence the opportunity to resume a normal life regardless of the destinies they have met in the first dénouement. This reparative re-set no doubt carries a warming feel-good factor, yet it does not ask us to forget the complexity of the foregoing drama and the depth of both the personal traumas and political evils explored therein. Thus, *Mai-HiME*'s cinematic magic could be said to reside, in the final analysis, with its ability to indulge in a fairy-tale resolution but nonetheless preserve the gravity of the magic missions at its core.

It will be immediately clear to viewers approaching *Mai-Otome* on the basis of previous familiarity with *Mai-HiME* that one of the later anime's greatest strengths lies with its flair for metamorphic magic in the handling of the characters instrumental to the advancement of its distinctive magic missions. Indeed, most of those personae are overtly redolent of members of *Mai-HiME*'s original cast in their physical appearance or even their names, yet tend to evince novel personalities and are placed at the center of quite different dramatic circumstances. For example, Mikoto is now reproposed both as a literal cat and as a feline deity, Natsuki is cast in the role of headmistress of "Garderobe Academy," Takumi is reinterpreted as the son of the *shogun* of Zipang and said to be traveling to the anime's chief location, the "Kingdom of Windbloom," on a diplomatic mission, while a Yuuichi lookalike renamed Sergej Wáng is put in the role of a military commander. *Mai-Otome* is not a direct sequel to *Mai-HiME*, therefore, but rather an independent yarn set in an alternate universe in which several of the faces that will look familiar to fans of the first anime fulfill functions and pursue quests that are unrelated to those associated with their ostensible predecessors or only tied with them in an elliptical sense.

Set on planet "Earl," putatively colonized by immigrants from Earth centuries earlier, Obara's later series employs its titular "Otomes" as female bodyguards for the aristocracy and royalty of various realms, held to be equipped with an old technology inherited from a bygone age. The protagonist, Arika Yumemiya, travels to Windbloom in the hope of gaining admittance to the prestigious Garderobe Academy, where prospective Otome are raised and trained, and thus emulating the model set by her lost mother, whom Arika knows was an Otome. However, many seemingly impervious obstacles stand in her way — not least a humble backwoods upbringing, which snooty trainees look down on with shameless arrogance. As Arika exhibits her budding Otome abilities in the course of a confrontation with a *mecha* that is after the princess of Windbloom herself, the rustic girl's potential usefulness is recognized but it will take several installments — and corresponding adventures — for her determination, adaptability and sheer fervor to gain her the respect of peers and superiors.

Mai-Otome echoes *Mai-HiME* in its overall narrative trajectory by incrementally disclosing the sinister schemes afoot both within the heroines' immediate contexts and the world at large. However, it is noteworthy that the second series also introduces a clever twist into a narrative structure that otherwise mirrors closely the framework previously established by *Mai-HiME*. This dwells with its mock-technoscientific explanation of the reason for which the Otome ranks consist exclusively of female warriors. It is thus proposed that the nanomachines injected into the girls' blood from which their magical abilities ensue are vulnerable to the "prostate-specific antigen" (PSA), a protein produced by the cells of the prostate gland. Contact with this substance would cause an Otome's body to become immune and hence totally unresponsive to the existing nanomachines and to any further injections, rendering the girl irrevocably powerless. For this same reason, the Otome warriors cannot engage in sexual relationships with males. Although this rather byzantine hypothesis may sound amusing at first, its dark implications become progressively evident as the series develops. Windbloom is said to be the only place on planet Earl to have "preserved most of the Earth's technology." Akira is greatly impressed by the massive monitors, planes and holographic displays around her but to the rural girl, the term "technology" means precious little and she rapidly comes to describe her new reality as "magic." The coalescence of magic and technology is thus brought to our attention right from the start. Although most of its subjects are not aware of it, the entire realm is in thrall to its rulers' manic desire to develop increasingly powerful technologies which, by and large, are geared toward the satisfaction of their warmongering proclivities. Sophisticated technology is also brought into play with the cyborgs of "Aswad," a fighting group led by the character of Midori, who seeks to recover the ancient technology.

At the same time, however, the Kingdom of Windbloom is traversed by magic in the form of myths and legends that still carry great authority despite their relegation to the shelves of awesomely streamlined libraries. Most influential among them is the relatively recent tale known as "The Fire String Ruby." This consists of a magic-coated retelling of Mai Tokiha's story in the form of a legendary event. *Mai-HiME*'s heroine is here portrayed as an Otome endowed with tremendous powers that was meant to become one of the "Five Pillars" and hence take on "a renowned job, protecting the existence of Otome" but was torn between these supernatural duties and her love for an ordinary man. "To decide her future path," the legend recounts, "in frustration she went to the Sprites' Forest, where the future-telling god resides. But in the end, she never emerged from the forest again. People say that her soul still wanders in that forest." Mai, in fact, is still very much alive and climactically revealed to be leading an idyllic existence with Mikoto the Cat Goddess in a "warp in space" known as the "Black Valley" amid verdant meadows and sapphire skies. The place is at one point described as "the holy ground of the Lost Technology. The technology of the Otome" was "created here." Thus, Mai's new home seamlessly blends magical and technological ingredients in its filmic brew. Alongside the "Ruby" legend, the other pivotal source of narrative magic consists of the story revolving around Akira's mother, Lena. Having inherited Windbloom's "Sapphire of the Azure Sky," Lena held on to it for a decade, faithfully serving the country's monarch all the while. However, "one day she decided to take off that gemstone. It was so she can be with the one she loved." The woman went missing fifteen years earlier alongside her baby daughter when insurgents attacked the Windbloom castle. This narrative exudes the classic magic of fairy tale at its purest as it discloses, perhaps not surprisingly for the seasoned fantasy audience, that the baby in question was Akira and that the heroine, moreover, is now the realm's legitimate queen.

Like both *Mai-HiME* and *Mai-Otome*, the anime *Sailor Moon* (TV series; dirs. Junichi Sato *et al.*, 1992–1997) chronicles a magic mission of heroical distinction by employing a seemingly ordinary girl as its pivot. *Sailor Moon*'s heroine, Tsukino Usagi, is initially portrayed not merely as ordinary but also as inept, weak and both practically and emotionally disorganized. Her life unexpectedly takes a different direction when a charismatic cat named Luna approaches her and informs her that the world is under imminent threat by a dark Kingdom that made its appearance once before but was vanquished by the heroic efforts of the "Kingdom of the Moon." It is now up to Tsukino to let her abeyant magic powers awaken and assume the role of "Sailor Moon" to protect the Earth from the malign forces aiming at its destruction, thereby encountering an almost endless procession of allies and foes, and obtaining preternatural insights into the future of the Solar System. Immensely popular both on home turf and in the West for a long time as the very epitome of the "Magical-Girl" show, and bolstered not solely by a phenomenally extensive run but also by a plethora of spin-offs and ancillary merchandise, *Sailor Moon* is also notable, in the present context, as an instance of anime's knack of channeling the magic of its distinctive visual vocabulary into the construction of magical multimedia worlds of enduring global appeal.

Magically endowed young protagonists that are initially oblivious to their abilities but gradually turn out to exceed in stature many of their peers and superiors alike abound in anime. Deployed to great effect in both *Sailor Moon* and *Mai-HiME*, this character typology is no less central and beautifully dramatized in *Shakugan no Shana* (TV series; dir. Takashi Watanabe, 2005). The show's protagonist, high-school student Yuji Sakai, is suddenly informed that he has been dead for some time unbeknownst to him and endured as a "Torch" in a state of apparent aliveness alongside myriad other humans. Torches are merely provisional replacements for erased humans, being bound to evaporate altogether from the world and from others' memories of their existence. Yuji, however, is not an ordinary Torch but a "Mystes" since he hosts a special power known as "Treasure Tool" (*hougo*). These unsettling revelations are proffered by Shana, a sword-yielding girl with flaming hair and eyes who agrees to protect Yuji in exchange for his services in an epic battle against the "Crimson Denizens," evil entities seeking to extract the "Power of Existence" imbued in all sorts of both organic and magical forms and exploit it to their selfish and depraved ends.

A further illustration of the Magical-Girl convention is yielded by *Magical Girl Lyrical Nanoha* (TV series; dir. Akiyuki Shinbou, 2004). The adventure charted in this series stems from the titular heroine's rescue of an injured ferret whose plea for help she has magically captured by telepathic means. The Shinto-based belief in the interpenetration of diverse living forces across the cosmos is thrown into relief as it transpires that the animal is actually a wizard and archeologist named Yuuno, who has inadvertently dispersed the hazardous "Jewel Seeds" all over the planet. Equipped by the ferret with a gem that allows her to use magic to combat the monsters unleashed by the baleful Seeds, Nanoha makes it her mission to collect the objects in the face of all manner of antagonists. A further magic exploit using the venerable symbol of the jewel, ubiquitous in tales of sorcery and esoteric knowledge across disparate media and cultures, is articulated in the TV series *Night Wizard* (dir. Yusuke Yamamoto, 2007). The quest here entailed revolves around people enjoined to guard the world from impending darkness — among them are high-schoolers Renji Hiiragi and Kureha Akabane, soon joined by transfer student Elis Shiho when she discovers that she also has the power to rise to the status of a "Night Wizard" after collecting the "Jewel of Affection." Six more gems must be retrieved in the battle against sempiternal gloom.

Yielding an intellectually challenging approach to the topos of alternate realities, the TV series *Ghost Hound* (dir. Ryutaro Nakamura, 2007–2008) articulates a multilayered quest in which mystery and magic collude with the generic priorities of psychological drama. Set in a remote region in the Japanese island of Kyuushuu, the anime charts the vicissitudes of three boys connected by traumatic childhood experiences and related ability to migrate psychically between the real world (*utsushiyo*) and the spirit world (*kakuriyo*) as both dimensions undergo changes caused by the latter's infiltration by ghosts emanating from the latter. The axial event linking the main characters' destinies is the kidnapping of one of the boys, Tarou Komori, alongside his sister Mizuka, held to have occurred eleven years prior to the beginning of the story chronicled by the anime itself. Following the kidnapping, Tarou has been beset by out-of-body experiences (O.B.E.s), or astral projections, during his sleep — a state into which Tarou's narcoleptic tendencies plunge him with somewhat pathological regularity. Keen on recording the visual content of his O.B.E.s in a desperate effort to grasp their true significance, the boy yearns to meet Mizuka again in the spirit world in the hope of obtaining some insights into the past's nefarious legacy. His quest is repeatedly frustrated by a localized form of amnesia, whereby Tarou harbors no clear recollection of the kidnapper's mien and seems only able to visualize the figure snatching his sister away in the form of a dark giant. The specifically magical component of Tarou's mission is reinforced by his vulnerability to possessions, and his ability to take the shape of a dog-like phantom when, in the course of an O.B.E., destructive emotions hold sway and the boy's characteristically gentle personality is temporarily displaced by hatred and ire. As the series unfolds, Tarou develops deep feelings toward Miyako, a girl who has the power to perceive ghosts, as well as Tarou's own spiritual shape during his O.B.E.s, is periodically possessed by supernatural agents, and often assists her father at the local shrine in the performance of exorcisms and other para-normal practices. Tarou is convinced that Miyako is his lost sister's reincarnation.

It will already be evident from this cursory portrayal of just two personae out of the anime's extensive cast that numerous motifs associated with the magic arts and their underlying belief systems hold great importance in *Ghost Hound*. Makoto Oogami, another protagonist, shares with Tarou a propensity for O.B.E.s in the course of which he is capable of morphing into a wolf-like hound. His affiliation with the supernatural is complicated exponentially by his belonging to a powerful family that prides itself on the creation of a whole new religion, of which Makoto's grandmother is the current leader. To his chagrin, the boy is expected to succeed the matriarch as the head of the sect. Makoto's predicament is further problematized by painful memories of his discovery of the body of his dad in the aftermath of the latter's violent and mysterious death, and by his occasionally murderous feelings of resentment toward his mother whom he blames for remarrying and thus leaving him behind. The third of the central boys is Masayuki Nakajima, a character also said to experience O.B.E.s and to have an interest in the kidnapping incident. Masayuki's psychological makeup is additionally shaped by the tormenting memory of his responsibility for the suicide of a former school mate and partial addiction to a virtual-reality game he plays in his spare time and whose weaponry he is at one point able to deploy in his spirit form during astral projection.

While possessions, exorcisms, visions, reincarnations, psychic migrations, curses, specters and ectoplasms of the first water, and attendant references to indigenous lore (most pointedly, Shinto traditions) abound throughout *Ghost Hound* and generally fuel its magical infrastructure, it is also noteworthy that the supernatural has a flair for invading not only the ordinary world but also domains of scientific research that could logically be expected to be immune to otherworldly incursions. This is patently attested to by the O.B.E. sequence where Tarou detects spirits in a biotech facility pivotal to the story. *Ghost Hound*'s specters are particularly memorable, gliding into view and fading from the screen with eerily enchanting fluidity. However, it must be stressed that *Ghost Hound* is pervaded by references to scientific or quasi-scientific concepts inspired by a wide variety of disciplines, including psychology, physics and biology. This is borne out by many of its episode titles, including "Hopeful Monster," a colloquial phrase used in evolutionary biology to designate the emergence of a new major evolutionary group; "Negentropy," what a living system relies upon to remain alive; "Stochastic Resonance," noise added to a system to enhance its performance — as well as "Lucid

Dream," "E.M.D.R.: Eye Movement Desensitization and Reprocessing," "Brain Homunculus" and "L.T.P.: Long Term Potentiation." While invoking concepts derived from actual sciences, however distortedly, the anime also draws from a wide frame of literary reference. For example, Lewis Carroll's nonsense poem *The Hunting of the Snark* (1874) is explicitly brought into play in the episode titled "For the Snark was a Boojum, you see." This heading is inspired by Carroll's proposition that, should a hunter capture a Boojum, he will inevitably disappear never to be seen again. This reference is undoubtedly very apposite to *Ghost Hound*'s merry-go-round of varyingly final vanishing acts.

For a significant proportion of the show, the three protagonists' missions progress along a path so tortuous as to often seem to preclude any realistic hopes of resolution. A crucial turning point in the adventure is the installment in which the three protagonists travel to an abandoned hospital situated near a dam tinged with ominous connotations, where Tarou and Mizuka were apparently held after being kidnapped, and discover that the location is saturated with supernatural energies and thus provides something of a metaphysical channel linking *utsushiyo* and *kakuriyo*. From this point onward, several crucial revelations concerning the relationship between the two dimensions are gradually proffered. The fulcrum of those incremental disclosures lies with latent connections among the development of an electronic brain, the aforementioned religious sect (and the status of cultism in general), the ethics of bio-engineering, illegal organ trade, and mysterious child abductions. At times, it should be noted, the story tends to meander somewhat in its prioritization of character development to narrative thrust. However, as emphasized by *The Nihon Review*, the anime's overall tempo is extremely effective insofar as its is capable of "advancing enough of the plot without revealing too much of the mystery too soon," which serves to draw the audience into Nakamura's distinctive world, yet give it "time to ponder and speculate over the whole affair. It also doesn't hurt that the characters have interesting, varied backgrounds and personalities, and that watching their interactions to discover more details about them and shed light on the overall mystery is something to look forward to in each episode" (zzeroparticle). Visually speaking, *Ghost Hound*'s magic ensues from its knack of magnetizing the audience's attention through the buildup of its macabre and creepy atmosphere. The blurred camera work and somber hues, allied to electronic sound effects replete with distorted voices and buzzing or whirring noises, are dexterously employed to cloud the actual nature of the mysteries at the heart of the anime and hence keep the spectator in a suspenseful state of tension and anticipation right through to the end.

It should also be noted that *Ghost Hound* shares some major narrative themes with the TV series *When Cicadas Cry* (a.k.a. *When They Cry — Higurashi*) and its sequel *When Cicadas Cry — Solutions* (dir. Chiaki Kon, 2006–2007), another anime in which elements of mystery and the supernatural collude in the molding of a highly original psychodrama. Most conspicuous among those themes are the dynamics of power associated with a prestigious family and its matriarch, the vicious machinations embedded in state-of-the-art biological experimentation, the curse-ridden dam, and the reincarnation topos. In addition, the concepts of *utsushiyo* and *kakuriyo* also play a key part in the hugely popular role-playing game *Magic: The Gathering*, a ludic package based on a traditional card-based system (*Magic*) and set in the "Dominia" game universe. The cards themselves represent legion spells, supernatural creatures and strategies for controlling *mana* (a supernatural energy residing in humans, other animals and even apparently inanimate objects). Dominia is the comprehensive designation for the vast ensemble of "planes" (i.e., universes) that make up the multiverse in which the tales of *Magic: The Gathering* unfold. Natural and artificial planes coexist in parallel, partitioned by the "Æther." Out of all the available planes, the world of Kamigawa constitutes the farthest and most separate, and is divided into the *utsushiyo* (material world) and the *kakuriyo* (spiritual world). The creatures inhabiting the *utsushiyo* are essentially human, whereas the *kakuriyo* hosts an incredible variety of spirits ideated along fundamentally Shintoist lines (*kami*). Corrupted spiritual forces that embody evil and suffering are known as demons (*oni*).

The double-reality perspective elaborated by *Ghost Hound* has been frequently invoked in recent decades in the contexts of animation, live-action cinema and cyberpunk fiction. Larry and Andy Wachowski's live-action movies *The Matrix* (1999) and its sequels, *The Matrix Reloaded* (2003) and *The Matrix Revolutions* (2003), are undoubtedly among the most popular instances of that topos (alongside some popular ludic adaptations of the movies). In the specific domain of anime, a relatively early interpretation of that theme comes with the three-part OVA series *Megazone 23* (dirs. Noburo Ishiguro, Ichirou Itano, Shinji Aramaki and Kenichi Yatagai, 1985–1989). As the OVA's protagonist, Shogo, finds himself inadvertently embroiled in a chain of uncontrollable events, it gradually emerges that his entire reality is actually a simulation maintained by a twenty-fifth century supercomputer. In the TV series *Zegapain* (dir. Masami Shimoda, 2006), the protagonist, Kyo Sogoru, is likewise inserted in a simulated world and is enjoined to protect the people that inhabit that pseudo-reality while also striving to save its genuine counterpart. Although neither *Megazone 23* nor *Zegapain* explicitly engage with the esoteric and the supernatural, both anime feature magic on the metaphorical plane as a crucial attribute of their speculative versions of technoscience.

The symphonic combination of mystery, magic and psychological drama found in *Ghost Hound* also resonates throughout *Sola* (TV series; dir. Tomoki Kobayashi, 2007). The anime's heroine, Matsuri Shihou, is a *yaka*, a magical creature that has lived for hundreds of years, hosts a whole range of supernatural powers (including portentous healing skills and the ability to cause the objects she touches to rapidly decay) and cannot endure daylight. In other words, Matsuri evinces many of the standard attributes of the classic Undead but is refreshingly devoid of blood-drinking proclivities — even though she is, in principle, capable of transforming humans into creatures of her ilk by inflicting the legendary bite. Her archenemy — a sword-wielding man named Takeshi in charge of a doll-like child, the *yaka* Mayuko Kamikawa — brands the heroine a "woe of the night" and wants nothing but her death, which he regards as a sacrificial immolation necessary to restore Mayuko's humanity. (Mayuko herself, however, will eventually endeavor to protect Matsuri from Takeshi's fierce onslaughts.) The male lead, fifteen-year-old high-school student Yorito Morimiya, conversely, is more than willing to shelter Matsuri and indeed treat her, as far as possible, like the ordinary human teenager she superficially appears to be.

An endearing aspect of the relationship between Matsuri and Yorito, established right from the start and reverberating throughout the series, lies with the tension between the *yaka*'s aversion to daylight and Yorito's almost compulsive fascination with the sky in all of its conceivable configurations, which he nourishes by both endlessly gazing at it and taking photographs of it at any time of the day or the night. Deeply drawn to the daytime sky which her nature forbids her contact with, Matsuri experiences that vast unknown dimension vicariously via Yorito, his pictures, his enthusiastic accounts of all manner of lighting effects and cloud formations, and the photorealistic painting of an azure sky flecked with roaming clouds covering his bedroom's entire ceiling. "The skies you saw, the skies you chased," Matsuri confesses to Yorito in the show's climax, "I saw them though your eyes." The centrality of the sky in the anime as a whole is succinctly confirmed by its title, "*sola*" being a slightly distorted transliteration of the Japanese word for "sky" — namely, "*sora*" — based on the phonetic overlap in the Japanese language between the sounds "l" and "r."

Yorito first chances upon Matsuri while setting up his photographic equipment by a bay to take a picture of the impending dawn over the sea and the *yaka* herself is busy bashing a vending-machine that stubbornly refuses to dispense the can of tomato juice she has already paid for. It is upon the main characters' second meeting, set in torrential rain this time, that they get round to introducing themselves properly and that a shared attraction to the sky transpires. The third encounter marks the decisive turning point in their budding connection, as Yorito witnesses Matsuri's vicious attack by Takeshi, hell-bent on her annihilation, and resolves to take her into his life: an act he elects as his personal magic mission. Up to this moment, *Sola* exhibits many features common in average anime series centered on an ordinary youth and his preternatural protégée. Also quite conventional is the portrayal of Matsuri as overly eager to undertake household chores of which she has no adequate experience with confidence and panache but almost invariably with disastrous results for the appliances or food items involved. The script reveals a self-conscious stance toward accepted anime formulae — as patently demonstrated by the scene in which Yorito attempts to explain Matsuri's provenance to his friend Mana in overtly parodic terms, first by claiming that the girl was a cat when he found her and then morphed magically into a human, and subsequently declaring that she actually comes from the future. This ruse indicates that *Sola*'s initial adoption of well-rehearsed generic conventions is quite deliberate. Moreover, it contributes crucially to the show's dramatic impact since, when those conventions are relegated to a peripheral position and then excised altogether from the diegesis to make room for an imaginative and original yarn, the audience's appreciation of this shift is likely to be heightened by its awareness of the formal substratum whence it is intentionally departing.

The first part of the anime, though punctuated with stirring flashes of dynamism, is methodically paced and gives priority to character presentation, enabling viewers to become acquainted gradually with both existing and evolving liaisons. Alongside the bond developing between Yorito and Matsuri, we witness the boy's interactions with his elder sister Aono, who lives in a hospital supposedly due to chronic poor health, and the aforementioned Mana, a spunky high-school girl with no interest in girly or romantic matters and a part-time job as a waitress that supplies the plot with subtle opportunities to link the scenes involving the protagonists with those following Matsuri's foes' parallel movements. As the series unfolds, its true magic incrementally comes to the fore, and the full stature of the missions therein at stake accordingly asserts itself. Although the overall storyline remains relatively straightforward and gracefully unlabored, the authentic significance of the *yaka* concept eventually emerges and the adventure accordingly acquires both momentum and pathos. At this point, insights into Yorito's occluded past compounded with a sensitive portrayal of the conflict between Matsuri and Aono concur to invest *Sola* with unprecedented dramatic richness. Concomitantly, the status of the protagonist's initial, self-appointed task is redefined as just one piece in a broader puzzle of interrelated magic quests. It is in the course of the final third of the anime, in particular, that its various narrative strands are dexterously braided together through intelligent plot twists and a shocking finale packed with swirling, adrenaline-soaked and even undilutedly violent action. Central to *Sola*'s climactic events is the revelation that Aono is also a *yaka*, having been made into one by Matsuri in days gone by when she tried to commit suicide after the version of her brother Yorito from that time was killed. Insofar as her dormant powers are reawakening, Aono will now stop at nothing to ensure that nobody stands between her and her beloved sibling and does not hesitate, to this end, to manipulate Yorito's psyche and even temporarily possess his body in order to induce him to hurt Matsuri on her behalf. No less unsettling is the disclosure that the present-day Yorito is not, after all, a human adolescent but a construct, a paper simulacrum created by Aono on the basis of her memories of the real Yorito from the past through the deployment of her magical power over paper in all its forms. (The art of *origami*, incidentally, is used throughout *Sola* as a pivotal symbol.) In the wake of Yorito's exposure to this profoundly disturbing truth, his chimeric identity is confirmed by the fact that everybody — the unflinchingly loyal Mana included — quickly forgets he ever existed.

As is often the case with anime produced by Nomad, *Sola* benefits considerably, in drawing the audience into its unique universe, from its character designs. These are invariably bolstered by meticulous attention to details, whereby even seemingly stereotypical features gain unmistakable individuality. For example, the heroine's dark locks and deep-hued eyes, while they might not instantly come across as especially original in themselves, derive unequivocal distinctiveness from their juxtaposition with a pale complexion intended to emphasize Matsuri's affiliation with the realm of the night. At the same time, details are deployed as a means of communicating a wide spectrum of emotions through subtle shifts of mood and expression. The sky, as central to the anime's artwork as it is to Yorito's own life, offers a perfect backdrop to these sensitively modulated character portrayals, its incessant changes in color, light, density and levels of dynamism mirroring the actors' fluctuating emotions. As noted in the *Minitokyo* review of Kobayashi's show, characterization is its major quality, to the point that "some of the characters' personalities alone make this a show worth watching. Mana is a strong character and a great friend. Koyori [Mana's kid sister] is quite possibly the most adorable character in creation. Matsuri is a misunderstood, lovely character.... You genuinely have a sense of the characters' emotions and can truly empathize with them. When they're angry, you feel that. When they're sad or crying, you get teary-eyed. You find yourself truly vested in the characters' ups and downs and their rollercoaster ride to the end" (shoujoboy).

Many viewers are likely to regard the TV series *Magikano* (dir. Seiji Kishi, 2006) as comic relief within the comprehensive galaxy of anime at large. There is unquestionably a generous dose of humor running through Kishi's entire series, its generic frame of reference incorporating the conventions of harem comedy, erotic dalliance, mock-heroic battle, farcically inept forays into witch-hunting and even fashion shows. To this extent, the magic mission dramatized in the anime is essentially driven by the cultural and ethical priorities of unexacting entertainment. This is not to say, however, that *Magikano* in any way fails to engage its audience in some assiduously engaging — and sometimes uplifting — action. In fact, the series instantly absorbs us into its imaginary world by presenting the emotional ties and energies that draw its protagonists together with sparkling lucidity. Central to the story is the character of Ayumi Mamiya, a witch doomed to lose her magical powers as a result of a dark spell which only one boy, Haruo Yoshikawa, has the hidden ability to break. Unfortunately for Ayumi, Haruo is entirely oblivious to his possession of wizardly skills and has never thought of himself as anything other than a boringly average school kid — his major goal in life, the character announces at the very start, is as trivial as a flawless attendance record. Haruo has indeed been raised by his supernaturally gifted sisters — the motherly Maika, the fitness-obsessed Chiaki and the grabby Fuyuno — in complete ignorance of the very existence of magic. While Ayumi is hell-bent on awakening Haruo's abeyant capacities to secure her survival as a witch, the boy's sisters will stop at nothing to interfere with Ayumi's scheme. Concurrently, whereas the endangered witch shows no restraint in flaunting her prodigious talent in public, the Yoshikawa girls prize the value of secrecy virtually above all other assets to be expected of an orthodox and polished practitioner. Within the privacy of their house, however, they show no scruples, and whenever their brother comes anywhere near witnessing magic, they do not hesitate to deploy vicious memory-erasing "hammers" to perpetuate his blindness to the cryptic arts.

Haruo is abruptly plunged into this preposterous war as, having caught a brief but memorable glimpse of Ayumi on his way back from school, he finds himself facing the prospect of protracted cohabitation with the creature when she prepotently installs herself in the Yoshikawa household in the capacity of a live-in maid with the intention of seducing the innocent boy. Hence, Ayumi effectively seals him within a contract of sorts (thus harking back to the topos discussed in Chapter 2), neither the conditions nor the exact nature of which Haruo is able to comprehend. It will not be hard to surmise, in light of this information, that the magic pact at the heart of *Magikano* is a rather one-sided one, given that most of the time, Haruo is unaware of the very existence of that bond — not to mention the momentous mission and attendant beliefs, customs and rites underpinning its undertaking. As the action progresses, complications rapidly proliferate, to culminate with the revelation that Haruo is actually the current "avatar for the Demon Lord" — an evil force seeking to sap the world's energy until it has reduced it to "zero" that has awakened several times in the past and has always been contained, however precariously, by the efforts of "artificial humans" constructed specifically for that purpose. At this level of the narrative, *Magikano* overtly brings magic into collusion with technology by highlighting the inextricability of supernatural occurrences rooted in an ancient tradition from science fictional motifs and futuristic imagery. This time around, the task of taming the Demon Lord poses greater challenges than has ever been the case before and hence exceeds the ability of the charismatic automaton Miss Hongo placed in charge of its successful accomplishment. It is therefore up to all the people that have ever cared for Haruo and whose memories are still engraved in his unconscious to work together and "synchronize with him" in order to "reverse the flow of time" to the point where he can exist as an ordinary kid. The bond initially established between Haruo and Ayumi, as argued, is fundamentally one-sided. In the show's climax, the situation is reversed, as the waning witch has a chance to play a major role in rescuing the boy from his abysmal preternatural fate and repay him, so to speak, out of sheer generosity and affection.

One of *Magikano*'s most remarkable features consists of a sustained reconceptualization of many of the narrative formulae and theatrical set pieces often found in romantic comedy. This is intended to integrate those elements in a magic-imbued mold of the anime's own making. Hence, while indulging in a relatively stereotypical treatment of situations such as the school's Culture Festival and Sports Day, the Christmas party and the New Year visit to the local shrine, the show elegantly incorporates at each opportune juncture dramatic occurrences dominated by intrinsically magical imagery and symbolism. These include Ayumi's generation of a dream world inside Haruo's psyche which several other characters are allowed to enter, thereby experiencing their ideal dreams first-hand; Ayumi's and the Yoshikawa sisters' journey back in time by means of an exclusive form of travel (for which Ayumi possesses a rather dodgy license) dubbed "Time Highway Magic"; a tale of haunting centered on a local swimming-pool and its otherworldly inhabitant traversed by vestiges of ancient Japanese lore; an adventure set in a castle located in a mystical forest replete with fairy-tale villains that tersely corroborates the alliance between magic and fairy tales discussed in Chapter 1. As the review of the anime published in *Anime Source* points out, *Magikano*'s "plot opens up plenty of opportunity to showcase some touching romance, suspenseful action, incredible and clever sequences involving the use of magic, and plenty of side-splitting humorous situations." However, the field in which it truly shines is "the magic. Magic is used really well and is integrated into each episode side-story perfectly. There is a perfect blend of reality and fantasy in every episode. It never feels like this is a show ABOUT magic and witches" (xenocrisis0153).

An eminently text-driven mission informs the TV series *Kagihime* (dir. Nagisa Miyazaki, 2006). (The anime's full original title, incidentally, is actually *Kagihime Monogatari Eikyuu Alice Rondo*, which translates literally as "Key Princess Story: Eternal Alice Rondo.") The anime pivots on the character of Aruto Kirihara, an avid reader of the *Alice* adventures that is enabled by his sheer fascination with that world to access the magical domain of "Wonderland Space," a "pocket dimension" in which girls dubbed "Seekers of Alice" (a.k.a. "Alice Users") are engaged in a complex tournament. The ultimate objective of all Seekers of Alice is to defeat each of their opponents in order to complete a story known as *The Eternal Alice*. This aim can only be accomplished, we are informed, "by gathering the stories girls keep hidden within their hearts.... The girls try to take each other's stories, placing their own at risk, so that they can complete the story that those stories are a part of." As a reward, the winner will be granted a wish, as is often the case in anime dedicated to the dramatization of magic missions. Through this strategy, *Kagihime* posits narrative deferral, enchainment and embedding as staple ingredients of good storytelling, positing them as creative and aesthetic tools imbued with ineffable magical power. At the start of the series, Aruto is busy writing his own Alice-based story when he sees a girl whom he believes to be the character he is so obsessively engrossed with leaping through the night sky just outside his window and decides to chase her.

The pursuit takes him to a stately library where he witnesses a duel between the girl and another young female. Upon winning the fight, Aruto's intended prey steals her antagonist's story and vanishes. The elusive girl later discloses her identity as Arisu Arisugawa, a Seeker of Alice capable of morphing into a *kemonomimi* (i.e., a humanoid figure with animal characteristics, in her case those of a bunny) that uses magical "keys" in her fights to unlock the tales stored in other Seekers' depths. The adventure takes a decisive turn as the male lead's little sister, Kiriha, reveals her own status as a Seeker and challenges Arisu to a fight. Not wishing to see either party conclusively vanquished and hence deprived of her story, Aruto breaks up the fight and proposes a truce whereby the three of them end up working together to complete *The Eternal Alice*. The bulk of the anime thence proceed to chronicle the trio's exploits together.

Kagihime may not constitute the most imaginative or thought-provoking of anime shows. It is, in fact, quite formulaic and, once the three-party alliance mentioned earlier has been established and the inceptive crisis accordingly surmounted, it also becomes rather mechanical in its presentation of events. There are, however, two important factors that elevate *Kagihime* above the basic level of shallow entertainment. First, its settings consistently work their magic on the action, instilling it with a sense of bewitchment and wonder. With the preliminary depiction of Aruto writing away at his desk by the window at night in the dusky solitude of his chamber, the anime vividly echoes several classic visual motifs enshrined in the history of magic fiction. These include the image of the young wizard working secretly in the nocturnal stillness of his bedroom, immortalized by the *Harry Potter* novels, or even the image of the mighty but disaffected magician alone in his study and about to establish a relationship that will change his life forever of the kind commonly associated with the Faust story. Another effective location used recurrently throughout the show is an old library redolent of Jorge Luis Borges' writings and, specifically, of their ideation of the cosmos at large as a hypothetical library whose volumes seem to consist of words randomly clustered together by sheer accident, yet are capable of periodically disclosing a modicum of meaning. It should also be noted, in this regard, that books as material objects no less than as the receptacles of abstract ideas or chimeric narratives play a key role in *Kagihime* and contribute vitally to the enhancement of its distinctive magic. This is most exuberantly borne out by the climactic sequence in which an old tome suddenly flies off out of Aruto's hands, the words therein begin to glow, unfurl as ribbons of light, and eventually envelop the protagonist and his sister in a stupendous cocoon to plunge them into a veritably Carrollian tunnel whence the two characters, in Aruto's own words, get "wrapped in a series of really strange events." This comes across as something of a diorama combining myriad references to the worlds of traditional fairy tales interspersed with *Alice*-centered iconography. It is also worth noting, in this context, that *Kagihime*'s old library occasionally echoes the similar edifice portrayed in *Yami to Boushi to Hon no Tabibito* (a.k.a. *Darkness, Hat and Book Traveler*; TV series; dir. Yuji Yamaguchi, 2003).

Second, *Kagihime*'s affective strength lies with its characters, who are generally portrayed with remarkable care for their psychological nuances even when they serve fundamentally functional, supporting roles or else are introduced into the action solely for the purpose of comic relief. The protagonist himself is especially remarkable, within the anime's gallery, as a subtle character study. Distinguished by a magical ability not only to copy and transcribe the stories locked in other people's hearts, which is no mean feat in itself, but also to enable the characters from those stories to appear in the real world, Aruto never exploits his supernatural skills to his personal advantage. In fact, his sensitive and generous disposition typically induces him to return the written tales to their legitimate owners in the Wonderland Space in the conviction that he has no right to appropriate such private accounts as his own literary dominion even though the girls that have been sapped of their hidden narratives are not allowed to reenter the magical Wonderland. Arisu, who rapidly asserts herself as the anime's female lead by virtue not only of her dramatic centrality but also of her inherent charisma, owes much of her allure to the enigmatic aura surrounding her identity and origins. The girl's past is indeed shrouded in mystery, not least due to her lack of any conscious memories preceding her encounter with Aruto. This fact becomes increasingly evident as the narrative develops. It eventually transpires that Arisu is actually a product of Aruto's own imagination, created as a replacement for Kiriha, whom he does not feel entitled to love in any fashion other than a purely brotherly one. A touching facet of Arisu's personality consists of her deliberate self-restraint. Indeed, even though she is a uniquely accomplished and devoted Seeker, she is prepared to distance herself from her mission by befriending two humans who, as potential finishers in the race for *The Eternal Alice*, she logically ought to consider her enemies. Aruto's little sister, for her part, is made intriguing by a bundle of inner conflicts produced by her feelings toward Aruto. Loving the boy as a lover rather than an elder sibling and intending to complete the *Endless Alice* to get Aruto to cherish her in return in analogously romantic terms, Kiriha has no choice but to cooperate with Arisu to advance her personal mission, yet deeply resents the girl as a threatening competitor for Aruto's affections.

The author of the two original *Alice* stories, a man named Takion, reputedly lost all of his "creative energy" after completing those works. It was at this point that the idea of *The Eternal Alice* was first formulated — not by the writer himself, for obvious reasons, but rather by a girl invented by Takion in Alice's image who feared that the author might be losing interest in her when he stopped telling her stories in the way he had been wont to do. Portrayed as the alternately suave and tyrannical villain of the piece, Takion aims to get hold of all of the stories belonging to the Seekers of Alice to assemble *The Eternal Alice* — which he proprietorially appears to consider his own legitimate right — and exploit the book's wish-fulfilling power to achieve immortality. [1]

The anime *Natsume Yuujinchou* and its sequel *Zoku Natsume Yuujinchou*

(TV series; dir. Takahiro Ohmori, 2008–2009) share with *Kagihime* a distinctive approach to the theme of the magic mission as a task governed by time-honored beliefs. The two shows' protagonist, Natsume Takashi, has been cursed since infancy with the ability to perceive spirits — a talent he has inherited from his late grandmother Reiko and carefully kept "an absolute secret." The boy's commitment to secrecy at any price receives an unexpected blow when he finds that the "Book of Friends," a highly valued item in the spirit world bequeathed to him by Reiko as an heirloom upon her death, hosts the names of all the spirits she vanquished in her lifetime and forced into servitude by means of preternatural laws. Natsume thus realizes that the reason for which innumerable otherworldly entities have been pestering him for as long as he can remember is that they are desperate to enlist his help in their quest for freedom. Hence, while Reiko spent a significant portion of her earthly existence trapping the hapless entities within the pages of a magical volume, Natsume's principal objective becomes, in the wake of that discovery, to release the spirits that come to him for assistance by returning the names contained in the formidable book to their legitimate owners and thus dissolving the old ties. Natsume undertakes his mission in the company of a cutely cynical, occasionally spiteful and always argumentative cat named Madara — whom the boy addresses as Nyanko-sensei, i.e., "Mister Little Meow" — that fulfills a double function as both a spiritual counselor and a magical bodyguard (the latter role being rendered necessary by the fact that even though Natsume is dedicated to the trapped spirits' welfare, some of them are intrinsically malicious and therefore want him dead). As in *Rental Magica*, the figure of the magical feline assistant is truly pivotal to this anime. Moreover, Nyanko-sensei's attitude at times recalls the portrayal of another eminent anime cat, Jiji from the movie *Kiki's Delivery Service* (dir. Hayao Miyazaki, 1989), here also addressed in Chapter 5.

Natsume's shamanic powers are brought into play in the course of the two shows on disparate occasions. At one point, a local deity turns to him for help when a lamentable dearth of devotees threatens to erode not only its spiritual authority but also its very survival as an object of worship. Furthermore, the youth is beseeched to assist entities in the process of being exorcized, and then asked to detect a spirit, Shigeru, haunting an abandoned school and furious at the prospect of its impending demolition. Shigeru reappears in a subsequent adventure when he requires Natsume to obtain teacups from a nearby pottery on his behalf. This vignette shows that Natsume, for all his prodigious powers, does not seem to mind being treated as a bit of an errand boy. Nor does he evince a hierarchical or otherwise elitist mentality, as demonstrated by the installments where he befriends the dim-witted spirit

Santo and a little fox spirit that grows very fond of the youth after receiving his help. At times, Natsume does not come across as merely open-minded but also touchingly kind, as attested to by the scene in which, following a bath at the hot springs, he tries to dry off a *youkai* (demon) to ensure she will not catch a cold even though, as his spiritualist friend Natori Shuuichi reminds him, her kind is not vulnerable to that danger. Natori, incidentally, is a popular actor who, being endowed with powers analogous to Natsume's, holds a side job as an exorcist. (This character recalls Housho from *Ghost Hunt*, who is also a performer-cum-spiritualist, as noted in the previous chapter.)

At another stage in his spirit-infested adventures, Natsume is possessed by a swallow spirit yearning to meet a human that once helped her, agrees to deploy his powers to abet her nostalgic quest and then endeavors to obtain a magical kimono deemed capable of transforming a spirit into an embodied person for just one day. Natsume gets to experience indirectly what it is like to possess psychic abilities and then suddenly lose them when he hears from a spirit about a human victim of this very predicament. Additionally, he encounters potentially kindred souls with the characters of Tanuma Kaname, a boy who also senses spirits though not as acutely as Natsume does, and Taki Tooru, a girl from a family of *onmyouji* that is able to perceive *youkai* with the assistance of a mysterious diagram redolent of a magician's circle, and strives to lift a curse intent on inscribing characters on Natsume's body in order to slowly destroy him. Taki also plays an important role in the hero's life as the first person ever to have said complimentary things about his somewhat notorious grandmother and her Book. Other creatures encountered by Natsume over the two series involve a sick *koto* player (the *koto*, incidentally, is a Japanese stringed instrument akin to a zither), an evil force sealed into a tree, a forest guardian inhabiting first a statue and then a snow bunny, a mermaid with cannibalistic tendencies, and a demonic force sworn to kill Natori — which causes Natsume to face the most unsavory ethical question which any human mage that honestly respects the non-human domain would pay to evade: that is to say, whether to side with the human world or with its demonic counterpart.

At one point, Natsume and Nyanko-sensei have to confront the uncanny reality of a painting accommodating a trapped *youkai* and gradually acquiring a power so great as to spread into the space that surrounds it and then appearing to merge with the natural realm itself. An especially moving adventure revolves around a specimen of the *tatsumi*: namely, a class of spirits intrinsically akin to birds or dragons but bound to "change into the first creature they see when they hatch." However, they are eventually bound to "return to their true forms and leave." The *tatsumi* whom Natsume hosts for a while in the safety of his own bedroom, addressing him as Tama (literally, "soul"), at first evinces the appearance of the cutest of dolls, recalling an angel-like Christmas-tree decoration with diminutive antlers. As Tama grows older, he is so loath to depart as to refrain from eating in order to delay his ineluctable separation from his protector. Finally, when his true form can no longer be kept at bay, Tama burgeons into one of the most formidable bird-dragons ever to have regaled the screen and has no choice but to leave Natsume behind. The boy comforts Tama by sharing with the bereft creature his own memories of the loneliness he had to endure as a parentless kid, thus lightening his heart at least for a while. At the levels of action, imagery and dialogue, the scene in which this affecting moment of communion takes place is vividly redolent of the climactic sequence from Miyazaki's film *Spirited Away* (2001), also referred to in Chapters 5 and 6. In this sequence, the protagonist, Chihiro, breaks the spell that besets her friend Haku, a river spirit robbed of his rightful memories, and thus enables him to recuperate his past and his identity. This movie, incidentally, relies on the idea of a magic mission ruled by a stringent magic contract as its diegetic pivot, thus bringing together two of this study's principal concerns. Chihiro is indeed forced to work for the witch Yubaba on the basis of a supernaturally summoned document if she is to accomplish the task of restoring her parents, morphed into pigs for behaving disrespectfully toward the local deities, to human form and, having been labeled "Sen" by the hag, to regain her rightful given name.

As noted, Natsume cultivates a pointedly non-hierarchical world view. As a result, his abilities never cause him to become so pointedly larger-than-life as an anime character as to cease to communicate a heartwarming sense of youthful humanity. Concurrently, he does not even appear especially scared of the spirits he encounters irrespective of their intentions, nor does he feel inclined to engage in spectacular ghostbusting feats whenever he comes across such a creature. In fact, as noted in the *Anime-Planet* review of the series, "Natsume's relationship with them is one of mutual curiosity and respect; he approaches them with the sympathy he would give to any human being. This in turn goes a long way to humanising the spirits and making their predicaments emotional as well as entertaining" (VivisQueen). Thus, the boy characteristically exhibits a quiet, composed and earnest attitude to his mission, steering clear of emotional outbursts and preferring instead to observe keenly the world around him before drawing any conclusions or opting for any one specific course of action. Furthermore, as the confinements sanctioned by the Book of Friends are gradually unveiled and repealed, the anime concomitantly chronicles its protagonist's voyage of self-discovery, tracing his development from a solitary orphan silently consumed by a touching desire to belong to a self-confident and affectively robust young man capable of capitalizing on his inner strength without ever yielding to arrogance or conceit.

As a result of its protagonist's typical conduct, the anime as a whole comes across as dramatically sedate and enchantingly mellow. The character designs adopted for the human actors are, by and large, so delicate and subtly nuanced as to appear simplistic at first. The style deployed in the portrayal of the spirits, by contrast, consistently evinces a preference for marked visual individuation compounded with a liberal allocation of eccentricities and grotesqueries that render those characters instantly appealing. In addition, while some creatures are so flamboyantly weird as to verge on the absurd, others are nightmarish in the most genuine sense of the word, bringing to mind the sinister incubi and succubi permeating Gothic-leaning Romantic art and literature. The character of the "shadow man," an amorphous blob capable of swiftly materializing and dissolving in its struggle to devour the hero, is arguably the most unsettling of these murkier types. Other entities bear witness to a healthy appetite for the bizarre on the part of Character Designer and Chief Animation Director Akira Takata. (These often hark back to the multifarious spirits that patronize the bathhouse run by the tyrannical and profit-obsessed sorceress Yubaba in *Spirited Away*.) This strategy enables the series to celebrate the uniqueness of magic through the actual portrayal of its supernatural personae, without requiring it to pander to any of the standard formulae associated with magic-oriented cinematography and their classic onslaughts of vivid hues or blaring transformation scenes. It is noteworthy, moreover, that the anime's aversion to sensationalism impacts on the nature of the magic missions at its core, as these tend to derive both narrative intensity and spiritual value not so much from their singular intrinsic substance or from the specific conflicts they give rise to as from their progressive accumulation across the anime's entire span.

Both *Natsume Yuujinchou* and *Zoku Natsume Yuujinchou* fully endorse the proposition, advanced earlier in this chapter, that magic-oriented anime fosters a notion of the self as a fluid entity and frequently conveys this idea through its representation of space. Ohmori's two-part anime does not overtly foster geographical diversity. In fact, the action consistently revisits the same or very similar locations: lyrically refined landscapes registering the passing of the seasons with remarkable symbolic incisiveness, and provincial everyday realities whenever urban architecture and amenities are brought into focus. Infiltrated by magic agencies, these basic places are regularly invested with a numinous aura and hence attain to their full standing within the metaphysical fabric of the narrative. Therefore, the sense of spatial richness yielded by both the original *Natsume* and its sequel does not originate in the anime's setting per se but rather in that hypothetical dimension where nature and art collude into metaphors — the sometimes hostile, sometimes playful and most often invisible elsewhere whence magic itself stems. In other words, the space created by the anime only achieves its full, authentic proportions by and through magic.

In so doing, the anime echoes the proposition, advanced by Yi-Fu Tuan, that as a "material environment," in its own right, "geographical place" is at once "natural" and "artifactual." No less importantly, according to Tuan, "artworks such as a painting, photograph, poem, story, movie, dance, or musical composition can also be a place" — a place by which we can be "nurtured" in much the same way as we are "nurtured by the towns and cities and landscapes we live in or visit" (Tuan 2004, p. 3). The concept of nurture is crucial, in this context, since it alerts us to the continually transforming impact which space is bound to have upon our bodies and psyches and therefore, once again, to the idea that the "self ... is not fixed" (p. 4). As artworks that do not communicate spatial profusion as a given but rather as an outcome of the ongoing interplay of nature and art effected by magic, Ohmori's shows pithily capture Tuan's outlook insofar as they posit the virtual space evoked by their adventures as a nourishing ground where the self is always susceptible to transformation and unanchoring. The protagonist's own maturation exemplifies this point with unobtrusive power. Natsume's self is indeed portrayed as pointedly fluid insofar as the youth is simultaneously rooted, both in a familiar semi-rural ambience and in a chain of quest-driven obligations, and rootless, perpetually journeying from one task to the next, one spirit's ordeal to the next. As a corollary of this split, which Tuan would term a "bipolar tug" (p. 7), Natsume senses at once "the call of open space" and "the call of home" (p. 8).

As an earnest explorer of the spirit world continually engaged in expeditions into its remotest nooks, the character needs the concept of home as a stable point of reference. Yet, home never offers a sealed area of safety into which Natsume may conclusively seek refuge but rather the launching pad for varyingly daring forays into the magical Beyond — and inevitably so, since even when Natsume does not physically leave his home to embark on a spirit-related adventure, the spirit world finds ways of reaching out to him and infiltrating the seemingly mundane compass of his bedroom. This is clearly evinced by the aforementioned installment in which a painting hosting a spirit spreads to its surroundings: the very walls of Natsume's unassuming chamber get progressively covered in cherry-tree branches as the story advances and the impassioned otherworldly force at its hub grows increasingly desperate to achieve its goal. Natsume's dual positioning enables him to retain a fine balance between kinesis and stasis, composure and adventurousness, preventing him from either becoming ossified or disintegrating into myriad identity shards. As a result, the character gradually achieves both consistency and strength, yet always remains open to the possibility of development. As Tuan applicably emphasizes, "rootedness ... sets the self into a mold too soon," while "Mobility carried to excess ... makes it difficult, if not impossible, for a strong sense of self to jell. A self that is coherent and firm, yet capable of growth, would seem to call for an alternation of stillness and motion, stability and change" (p. 4).

One of the most thought-provoking factors distinguishing both of the *Natsume* series is their recurrent intimation that humans might be quite misled when they strive, as insistently as they do, to locate magic and the threats it is deemed to pose solely with extraordinary entities and phenomena. In so doing, humans force various mysterious creatures, such as demons and spooks, to serve a consolatory purpose, to fuel the illusion that the ordinary world is immune to the influence of those entities and may therefore be exempt from the burden of fear. Yet, the real challenge, the *Natsume* shows suggest, actually arises from being in the world, *this* world. As the character of Terry Dare from William Peter Blatty's "Elsewhere" maintains, by turning to supernatural threats, human beings struggle to exorcize the terrors and horrors of the everyday and the mundane, acting "as if living on a spinning rock hurtling through the void dodging asteroids and comets weren't challenge enough, not to mention tornadoes, death and disease as well as Vlad the Impaler and earthquakes and war" (Blatty, p. 576). The corollary of these reflections, as the character of the psychic expert Anna Trawley from the same novella observes, is a frank acknowledgement of fear as inherent in human existence at large: "Fear, if we correctly observe our situation, is our ordinary way, like feeding, like dying" (Blatty, p. 629).

Like *Natsume Yuujinchou* and its sequel, the TV series *Shigofumi: Letters from the Departed* (dir. Tatsuo Sato, 2008) establishes a powerful connection between textuality and the supernatural. Sato's anime dauntlessly breaches the barrier supposedly separating the prosaic and the spiritual by disrupting the boundary between life and the afterlife. This ruse is effected through magical missives from the dead directed to the living. The letters are dispatched by an austere girl named Fumika and her talking staff Kanaka (which is wont to turn into an exquisite pendant matched by no less splendid a set of glowing wings whenever the courier requires transportation). In the logic of the show, the body retains a modicum of sentience and volition in the immediate aftermath of a person's death. It is also at this juncture that humans have a chance of communicating their feelings most freely and truthfully even if, while alive, they have been normally furtive or even deceitful. The deceased characters responsible for authoring the letters which Fumika ceremoniously delivers to their addressees use that liminal realm precisely to express occluded emotions, reveal their secrets and provide clues to the unraveling of unsolved riddles, thereby situating the written word as a vital bridge to the otherworld and its magic.

The partnership of textuality and the supernatural is further reinforced by *Death Note* (TV series; dir. Tetsurou Araki, 2006–2007). This anime's protagonist, Yagami Light, is a first-class student with brilliant prospects that deeply resents the ostensibly unrelenting escalation of crime and corruption in his society. Light unexpectedly finds himself in possession of a magical instrument capable of satisfying his yearning for a better world when he chances upon the "Death Note," a notebook originating in the mythical realm of the "Death Gods" that claims to hold the power to destroy any person whose name is inscribed therein. Although the youth initially doubts the artifact's reliability, empirical experimentation rapidly demonstrates the utter authenticity of its claim. Following his encounter with the notebook's previous owner, a *shinigami* ("Death Spirit") named Ryuk, Light takes it upon himself to create an ideal world utterly devoid of either iniquity or malefactors. Eventually, however, the Death Note's power boomerangs and the self-appointed hero becomes a victim of the portentous object's magic as Ryuk strategically deploys it to dispose of him.

The anime here employed to elucidate the theme of the magic mission offer novel interpretations of the concept of the "ghost in the machine." This was formulated by Gilbert Ryle in *The Concept of Mind* (1949) to criticize the stridently dualistic character of the Cartesian system, where the body is viewed as a purely mechanical apparatus, and the spirit or soul supposed to inhabit and govern it as an utterly incorporeal entity. The titles under scrutiny in this chapter radically question Descartes' model by proposing that both the body and the spirit or soul participate at all times in the province of the mechanical and in that of the spiritual. They do so, most pointedly, by portraying mechanical instruments and automated systems that cannot be approached as entirely material entities but are actually continually traversed by impalpable, otherworldly forces akin to magic. Both their indigenous vocabularies and their visual rhetoric serve to reinforce this perspective. The magical dimension is further strengthened by the inclusion of Gothic elements, especially in the representation of settings that irreverently defy gravity and thus evoke a distinctive sense of space readily associated with Gothic architecture. "The word 'Gothic,'" James Rollins maintains, "comes from the Greek word 'goetic.' Which translates to 'magic.' And such architecture was considered magical. It was like nothing seen at the time: the thin ribbing, the flying buttresses, the impossible heights. It gave an impression of *weightlessness*" (Rollins, p. 406). The etymological explanation for the term "Gothic" adopted by Rollins is not universally shared but is undoubtedly most apposite to the present context given its overt link with magic. (The Greek word, as seen in Chapter 2, is also deeply relevant to *Rental Magica*.)

Therefore, though crisscrossed by highly sophisticated machinery, the hypothetical technologies portrayed in the anime nonetheless exude an esoteric feel that draws them into closer proximity to the realm of ancient magic than to the domain of advanced science. Ryle uses the idea of the ghost in the machine in essentially figurative terms. The anime under scrutiny, while preserving its metaphorical import, also strive to literalize it by presenting situations where technology is infiltrated by supernatural agencies — where the machine, in other words, is invaded by the ghost. Thus, the magic missions dramatized in the chosen anime are principally metaphors for a sustained and variegated investigation of the relationship between magic and technology: a partnership already highlighted in Chapter 1 and also seen to play an interesting role in both *Ghost Hunt* and *Darker than Black* in Chapter 2.

The interplay of magic and technology reminds us that even tough people are often inclined to associate technology with the application of scientific findings, and hence with rationality, efficiency and functionality, this stereotypical grasp of technology does not properly acknowledge the word's etymology: the Greek word *techne*, namely "art." Recognition of this lexical connection entails a reevaluation of the relationship between technology and art. Indeed, the semantic imbrication of technology with art entails that it cannot be tied up unproblematically with the realm of the empirically demonstrable, as imagination and fantasy will inevitably penetrate its equations. Relatedly, *techne* does not merely refer to the production of objects endowed with practical functions but to production in the broadest imaginable sense of the term, and therefore encompasses the conception of hypothetical realities through literature, painting, music and several other practices. This list must logically include magic, too, as a quintessential manifestation of human creativity — a creativity so hearty and unbridled, in fact, as to extend to the ideation of entire realities virtually from scratch. In other words, if technology is also art, and magic can be regarded as an art, then technology and magic cannot be posited as mutually exclusive polar opposites. Richard Stivers pursue this line of thought by arguing that technology has become akin to magic in the sense that "our expectations for technology have become magical and our use of it increasingly irrational" (Stivers, p. 1). That is to say, human beings have been progressively forging multifarious technologies that operate analogously to magic rites, particularly in the areas of psychology, administration, the advertising industry and the mass media, whose ultimate goal is the establishment of structures of human adjustment and control that may be capable of linking symbolically a plethora of consumer goods and the utopian ideals of success, pleasure and wellbeing.

It seems also worth noting, in this respect, that the interpenetration of magic and technology in contemporary culture is pithily confirmed by the rampant infiltration of numerous aspects of popular fantasy technologies by appropriately fictionalized facets of medieval and Renaissance history and lore replete with wizards, warlocks, spells, enchanted weapons and, most crucially, magic missions. Videogames of the role-playing adventure type are the most blatant instance of this trend. Also notable, as an illustration of contemporary technoculture's interaction with magic-imbued epochs is the *Annual Renaissance Pleasure Faire*. Held in California over six weekends every Spring and comprising theatrical and swordplay performances, folk dances, maypole carousels, amateur archery contests, juggling, parades and processions, as well as stalls selling household artifacts, swords and chain mail and a jousting arena for armored knights. Eddo Stern's depiction of the motley crowd in attendance at the *39th Annual Renaissance Pleasure Faire* (San Bernardino, 2001) vividly captures the convention's characteristic atmosphere: "The creatively anachronistic Renfaire crowd is comprised of a colorful band of jolly Anglophiles, mediaevalists, woodworkers, elves, druids and wizards selling handmade crafts, performing jousts, drinking mead and offering an all out sun-beaten Californian version of new-age virtual reality" (Stern, p. 258).

In *Mai-HiME* and *Mai-Otome*, the coalescence of magic and technology is attested to by the portrayal of the key characters' supernatural abilities. These are frequently referred to in technological or cryptotechnological terms. At the same time, cybernetic apparatuses can be seen to hold an authoritative status in the maintenance of the balance of power at stake in their respective stories. Yet, there can be little doubt that the technology on which the heroines and both their associates and their antagonists rely in the performance of their missions is pervaded by forces of an inherently magical nature.

In both series, magic and technology collude to give rise to myths, rituals and, most crucially, metaphors enabling people to interact with their natural and social milieux. Concomitantly, the creative energies unleashed by that collusion facilitate the emergence of alternate imaginary realities within such contexts. For instance, the nanomachines central to *Mai-HiME* and *Mai-Otome*, operating simultaneously as magical instruments and as technological equipment, come to represent parallel worlds unto themselves—

dimensions governed by rhythms that resemble the workings of nature and society alike insofar as their survival depends on the maintenance and respect of certain fundamental laws. Those worlds could be figuratively described as "magic villages"— bearing in mind that neither in the universe of Oriental lore at large nor in the realm of anime of the more mature ilk could such a phrase be deemed coterminous with a halcyon fairyland guaranteeing unlimited leeway for the satisfaction of dreams of wish-fulfillment. In fact, darkness, fear and even horror are never conclusively excised from the picture, as evinced by the tragic fate looming over an Otome should she wish to contravene the technomagical laws by which her breed is meant to abide.

The state of affairs dramatized in Obara's anime finds a direct parallel in *Sola* with the interplay of the magical and the technological elements surrounding the otherworldly species to which the heroine is said to belong. On the one hand, this is steeped in ancient lore and hence seemingly impenetrable by technoscientific investigation. On the other hand, it constitutes a technology in its own right to the extent that it is ideated as a specific body of knowledge, matched by an appropriate set of skills, methodologies and tools, regulating that species' functioning. This interplay creates a context within which Matsuri and Yorito can interact with each other vis-à-vis their shared natural environment and their societal circumstances. At the same time, the interactions centered on the protagonists and their friends and foes (where unforeseeable shifts of allegiance abound) give rise to an alternate world of a distinctively magical stamp. In this context, the pleasing (wish-fulfilling) capacities of magic are encapsulated by the quasi-romantic relationship that gradually develops between Matsuri and Yorito. This heartwarming prospect is, however, ineluctably held in check by dark omens presaging and ultimately decreeing a fate of separation and loss.

A further interpretation of the synergy of magic and technology is yielded by *Ghost Hound* and *Magikano*. In these anime, technological motifs pivoting on either bio-engineering or the production of artificial humans carry magical connotations insofar as they function as metaphors for the power ascribed to magic in traditional cultures to influence or even reshape nature. As Chapter 4 will show in some depth, magic has been historically harnessed to the investigation and, where appropriate, stabilization of unruly forces pervading the natural domain. Technologies of the kind we see hypothesized in *Ghost Hound* and *Magikano* take it upon themselves to undertake the missions assigned to magic itself in cultural contexts more intimately connected with nature — that is to say, older or more lore-oriented societies. Nevertheless, the emplacement of technology as an agency capable of affecting nature by quasi-magical means does not unproblematically emblazon it as an object of uncritical worship. In fact, we are constantly reminded of the destructive potentialities inherent in the use of technology as a way of working magic and, by implication, of nature's resistance to conclusive policing. The tribulations to which *Ghost Hound*'s principal characters are fated as inevitable concomitants of their dimension-crossing abilities bear witness to this unpalatable reality with uncompromising honesty. The tenebrous destiny potentially in store for the entire Earth in *Magikano* should its protagonist's preternatural powers be allowed to run amuck corroborates the message. Simultaneously, *Ghost Hound* underscores the inextricability of magic and technology through the proposition that even the most advanced forms of scientific experimentation are ultimately sustained by otherworldly agencies and mysterious psychosomatic interactions with the inscrutable Beyond. In *Magikano*, the inextricability of supernatural phenomena and technological themes is couched in more explicitly science fictional overtones.

In *Kagihime*, the technological dimension takes the specific form of a textual technology and preeminently the concept of hypertext — a term here broadly understood as a system of writing that enables different portions of a text to be linked nonlinearly with a potentially indefinite number of other texts. Indeed, the anime is one among a plethora of works in diverse media to have been influenced, more or less directly, by Carroll's narratives. Those works are not explicitly referenced in the series itself, which could not be logically expected of a show of its scope and tenor. Nevertheless, they could be said to be implied or inferentially alluded to by the anime, and any number of them might spring into the spectator's mind depending on the breadth of the frame of intertextual references which he or she brings to bear upon the viewing experience. In the two *Natsume* series, technology likewise comes to the fore on the textual level insofar as the show's own technology — broadly understood as the system of knowledge, tools and methods used to create the medium in which the text exists and through which it is conveyed to its audience — is inseparable from the notorious tome that effectively defines the protagonist's identity, interactions and psychological development.

Another popular exemplification of the marriage of magic and technology worthy of notice in this context is supplied by the TV series *MoonPhase* (dir. Akiyuki Shinbou, 2004–2005). One of the show's principal personae, Kouhei Morioka, is indeed presented as a photographer of supernatural phenomena that spends much of his time capturing the otherwise elusive or even invisible apparitions of creatures such as specters, demons and poltergeists by recourse to cutting-edge equipment on behalf of a specialist journal. What enables the youth to undertake this unusual task, ostensibly, is his total unreceptiveness to paranormal phenomena and attendant immunity to their influence. According to his grandfather, a mystic, this makes Kouhei "spiritually retarded." Yet, it eventually transpires that he is, in fact, endowed with the rare powers of a "Vampire Lover," a human being immune to the consequences of the mythical blood-sucker's lethal bite. As a character initially portrayed as utterly ordinary or even fairly mediocre later revealed to possess formidable preternatural abilities, *MoonPhase*'s male lead echoes some of the protagonists of other series discussed in this chapter as focal studies.

Ultimately, all anime — and, most pointedly, anime that engages at a deep level with the interplay of magical and technological motifs — operates as a potent testimony to the intrinsically technomagical character of the art of animation as a whole. It indeed emphasizes with peerless vigor that art's capacity, through the utilization of specific kinds of *techne*, to perform tricks, dramatic rituals and metamorphic ruses similar to those traditionally enacted by stage magic. As Richard Williams maintains, "seeing a series of images we've made spring to life and start walking around is already fascinating," and "seeing a series of our drawings talking" ascends to the level of "a very startling experience." When animators finally see pictures they have executed "actually go through a thinking process," in the awareness that they have been "creating something that is unique, which has never been done before," they are rewarded with "the real aphrodisiac" — with sensations, therefore, akin to the feelings of bewitchment, rapture and sheer *jouissance* with which magic is famously associated (Williams, Richard, p. 11).

Chapter 4

Magic Natures

*The universe is full of magical things, patiently waiting
for our wits to grow sharper.* — Eden Phillpotts

*Break open a cherry tree and there are no flowers, but the
spring breeze brings forth myriad blossoms.* — Sojun Ikkyuu

The concept of place again plays a key role in the treatment of magic
natures as it did in the handling of contracts and missions of a likewise preternatural ilk. The anime here explored varyingly emphasize that the practices, tools, emotions, images and ideas unfolding within the universe of magic
derive both dramatic and symbolic meaning from the locations in which they
are set. In fact, the phenomenon of magic in the broadest imaginable sense
of the phrase could be metaphorically ideated in architectural terms as a spacious edifice accommodating various levels of both practical and abstract
engagement. One level, comparable to an adaptable storeroom, houses the
materials underpinning the activities and techniques associated with the performance of magic. A further level holds the affects that both trigger and sustain its employment: this equates to the more intimate portions of a home,
such as the bedroom or the kitchen. Another level, something like the magic
building's study or library, provides a setting for the moments of reflection
and analysis necessary to complement the performance per se with introspective awareness of its likely roots and consequences. At the top of the edifice,
a loft offering a generous view of the sky above hosts the imagination, while
at the bottom, a shadow-mantled cellar gives shelter to dreams. Taken in tandem, the imagination and dreams supply the catalysts capable of bringing all
of the other layers together in a variety of combinations and patterns. The
house of magic thus conceived posits space as a center of meaning.

As the titles here under scrutiny indicate, the contingent magnitude of
the space involved is immaterial compared to its resources as a signifying
force. Therefore, no less substantial a volume of meaning may be generated
by a modest straw mat or a flimsy folding screen than by an entire household,
school, sprawling city or empire. In all its manifestations, space molds experience on both the sensory and the intellectual planes, at times allowing for

hands-on communion with its materials and at others engaging us conceptually through symbols and mental images. As artworks, all anime productions constitute virtual places fostering the formation of meanings and experiences wherein the actual and the imaginary seamlessly blend. When anime intersects with magic, the scope for constructing hypothetical places in which reality and fantasy meet grows exponentially. The world and the self alike are thereby conceived of as continual work-in-progress — as processes defined by people's interactions with myriad spaces and places as they endeavor at once to establish roots and to move on, to belong and to "ex-ist," to feel at home and to outgrow home. In the realm of magic, the journey itself is ultimately more defining a trait of its inhabitants than the desire to be anchored. Magic, in other words, is the boundless land of the eternal wanderer.

Places, in these shows, do not lay out their meanings overtly or even visibly. In fact, and most pointedly when they coalesce with magic, they embed them cryptically in their nooks and interstices, scratches and indentations, ditches, furrows, honeycombs, subways and eaves, in a fashion reminiscent of the lines on the palm of a hand — namely, texts pregnant with stories always waiting to be discovered. It would be preposterous to assume, however, that one could ever grasp in its totality what that dense coating of signs might contain or conceal. Discovery remains an approximative and fragmentary achievement even after years of painstaking exploration. All one can hope for is a bundle of labile logogriphs, an inevitably precarious reward to be only attained, if at all, not by traveling in a straight line but rather in a zigzag of tortuous ramifications. Any one evident path is countered by at least a thousand hidden ones, any one solid route, by legion airy or liquid ones. This is the challenge of magic space and its ultimate beauty for those who value the voyage over and above any possible destination.

The representation of specifically natural environments traversed by magic forces provides anime with one of its most inspiring tasks. Unleashing countless life forms that mock or defy human understanding, let alone mastery, the anime here explored invoke the partnership of magic and nature as a means of exploding a vast array of anthropocentric and anthropomorphic myths with unparalleled energy. In engaging with life forms that intrepidly elude classification in classic scientific terms, the type of magic space here at stake expresses the non-things which populate the interstices between any two accepted categories, thus exposing the precariousness of the dividing line between presence and absence, worlds and anti-worlds. Whilst, as Edmund Leach remarks, the "taboo inhibits the recognition of those parts of the continuum which separate the things" (Leach, p. 47) the magical natures here portrayed invite us to acknowledge the life that lingers on the boundaries, and thus prompt us to face the taboo as a paradoxical source of fascination and revulsion at one and the same time.

Certain motifs influenced by both Eastern and Western sources recur with notable regularity in the shows under scrutiny and are therefore deserving of special attention. These include Shinto-based beliefs and rituals; the doctrine of *onmyoudou* and underlying associations with various philosophical ideas; and alchemy in the broad sense of the term. As one focuses on specific titles wherein these themes find articulation, a tantalizing range of magic natures comes to the fore. An especially significant role is played throughout by the spiritual principles of Shinto, as described in Chapter 1, and by the shamanistic practices based upon them. All of the titles under inspection resonate, albeit with variable degrees of explicitness and emphasis, with pantheistic motifs redolent of Shinto's perception of the cosmos as a symphony of ubiquitous spiritual forces. All manner of material objects, and most pointedly natural or semi-natural entities, are time and again posited as the receptacles of different *kami* capable of influencing human lives in both foreseeable and unexpected ways. In the depiction of the natural environment, rocks and trees, mountains and rivers, wild and domestic animals convey that message with arresting beauty. Household interiors and man-made architecture also exude spiritual powers, not only in conjunction with time-honored activities of ceremonial stature but also in the portrayal of day-to-day chores. The spirits of the departed likewise constitute pervasive and influential agencies. In all of these domains, one feels, as Michael Ashkenazi maintains, that there is "no effective limit to the number of *kami*" and that there is "no clear division between the mundane and the *kami* worlds" (Ashkenazi, p. 27).

The anime here explored reflect Shinto-based traditions in two major ways. At one level, they abide by the body of textually encoded myths that have come to be shared and sanctioned over the centuries as defining aspects of the Japanese nation, most notably the *Kojiki* (a.k.a. *Furukotofumi*, c. 712) and the *Nihonji* (c. 720). At another level, they capture local myths, both documented and imaginary, centered on demons (*oni*), forest goblins (*tengu*), ghosts (*gaki*), water spirits (*kappa*), and patrons, itinerant gods or saints spawned by the genius loci of each of a plethora of small communities. In addition, some of the *kami* alluded to in the shows are heavenly and other earthly, some recall officially recorded and nationally recognized spirits and others the contingent expressions of localized forces, all the time bearing witness to a markedly commodious attitude to mythology that makes the Japanese characteristically willing to integrate a wide range of mythical elements within their culture, and tends to result in a simultaneous dismissal of their contents as no more than old wives' tales and absorption thereof in the fabric of modern everyday existence.

The principles of Shinto are overtly prominent in *Mononoke* (dir. Kenji Nakamura, 2007), a TV series set in feudal Japan and pivoting on the exploits of an unnamed character known simply as the "Medicine Seller" (*shugensha*), as he deploys a variety of methods and tools to deal with pernicious spirits (the titular *mononoke*). This entails systematically unveiling their true "form" (*katachi*), the "truth" behind their manifestation (*makoto*) and the "reason" triggering their bizarre conduct (*kotowari*). Only after this investigative task has been completed is the character in a position to unsheathe his weapon and exorcise the spirits. The *mononoke*, it should be noted, belong to a broader magical species dubbed *ayakashi*, the term originally employed to designate a specter appearing at sea during a shipwreck and subsequently used also to refer to any demon that lingers unnaturally in the human world. The Medicine Seller describes the entities as "something that simply should not exist," adding that there are, however, "millions" of them "all over." "As long as darkness exists within the hearts of men," the hero later comments, "there will always be more.... No matter how they came to be, though, an *ayakashi*'s reason for being is beyond human understanding."

Many of the supernatural incidents recorded in *Mononoke* bring to mind salient aspects of Japanese mythology and lore. One of the most interesting instances consists of the *zashiki-warashi*— namely, a subset of the *youkai*, a category of supernatural beings ranging from the evil demon or ogre (*oni*), through the mischievous fox spirit (*kitsune*), to the ambiguous snow woman (*yuki-onna*) and the shapeshifter (*obake*). *Zashiki-warashi* are frequently associated with well-kept and ideally spacious old houses, supposedly bringing the residence good fortune as long as they occupy it and precipitating its fall into a rapid decline upon their departure. *Umibouzu*, entities reputed to dwell in the ocean and overturn the vessel of anyone bold enough to address to them, are likewise conspicuous presences in *Mononoke*'s multi-spirited realm. *Umibouzu* are commonly held to be drowned monks and to retain the shaven head and praying position appropriate to their earthly origins. In addition, the show features the uniquely intriguing *noppera-bou*, faceless ghosts that normally manifest themselves in human form. No less prominent are the *nue*, creatures of ill omen supposedly equipped with the head of a monkey, the body of a raccoon, the legs of a tiger, and a reptilian tail, in some legends also exhibiting the power to morph into a dark cloud and fly. As a result of its dizzyingly hybrid appearance, the *nue* is at times alluded to as a Japanese chimera.

Finally, the show truly excels in its interpretation of one of the most popular creatures of Japanese folklore, the *bakeneko* ("monster cat"), normally described as a feline endowed with supernatural abilities akin to those of the fox spirit (the aforementioned *kitsune*) or the raccoon spirit (*tanuki*). A cat may become a *bakeneko* as a result of its age, the particular number of years for which it has been kept, the specific size it has reached, or the retention of a long tail. The *bakeneko* typically haunts the house it inhabits, deploying all sorts of ruses to terrify its owners, from the summoning of spectral fireballs to the temporary assumption of a human shape or even the cannibalistic consumption of its owner in order to shapeshift and replace him or her. Stylistically, *Mononoke*'s greatest strength resides with its ability to commingle its supernatural themes with a narrative structure reminiscent of the murder mystery genre, elements of historical drama and a fair share of experimental flourishes.

A paradigmatic illustration of the Medicine Seller's characteristic modus operandi can be found in the arc focusing on the *mononoke* typology of the *umibouzu*. In this segment of the anime, the protagonist is called upon to investigate the case of a "ghost ship" said to be controlled by "the spirit of a sailor lost at sea on a stormy night." In the sequence where the demon's form is first drawn out, the show regales the eye with one of its most audacious experimentative moments. The ghost ship materializes as an ensemble of giant shells and fragments of marine fossils, using as attacking weapons no less massive fishbones that come shooting out of its crustaceous flanks like harpoons. The ship's sinister lines stand in stark contrast with the fluid, curvaceous and undulating rhythms that characterize the design of the vessel on which the Medicine Seller and his traveling companions are trapped.

As the protagonist patiently waits for the *mononoke*'s truth to reveal itself, a grotesque creature appears in the shape of a large fish with webbed hand-like fins, wearing a gorgeously patterned robe and playing an indigenous instrument akin to a Western lute, supplying director Nakamura with another splendid pretext for daring design. The figure's purpose seems to be to induce the passengers to bare their souls, and reveal what they fear most intensely, so as to expose the reprehensible feelings that could conceivably have occasioned the emergence of the ghost ship in the first place. Initially, the root of the problem would appear to be the restless soul of one of the travelers' sister — a maiden thrown into the sea within a sealed container (*utsurobune*) as a sacrificial offering intended to appease a host of angry water demons. Eventually, however, it turns out that the culprit is the girl's brother: a man determined to become the chastest of monks but tormented by an utterly consuming carnal longing for his sister. Having given up her life in place of her brother, who was actually the ritual's intended victim, the girl is said to have found peace in the depth of the sea. The would-be monk, conversely, has been harboring an especially malign *mononoke* within his soul ever since the immolation was performed as an incarnation of his own dark, repressed nature. It is only when the man is able to admit to his genuine emotions — and, above all, to his ruthless solipsism — that his soul can be cleansed and his human integrity restored by the Medicine Seller's portentous sword.

The purification motif pivotal to the Medicine Seller's magical duties likewise plays a key role in the two TV series *Neo Angelique — Abyss —* and *Neo Angelique Abyss — Second Age —* (dir. Shin Katagai, 2008). Set in the quintessentially magic world of "Arcadia," the anime pivots on the character of the ethereally beautiful girl Angelique. While this heroine seems quite satisfied with her peaceful routine as an ordinary schoolgirl without any need for otherworldly challenges, life-draining monsters dubbed "Thanatos" increasingly terrorize her land. Angelique's existence takes a new direction when she is approached by the "Purifier" Nyx, one of the very few men with the power to eliminate the Thanatos, and is urged to join his organization as possibly the only woman endowed with the necessary exorcizing talent — namely, the legendary "Queen's Egg." Angelique initially resists Nyx's pressing invitation, her objective being to follow in her father's footsteps and become a doctor of the secular ilk and not a traditional healer. She is, however, compelled to reassess her position quite drastically as her own school and classmates fall prey to the demons and her true vocation accordingly awakens.

The pull of ancient mythology, so intensely palpable throughout *Mononoke*, also works as the governing force behind the TV series *The Tower of Druaga — The Aegis of Uruk* (2008) and its sequel *The Tower of Druaga — The Sword of Uruk* (2009), both of which were helmed by Koichi Chigira. In this case, the body of legends on which the adventure relies for inspiration is not indigenous, however, but drawn from remote Sumerian culture. Chigira's anime woks on the premise that every few years, a supernatural phenomenon known as the "Summer of Anu" occurs, in the course of which the monstrous spirits associated with the eponymous edifice lose their powers due to the benevolent intervention of the sky-god Anu, the lord of heaven and all its constellations, of other deities and of all imaginable spirits and demons. This is a perfect time for the armies of the Kingdom of Uruk to launch their attack, annihilate those demonic forces, and climb to the Tower's upper levels to reach the legendary treasure reputed to be hidden at the very top: the "Blue Crystal Rod." The quest's ultimate aim is to conquer the Tower's entire magic environment — an enormous epic edifice redolent of Babylon — so as to vanquish conclusively the monster Druaga, the evil being that was once defeated by the mighty King Gilgamesh alongside the Tower itself but has since regained strength and now plagues the people within the regenerated building from its very summit. (The concept of level-by-level achievements in the incremental progression towards an ultimate goal betrays the anime's origin in a multilayered arcade game released by Namco in 1984.)

The figure of the medicine seller, so pivotal to *Mononoke*'s entire diegesis, holds considerable significance in the context of autochthonous Shinto-oriented traditions generally. A wandering character occasionally reminiscent of the figure of the witch doctor found in numerous cultures across the globe, the *shugensha* is renowned not only for his power to perform exorcisms and spells but also, on a more mundane plane, for his function as a divulger of news from the outside world to remote and isolated villages, as well as a cherished peddler of charms and trinkets. *Shugensha* are, typically, practitioners of *shugendou*, a synthesis of Shinto and Buddhism within which magic constitutes both a catalyst and an adhesive. It should also be noted, on this point, that Japanese history abounds with figures akin to the *shugensha*: namely, various outsiders and nomads associated with religious and supernatural motifs. At one end of the spectrum stands the roving outcast (*hinnin*); at the other, the visiting deity (*marebito*). In between these two categories, one finds the *kebouzu* and the *bikuni*, peripatetic monks and nuns specializing in the performance of conjurations, exorcisms and other cleansing rites. The rites performed by these and other traditional practitioners evince a reverential attitude toward all of the natural entities with which they typically deal — be they flora, fauna, water or rock, for example. In thaumaturgic contexts, this respect seamlessly extends to supernatural creatures and phenomena, and this implies that even when such presences have to be tamed or perhaps eliminated altogether from the scene, they are nonetheless accorded an existential status analogous to that of the familiar beings with whom they — more or less precariously and more or less hazardously — coexist or interact. Profound deference, relatedly, is displayed toward all manner of natural materials — particularly those that are deployed in the manufacture of ceremonial objects such as purificatory or summoning tools, of paper lanterns associated with ritual functions (*chochin*), of *shimenawa*, sacred straw ropes enshrined in the Shinto tradition, and of the paper streamers (*gohei*) normally attached to them for liturgical or divinatory purposes, whence the art of *origami* is held to have originated.

This stance reflects a very distinctive aspect of indigenous mentality that expresses itself most vibrantly with artisans and artists, as well as in pursuits embedded in daily life, such as garden design, flower arrangement, interior design and fashion design, the tea ceremony and various gastronomic practices, as well as both artisanal and industrial packaging. According to Lenor

Larsen, the value of the physical element is cardinal to the creation of all manner of artifacts within both traditional and contemporary Japanese society: "Craftmakers working within Japan's ancient traditions respond to the generations of passed-on knowledge. This collective memory includes a deep respect for material and process, and respect too for the intended user" (Larsen, p. 12). It is though this respectful approach to nature and its materials, ultimately, that magic practitioners teach us to see in nature beauties whose existence we could otherwise have barely dreamed, intimating that even a glance at the natural world out of the window of one's hut, castle or urban apartment (as the case may be) could inaugurate an enthusing adventure.

Mushi-Shi (TV series; dir. Hiroshi Nagahama, 2006) bears affinities to *Mononoke* in its adoption of an ambulant protagonist, Ginko, as an indefatigable investigator of latent primeval life forms known simply as *mushi* and the supernatural events supposedly connected with them. The *mushi* are quite simply posited as a breed of ethereal beings that "dwell, unseen, in the shadows — a host of creatures completely different from the flora and fauna familiar to us, an invisible world of life within our own." Like the classic wandering healer, the *mushi-shi* ("*mushi* hunter") Ginko repeatedly endeavors to assist people troubled by phenomena they cannot comprehend, though these are more intimately connected with the essence of life than any familiar plant or animal, and to teach them how to live in harmony with the unknown. Only very few humans are actually able to perceive the *mushi*, even though these peculiar entities are continually interacting with the ordinary world in more or less peculiar ways. While it is not normally in their nature deliberately to cause harm or discomfort to humans, their quintessential alterity often entails that whenever *mushi* and people come into contact, neither party is likely to benefit from the interaction. It is for this very reason that *mushi* hunters like Ginko have come into being.

Respectful of the creatures' inherently nonbelligerent disposition, the protagonist never seeks to either inflict damage to the objects of his research or oppose their efforts at self-assertion — unless, that is, the *mushi*'s interventions prove palpably detrimental to the lives of innocent villagers. On the whole, however, he is portrayed not so much as the stereotypical exterminator of villains and demons so frequent in action-adventure anime as a thoughtful detective or even a proto-scientist. Hence, installments incorporating battle sequences are dexterously interspersed throughout the series with episodes in which the investigation mode is predominant, allowing a narrative that might otherwise have come across as repetitive in its "one-creature-per-adventure" approach to retain a refreshing modicum of dramatic agility. Moreover, the show's reflective tenor is perfectly matched by the somber magic of its natural setting, where a palette composed almost entirely of green, brown and gray hues dominates. At the same time, as Tasha Robinson emphasizes, "The backgrounds are exquisitely rendered, luminous nature scenes; ... the contrast between detailed backdrops and simple, iconic characters is extreme. The storylines repeatedly emphasize that humanity is lost and small amid the diversity and intensity of primal life on Earth, and the animation brings that idea across by visually overwhelming the human characters with vibrant forests, mountains, snowstorms" (Robinson).

It is with the *mushi*'s astonishing diversity, ultimately, that the anime's true magic resides. The templates employed in the depiction of the bizarre entities stretch over an exceptionally broad visual repertoire, evoking birds, jellyfish, bamboo and rainbows — among legion more images drawn from the visible world of nature. The designs of some *mushi* reflect the preference for stylized ornamentation characteristic of traditional Japanese art, others bring to mind the decorative motifs favored by the postmodern Japanese movement known as Superflat, others still evoke Joan Miró's perplexing amoebas and doodles. *Mushi-Shi*'s magic nature, therefore, is of the order of a bewitching world-within-a-world that both departs radically from our familiar reality and recalls it by means of supple visual metaphors. Figures such as these eloquently demonstrate the relevance to the art of anime of E. H. Gombrich's contention, advanced with regard to images generally, that images can be most effectively "used to work magic" (Gombrich, p. 40). This function, according to the illustrious philosopher of art, is intrinsic to the most archaic of graphics — to "pictures of animals" of the kind that "primitive peoples" were wont to "scratch" on "rocks" in "the eerie depth of the earth" to appropriate metaphorically the "power" of the creatures represented therein (p. 42). The images invoked by Gombrich are so primordial as to constitute apposite visual correlatives for the *mushi* designs pervading Nagahama's anime.

A close graphic relation of *Mushi-Shi*'s speculative menagerie within the broader family of fantastic anime life forms is provided by a sequence from *Gunbuster 2* (OVA series; dir. Kazuya Tsurumaki, 2004). This show, it must be noted, cannot be termed "magical" in the purest sense of the term insofar as its primary frames of reference are science fiction and the coming-of-age tale, yet reverberates with poetic echoes of the fantastic and the otherworldly in its forays into some of the most spellbinding vistas inaugurated by contemporary physics. In the sequence in question, the character of the "Chief of Staff" Niigo attempts to elucidate some of the mysteries underlying the "Sol System" with the aid of cutting-edge technology (incredibly sophisticated monitors, multidimensional digital graphs, holograms), documenting the evolution of a complex set of life forms from a shape akin to a spermatozoon to a proliferation of figures that recall micro-organisms congruous with real-life specimens, yet are entirely fictitious and inspired by disparate aesthetic leanings. Concurrently, *Mushi-Shi* is redolent of *Kino's Journey* (TV series; dir. Ryutaro Nakamura, 2003) in its adoption of a nomadic adventurer eager to discover incessantly new places and cultures, and of *Mermaid's Forest* (TV series; dir. Masaharu Okuwaki, 2003) in its sensitive exploration of the difficulties issuing from the interaction of human and non-human agencies.

As *Mushi-Shi's* hero travels from place to place in his tirelessly inquisitive — and potentially infinite — journey through the unknown, he comes across all sorts of strange characters and situations. These include a girl whose eyesight has been impaired by *mushi* and is hence only capable of perceiving the glimmering river that symbolizes the source of all life but cannot withstand any other form of light; a man that inexplicably chases rainbows; a nearly-drowned woman that has turned into translucent jelly as a result of drinking water *mushi*; a coat apparently infested by *mushi*; a boy that has developed horns; a shrine held capable of granting people a second life; a man apparently supplied by *mushi* with prophetic dreams deleterious to the welfare of his village. Several of these cases echo, more or less explicitly, figures and situations enshrined in indigenous lore for time immemorial, held either to trigger the eruption of magical phenomena or to invite magical interventions on the part of professional or semi-professional practitioners.

Mushi-Shi also echoes the *Natsume* anime, *Shigofumi* and *Kagihime* (all of which are addressed in Chapter 3) in its association of potent magical energies with textuality. The anime's imaginary biology could be said to represent life at its purest and its entities are, as a corollary, amorphous and polymorphic at once. In one of the show's most memorable adventures, the physical portrayal of these fluid and resolutely unclassifiable creatures is deployed as a metaphor for the materiality, transience and inherent vitality of language itself— a system made up of minute characters which, like the *mushi*, can be conceived of as both devoid of form and potentially capable of acquiring the most vertiginous profusion of shapes imaginable. This metaphorical equation is effected through the rendition of pictographs that are actually capable of detaching themselves from the page on which the tale's protagonist studiously draws them and of acquiring animate, indeed exuberantly kinetic, existence. At the same time, the idea that typographic characters are inherently invested with vitality functions as a potent metaphor for the essence of animation as an art capable of bringing inert matter to vibrant life. In *Mushi-Shi*, textuality is also brought into play in the episode where Ginko visits a bizarre library containing *mushi*-related scrolls written by a girl whose entire family has been laboring for generations under a dark curse. This entails that one member of the family in each generation comes into the world with a "charcoal birthmark" indicating that a *mushi* is trapped within his or her body. The curse results from "a forbidden *mushi*" being once sealed in one of the girl's ancestors and then passed on with the ordinary human genes from one generation to the next. The only way to anesthetize the invasive entity and alleviate the physical pain caused in the bearer by its presence is to collect tales about *mushi* and write them down so as to seal the *mushi* within the boundaries of a scroll. If the *mushi* thus contained break loose, the sentences written in each scroll release themselves from the paper and fill the entire space of the library with an intricate net of character strings intersecting like the threads in a spider web, which it is then up to the cursed heroine to unravel, returning the sentences to their original scrolls with the aid of magical glue.

The natural realm in all of its multifarious manifestations is also conceived of as saturated with spiritual forces, in a fashion again reminiscent of Shinto principles, in the anime *D. C.—Da Capo*—(TV series; dir. Nagisa Miyazaki, 2003) and in its sequel *D. C. S. S.—Da Capo Second Season*—(TV series; dir. Munenori Nawa, 2005). The story's magical feel is sustained throughout by its setting on a crescent-shaped island, Hatsunejima, where all sorts of creatures appear to host unusual powers and cherry trees bloom all year long. Most revered among them is the monumental *sakura* held capable of fulfilling any wish, no matter how ambitious or bizarre. The anime deploys a large and subtly nuanced cast, according privileged roles to Jun'ichi Asakura, a youth able to peek into other people's dreams, though powerless to interfere with them, and to summon candy out of the blue, his beloved and adoptive sister Nemu, and the eternally childlike sorceress Sakura Yoshino. The action focuses on the dire repercussions of Sakura's tampering with the mighty tree's powers to satisfy her personal aspirations. While Jun'ichi and Nemu are the principal casualties of the witch's spells, numerous other characters see their lives fall apart as the fulfilled wishes on which those are predicated are abruptly revoked. These include non-human characters that have been allowed to gain human form and emotions by the preternatural *sakura* and have no choice but to return to their initial state once the tree's powers have been eroded. A positive variation on the theme of the supernatural cat, noted in the analysis of *Mononoke* with reference to the baleful figure of the *bakeneko*, is proposed in *Da Capo* through the recurrent appearance of magical cats of all shapes and sizes. Among the more remarkable of these creatures are a metamorphic kitten capable of temporarily assuming the shape of a human girl to appease its agoraphobic owner's longing to interact with the external world, and a cat-man attired in distinctive film-noir gear, whom Sakura dubs "Fushigi-san" (literally, "Mr. Mystery"). This enigmatic character tends to feature as a silent observer in several of the anime's surreal and dreamy scenes.

The image of the cherry tree — arguably an icon of Japanicity par excellence — features no less conspicuously in *Magic User's Club*, an anime whose story unfolds over an OVA series (1996) and a TV series (1999), both of which were directed by Junichi Sato. The anime revolves around a five-member school club which, due to its paltry size, has a hard time not only performing magic as its designation implies but also compete for meeting space with the infinitely more popular Manga Club. Both series evince an enticingly broad frame of visual reference, ranging from alien invaders to magical teddy bears, from the character type of the clumsy teenage witch to that of the exquisitely handsome gay wizard, all the while amalgamating Eastern and Western motifs in its dramatic potion. Following the defeat of its alien foes, the titular club has to deal with the emergence of a novel preternatural problem in the guise of a titanic *sakura*, rising like a skyscraper in the middle of Tokyo to the great discomfort of all of the city's inhabitants.

A curative function reminiscent of the tasks undertaken by *Mononoke*'s and *Mushi-Shi*'s protagonists in the trail of Shinto shamans is embraced by Touko and Rinko Mishima in *Yume Tsukai* (TV series; dir. Kazuo Yamazaki, 2006). Known as *Yume Tsukai* (a.k.a. "Dream Users"), the two girls take it upon themselves to tame the uncontrollable nightmares that ensue from people's dreams when the desires embedded therein spill into reality with potentially calamitous repercussions. When this happens, the baleful visions plague the everyday world in the form of paranormal phenomena that typically manifest themselves as poltergeist activity. Once they have apprehended the unruly nightmares and translated them into more tranquil dreams, Touko and Rinko seek to return them to their rightful originators. In doing so, however, they deliberately refrain from intruding upon the dreamers' ordinary lives. In other words, they act exclusively as exorcists and do not presume to take on the secular roles of counselors or psychotherapists, for their job rests on the belief that it is up to the nightmares' owners to identify their causes and, ideally, negotiate the consequences of their emergence. The show's magical infrastructure is felicitously buttressed by haunting music, and visually punctuated by images of children's toys intended to function as metaphorical "offerings," that are capable of morphing into shamanic weapons and monstrous creatures. The protagonists' dad is reputed to have introduced the toy-based practice into the job by replacing the established custom of using "religious objects such as mirrors or *magatama* [curved beads]" as offerings.

The theme of toys that magically come to life is a well-established component of both Western and Eastern fantasy. At one end of the spectrum, to cite a famous instance, stands E. T. A. Hoffmann's *The Nutcracker* (1816), with its armies of toy soldiers, sentient dolls and highly spirited eponymous figurine. At the other, as a further example, one finds Takeshi Kitano's film *Dolls* (2002), where the haunting power of the doll figure is dramatizes with unsettling potency with recourse to a Bunraku (puppet) show that reverses the standard puppet/spectator relationship by allowing the artificial creatures to observe the human audience with an uncannily dispassionate gaze. In the specific context of Japanese history, the most disquietingly attractive of all imaginable animated toys are the "*karakuri ningyou,*" mechanized dolls or puppets typically manufactured and treasured by the affluent classes in the eighteenth and nineteenth centuries. As the relevant *Wikipedia* entry explains, the term "*karakuri*" "means a mechanical device to tease, trick, or take a person by surprise'" and hence "implies hidden magic, or an element of mystery. ... '*ningyou*' is written as two separate characters, meaning person and shape. It may be translated as puppet, but also by doll or effigy" (*Wikipedia, the free encyclopedia — Karakuri ningyou*). Echoes of this tradition reverberate throughout Mamoru Oshii's movie *Ghost in the Shell 2: Innocence* (2004), where they are interspersed with both homages to Hans Bellmer's uncanny jointed dolls and daring forays into magic-tinged cybertechnology.

As these illustrations indicate, while it might be tempting to regard the figure of the magically animated toy as an incarnation of playful innocence, it is important to bear in mind that its treatment is frequently tinged with sinister connotations. *Yume Tsukai* fully endorses this proposition, using its toys in an unpredictable and often baffling manner. A striking example of this trend is provided by the sequence in which Rinko reveals that the *Yume Tsukai* are able to "become one" with the toys they handle as offerings and that, as a result, the toys let them "use their powers and abilities." In this particular case, Touko deploys a diminutive toy missile and, as she merges with the object's own spiritual energy, morphs into a flying machine bearing all the most salient attributes of rather an intimidating mythical bird of prey.

The close relationship obtaining between the play offerings and the *Yume Tsukai*'s physical bodies, posited by the anime as an integral aspect of Touko's and Rinko's tasks, brings to mind the notion of "sympathetic" magic, a phenomenon detected by numerous anthropologists, archeologists and sociologists across disparate traditional cultures. Originally outlined by Edward B. Tylor in *Primitive Culture* and subsequently developed to a substantial degree by Sir James George Frazer in *The Golden Bough* and by Marcel Mauss in *A General Theory of Magic*, the laws of sympathetic magic pivot on various principles, the most relevant ones in the present context being those of contagion and similarity. Frazer elucidates this proposition in Chapter 3 of his seminal text, devoted to the concept of "Sympathetic Magic," and specifically in its first section, where "The Principles of Magic" are outlined: "If we analyse the principles of thought on which magic is based, they will probably be found to resolve themselves into two: first, that like produces like, or that an effect resembles its cause; and, second, that things which have once been in contact with each other continue to act on each other at a distance after the physical contact has been severed. The former principle may be called the Law of Similarity, the latter the Law of Contact or Contagion. From the first of these principles, namely the Law of Similarity, the magician infers that he can produce any effect he desires merely by imitating it: from the second he infers that whatever he does to a material object will affect equally the person with whom the object was once in contact, whether it formed part of his body or not. Charms based on the Law of Similarity may be called Homoeopathic or Imitative Magic. Charms based on the Law of Contact or Contagion may be called Contagious Magic" (Frazer).

Thus, the law of contagion maintains that once separate entities have been in contact with each other for even a short period of time, they remain able (at least potentially) to affect or alter one another well beyond the end of the contingent contact. Numerous properties may thus be transferred across both animate and inanimate objects. In *Yume Tsukai*, this idea is spectacularly substantiated by the metamorphic sequences in which separate physical objects that have undergone a modicum of mystical contact in preparation for a mission influence each other so intimately as to literally fuse into a single being. The law of similarity, for its part, proposes that entities that resemble each other on the surface also bear deeper affinities of a spiritual nature. In the anime, this idea is corroborated by the existence of correspondences between the superficial appearance of the toys to be deployed as offerings prior to their magic transformation and the shape they thereafter acquire, which tends to be a more imposing variation on the initial form, enhanced by the Dream Users' own agency. The object resulting from the mystical fusion retains a resemblance to the original toy, it is intimated, because its essence bears a deep spiritual affinity with the essence of its antecedent. This implies, in accordance with the Shinto belief in the intrinsic spirituality of all entities, that the initial entity already harbored a spiritual substance despite its ostensible inertness.

It is also noteworthy that the terminology employed by *Yume Tsukai* to describe the protagonists' job is itself steeped in mythology. Claiming that the present-day dream tamers are the descendants of the ancient "Asobibe clan," Rinko explains to a novice that "the origin of the kanji for '*asobu*'" contained in the clan's name is the "character of god carrying a flag while charging onto the battlefront. The picture of god presenting himself for battle changed into the meaning for *asobi*, ... 'to play.' That's why when *Yume Tsukai* go to play, it means that we go to fight." With the girls' characterization, moreover, *Yume Tsukai* echoes several indigenous customs of magical significance. The hermit-like Touko, who appears to spend most of her time asleep in the eerie toyshop where the dream-exorcising business is based, [1] declares openly her association with the supernatural by donning unremittingly the Noh mask, modeled on the figure of the *kitsune*, that once belonged to her father, killed in the course of a mission before Touko took over the practice. The girl's most formidable power resides with her left eye, through which she can gaze into her clients' troublesome visions. Endowed with a lively and somewhat impetuous personality, Rinko comes across as infinitely more practical and dynamic than her elder sister and tends to be the first to jump into action when a fractious nightmare raises its head.

Yume Tsukai earnestly underscores, even at its most facetious, the collusion of disparate reality levels whose boundaries are no more substantial than gossamer webs. In this regard, the anime brings to mind the writings of the illustrious Jungian psychologist Hayao Kawai. Invoking a branch of Buddhist philosophy, Kawai maintains that "all things freely interpenetrate each other." Citing Toshihiko Izutsu, he further elucidate this proposition as follows: "nothing in this world exists independently of others. Everything depends for its phenomenal existence upon everything else. All things are correlated with one another.... Thus the universe in this vista is a tightly structured nexus of multifariously and manifoldly interrelated ontological events, so that even the slightest change in the tiniest part cannot but affect all the other parts" (Kawai, p. 33). This world view reverberates throughout both *Mushi-Shi* and *Yume Tsukai* through a felicitous admixture of gravity and playfulness.

Japan's fascination with dreams, their language and their symbolism is borne out by myriad aspects of both the more venerable artistic and performative traditions and popular culture. An especially apposite example, in this context, lies with Akira Kurosawa's live-action film *Yume* (*Dreams*, 1992). The section of the movie entitled "The Peach Orchard," moreover, shares with *Yume Tsukai* a fascination with the latent aliveness of inanimate objects in general and toys in particular, as a young girl's doll collection comes to life on the day of the time-honored *Hina Matsuri* festival. The ubiquity of oneiric discourse in Japanese culture is corroborated by the frequency with which the designation "*yume*" features in disparate areas thereof— including the *shoujo* manga magazine *Hana to Yume*, the TV drama show *Nagai Yume*, the song *Yume wa Yoru Hiraku*, the videogame *Yume nikki*, and the psychedelic rock band *Yume Bitsu*. (Please note that dreams are also profoundly relevant to the bildungsromans discussed in Chapter 5.)

Mononoke, Mushi-Shi and *Yume Tsukai* bear implicit similarities in their exploration of the repercussions of their protagonists' efforts to penetrate the world's pockets of darkness — a quest which all three shows present as immensely preferable to the colonialist endeavor to disavow those enigmatic regions in the name of reason. In doing so, they echo the perspective expounded in Chapter 2 by promoting an understanding of darkness as potentially enlightening. It is also noteworthy that the chosen anime's portrayal of darkness echoes a specifically psychoanalytical perspective associated with the concept of the *shadow*: the receptacle of all things that consciousness most deeply dreads and struggles to disown. In Jungian psychoanalysis, specifically, the shadow is described as the repository of affects that civilized society circumvents or suppresses. What is most threatening about the shadow is that it has an autonomous energy prone to express itself in the guise of monstrous or otherwise unsettling entities. Ironically, the more vigorously the shadow is avoided, the more powerful and energetic it tends to become — the more sonorously it vibrates with dynamism and creativity. Acknowledging these qualities as essential properties of the shadowy and the dark is paramount if we are to recognize that what is commonly demonized as evil may actually hold the power to open our eyes to very valuable, albeit submerged, reality levels.

There is something amusingly — and inexorably — circular about the magical exploits undertaken by the likes of *Mononoke*'s Medicine Seller, *Mushi-Shi*'s Ginko and *Yume Tsukai*'s Dream Users. This is a direct corollary of an important facet of magical thinking, which Richard Stivers has elucidated as follows: "Magic is effective only in relation to humans and only when they believe in it. Magic succeeds as a self-fulfilling prophecy: belief in magic makes it seem efficacious. In relation to nature, magic is only apparently effective. If my bear-hunting ritual is invariably performed before I hunt bears, then it is associated with successful hunts. Hunting failures can always be explained away, e.g., we did not perform the ritual correctly. Magical healing can be effective, however, as a placebo, a kind of emotional self-fulfilling prophecy. Placebos often do work, if only temporarily" (Stivers, p. 3). By extension, it could be argued that the rituals enacted by the Medicine Seller, Ginko and the Dream Users are not necessarily efficacious per se in influencing nature. They only become so when their performers are in a position to invest those rituals with the honest force of their belief in magic and, ideally, to harness the trust placed in their abilities by the lay people in need of their professional assistance.

In tracing the vicissitudes of the young Masahiro, the grandson of the legendary mystic Abe no Seimei, as he struggles to overcome his spiritual shortcomings with the assistance of the formidable *mononoke* Mokkun (a.k.a. Touda or Guren), *Shounen Onmyouji* (TV series; dir. Kunihiro Mori, 2006–2007) engages with one of Japan's most intriguing magic traditions, *onmyoudou*. This term designates a synthesis of esoteric cosmology and natural science influenced by practices brought into Japan by Buddhist monks; by the philosophy of *yin* and *yang*; by principles akin to those promulgated by present-day *feng shui* (*fuusui* in Japanese); and by a conception of the universe as a collusion of the Five Elements, which bears affinities to alchemy. Its principal objectives encompass divination, protection from evil spirits, and control of the *shikigami*—a concept parallel to the Western notion of the "familiar." (This is central to the anime *The Familiar of Zero*, here discussed in Chapter 5, where the doctrine of the Five Elements is also very prominent.) *Onmyoudou*, it will be recalled, also plays a part in *Ghost Hunt* and *Rental Magica* (please see Chapter 2).

For both many young Japanese and for most Westerners, *onmyoudou* is only known as a fruitful source of fictional entertainment. However, *onmyoudou* is fundamentally a spiritual journey meant to abet the achievement of balance within the self and between the self and its environment. The figure of Abe no Seimei invoked in *Shounen Onmyouji* is celebrated as one of the greatest practitioners of all ages, and accordingly placed at the intersection of myriad varyingly elaborate tales. The mystic's origin in the marriage of a fox spirit and a human, allied to his supposed affiliation with no less than twelve *shikigami*, has contributed significantly to the perpetuation of his mythical fame. As explained in the *Onmyoudou Awakening* website, even though "the Muromachi period saw closure of the schools formally teaching *onmyoudou* and the royal affiliation with *onmyouji*," the "the romantic ideal of *onmyoudou* persisted on, especially in the legends of the beloved Abe no Seimei.... It is through his adventures that many came to know about *onmyoudou* and *onmyouji*, and indeed the name Abe no Seimei is recognized by most Japanese adults and many Japanese children." Furthermore, while *onmyoudou* has influenced various practices and rites carried out by Shinto and Buddhism, it is often outside the strictly ceremonial sphere that it has survived most potently as a magnetizing force, particularly in "popular culture," where "the romantic concept of *onmyouji* lives on as youths in animated series call upon game cards that come to life and do their bidding just like an *onmyouji* would a *shikigami* in days past. So even if they have been unable to put a label upon it, they know the concept as they had been born into it" ("*Onmyoudou* Introduction").

While *Shounen Onmyouji* takes its *onmyoudou* background seriously, rooting it in the reality of feudal Japan with almost documentary accuracy, it also displays a refreshing flair for turning it repeatedly into a valid pretext for comic relief. This derives principally from the protagonist's dissatisfaction with his situation — which is perfectly understandable when one considers that whenever the boy manages to pull off a magical feat, people are only too eager to take his performance for granted, claiming to expect nothing less of Abe no Seimei's successor, and, conversely, whenever he fails, people are quick to sneer at his ineptitude in comparison with his venerable ancestor's brilliance. Plenty of humorous moments are additionally provided by the recurrent scenes in which Mokkun teases Masahiro and derisively addresses him as "grandson," exploiting to his advantage the fact that most of the time nobody else can perceive his presence. Comedy is also periodically generated by the scenes in which Masahiro's famed grandfather petulantly urges the boy to work harder, affecting operatic anguish at the tiniest of mishaps.

Shounen Onmyouji encompasses two arcs, the first of which focuses on Kyuuki, a winged tiger from China exiled after being vanquished by another demon, that aims to devour the imperial princess Fujiwara no Akiko to replenish his weakened constitution with the aid of a host of foreign demons. The second arc pivots on a vengeful spirit's persecution of the character of Yukinari Fujiwara. Over both arcs, *Shounen Onmyouji*'s greatest dramatic strength lies with its combat sequences. Although these are employed as regular fixtures throughout the series, they are prevented from becoming repetitious and predictable by the anime's dexterous diversification of the opponents' magic natures and attendant superpowers.

It transpires that as a kid, Masahiro possessed a magical talent known as "second sight," consisting of the ability to perceive demons and spirits that most ordinary people cannot even begin to sense. His grandfather, therefore, trained him to become an *onmyouji*, hoping to mold the boy into a worthy successor. At one point, however, Seimei decided to seal Masahiro's second sight in the belief that a proper mystic should develop his powers through hard work and study and not by merely relying on natural endowments. The Japanese devotion to the concept of "*gambaru*" — to do one's best, to persevere — is here pithily asserted. The show's initial emphasis on the ephemerality of its protagonist's talent also serves to indicate that supernatural powers can never be taken for granted as permanent possessions, since the sheer capriciousness of fate may snatch them away at a moment's notice. When Mokkun turns up and Masahiro is able to see him, the boy is tempted to believe that his perception of the spirit world has been restored. His expectations are frustrated, alas, as a giant monster threatens his town and Masahiro proves quite powerless to confront it.

A highly original interpretation of *onmyoudou* in recent anime is offered by *Magical Shopping Arcade Abenobashi* (TV series; dir. Hiroyuki Yamaga, 2002), a multiple-reality show centered on Sasshi Imamiya and his best friend Arumi Asahina, and the adventures on which they embark following Arumi's grandfather's seemingly fatal fall from the roof of the Asahina family diner. In the course of the series, the protagonists enter and interact with a tremendous variety of alternate worlds, each of which is thoroughly designed in accordance with the codes and conventions of specific genres, both cinematic and literary. These include the medieval role-playing game, *mecha* anime, the martial-arts live-action movie, the prehistoric-world cartoon, the film noir, hard-boiled detective fiction, the gangster film, the Sherlock-Holmes-inspired crime story, the dating-sim game, pulpy fantasy fiction, the war drama, the horror genre, the musical and the plane-hijack yarn (with additional hints at the likes of *Jaws*, the *Terminator* movies and Indiana Jones). Since this protean universe gives rise to prodigiously diverse realms governed by context-specific rules, Sasshi and Arumi are never allowed to take their situation for granted and must, in fact, struggle to recognize the sort of reality into which they have descended at each step of the narrative. The reason for this relentless world-hopping is initially unclear. The only obvious thing is that Arumi longs to return home, while Sasshi seems eager to continue traveling across disparate realms indefinitely.

The anime's climax reveals that Sasshi, a direct descendant of the acclaimed *onmyouji* Abe no Seimei, is actually the cause of his and his friend's wandering and does not wish to go back because he senses that if they return to normality, Arumi will have to witness her grandfather's death and does not wish to expose her to this harsh truth. Moreover, the boy knows that Arumi's family is just about to relocate to a remote region and the return to ordinary life would therefore be tantamount to his loss of the sole relationship he truly treasures. The power enabling Sasshi to pull off such a monumental feat emanates from *onmyoudou*'s belief that when problems appear most intractable, it may nonetheless be possible to bypass them by migrating from one reality to another. As argued by Arata Kanoh in the "Guided Tour" to the anime provided by *Newtype USA*, *Abenobashi*'s distinctive approach to *onmyoudou* mysticism indeed pivots on its presumed ability to "solve all your problems by hopping from world to world" (Kanoh, p. 61). In Yamaga's show, *onmyoudou* is brought into play right from the start — in the preamble to the opening episode, in fact — and symbolically associated with the pentagram (or pentacle): *Abenobashi*' logo and very possibly the most universal emblem for magic practices ever. The anime's deployment of ancient magical references no doubt provides scope for entertaining forays into parallel dimensions. However, it also dramatizes, in a pointedly metaphorical vein, the drama of growing up. In rejecting reality and its pain, Sasshi is effectively using his magical abilities to ensure his and Arumi's abidance in a kind of Neverland. In the climax, where the boy has no choice but to accept the return to reality as inevitable, Sasshi is also capitulating to adult imperatives. Nevertheless, the anime's finale does not unequivocally dramatize the protagonists' reinscription in their original reality, since the world in which they land following their esoteric peregrinations does not slavishly conform with that reality but rather appears to have magically altered for the better during their absence — and, arguably, as an oblique result of Sasshi's mystical ruses.

Moving on to consider some of *onmyoudou*'s most important affiliations, we must first of all take into account the concept of *yin* and *yang*. Imported from China, this advocates that seemingly conflicting forces are in fact interdependent, rooted in each other at all times, and hence capable of reciprocal transformation. The concept underpins various forms of Chinese science, medicine and philosophy, as well as the martial arts and most notably, among them, *taijiquan* (a.k.a. *tai chi chuan*). *Yin* and *yang* are held to have arisen in tandem from a state of quiescence and to move together until that state can be restored. *Tai chi* is supposed to mirror this process by cultivating patterns of motion which, through a balance of *yin* and *yang*, may lead to a condition of stillness. The relationship between *yin* and *yang*, famously captured by the emblem of the divided circle (the *taijitu*), is frequently ideated in terms of sunlight playing over a shady valley (*yin*) and over the brightly lit mountain slope rising above it (*yang*). By extension, *yin* is associated with tranquility, coldness, softness, the night and the feminine principle, while *yang* pertains to dynamism, heat, hardness, daylight and the masculine principle. Nevertheless, *yin* and *yang* do not represent mutually exclusive binary opposites and neither polarity, therefore, is ultimately conceivable of independently of the other.

The concept of *yin* and *yang* also structures the *I Ching*, or "Book of Changes," a symbolic divination system used to identify order in ostensibly random occurrences whose central cosmological assumption is the dynamic balance of opposites. In the *I Ching*, *yang*— posited as the creative principle — is emblematized by an unbroken line (______), while *yin*— the receptive principle — consists of a broken line (__ __). Unbroken and broken lines are combined into sets of three-line arrangements (*trigrams*) which lean more toward *yin* or *yang* depending on the number of lines of each kind they contain. Trigrams are clustered into more complex arrangements of six lines each (*hexagrams*) held to correspond to oracular statements. Some basic trigrams exemplifying the preponderance of either principle include the following:

Earth	Mountain	Water	Wind
— —	———	— —	———
— —	— —	———	———
— —	— —	— —	— —

Thunder	Fire	Lake	Heaven
— —	———	———	———
— —	— —	———	———
———	———	———	———

Another key influence behind *onmyoudou* is the Chinese doctrine of *Wu Xing*, i.e., the "Five Movements" or the "Five Elements" encapsulating the variable relations and interactions among phenomena. The five components of *Wu Xing* trace a creation cycle and a destruction cycle involving Wood, Fire, Earth, Metal and Water, and to each of these correspond different facets of nature, including specific colors, planets, seasons, climates, plants and animals, within a comprehensive cosmological system — as well as particular trigrams of the *I Ching*. Wood, for example, finds its cosmic correlatives in the color green, Jupiter, the spring, windy weather, the dog, the plum and wheat, as well as the trigram used in the *I Ching* to symbolize Wind. *Wu Xing* has influenced numerous aspects of Chinese tradition, from astrology and geomancy (*feng shui*), to medicine, music and the martial arts. Japanese philosophy has its own version of a system (heavily influenced by Buddhism) organized around the "Five Elements" (*godai*) — in this instance, Earth, Water, Fire, Wind and the Void. At times, Consciousness is also included as a sixth element. Frequently alluded to in both the context of indigenous martial arts and popular culture (anime and manga included), the theory of *godai* finds glorious expression in five-tiered Buddhist pagodas symbolizing the transition from Earth to the Void via the other three elements and a more modest, though no less memorable, manifestation in the stone lanterns adorning Japanese gardens. Earth (*chi* or *tsuchi*) emblematizes stability in both physical and psychological terms, while Water (*sui*) stands for the opposing pull of fluidity or flux, Fire (*ka*) represents dynamism, passion and desire, Wind (*fuu*) refers to expansive and joyful motion, and the Void (*kuu*) typifies the forms of pure energy that lie beyond the boundaries of human comprehension, creativity included. The doctrine of the Five Elements, as we shall see in Chapter 5, is cardinal to the entire diegetic structure of *The Familiar of Zero*. For the present purpose, it is worthy of attention both because of its connection with *onmyoudou* (via the aforementioned beliefs of Chinese provenance) and because of its implicit relationship with alchemy, one of the most renowned esoteric systems ever within Western civilizations.

In the West, alchemy is commonly associated with the medieval occultist, astrologer, botanist and physician Paracelsus (Theophrastus von Hohenheim, c. 1493–1541)—a major influence upon esoteric iconography and fantasy fiction for centuries to follow. Paracelsus subscribes to the classic Greek conception of the universe as a result of the interplay of the four elements (Earth, Water, Air and Fire)—according to which, incidentally, both the Western Zodiac and the symbolism of the Tarot are constellated. However, the medieval mage also posits an alternate configuration of the cosmos based on the *Tria Prima* consisting of Mercury, Sulphur and Salt. These substances are regarded as repositories of the universal principles ultimately responsible for both the latent essence and the visible shape of each and every object. Mercury symbolizes transformation, Sulphur a binding force, and Salt a solidifying agent. Relatedly, the three primary substances shape the human spirit—and, by implication, the magical powers lurking within it. Mercury lies at the foundation of the highest mental faculties, such as the imagination, whereas Sulphur begets the emotions and Salt the body. Paracelsus also held that Earth, Water, Air and Fire host elemental creatures—namely, the Gnomes, Undines, (or Nymphs), Sylphs and Salamanders respectively—that are regarded as soulless spirits nonetheless capable of assuming both angelic and corporeal attributes.

Alchemy as promoted by Paracelsus has been somewhat notoriously associated with an almost frenzied quest for immortality. It is with reference to this particular fantasy that popular culture has time and again enlisted alchemical symbolism to the portrayal of magical worlds—the ubiquitous concept of the Philosopher's (or Sorcerer's) Stone is undoubtedly the most illustrious of the available images. On Eastern soil, this thirst for immortality is shared by Daoism (a.k.a. Taoism), an ensemble of philosophical and religious traditions that have influenced various cultures for at least two thousand years. Promulgating the principles of moderation, humility and compassion, Daoism embraces the lessons of *Wu Xing*, ideating the human organism itself as a microcosm wherein the five elements constantly interact, and hence as capable of aligning itself to cosmic forces through rituals and spiritual journeys. As Jeannie Radcliffe explains, in the context of Daoism, "The body was seen as a furnace where the different energies were purified and raised to a point of focused perfection before ascending to the realms of the Immortals." The practitioner's primary objective was the conservation of the dynamic principle (*chi*), which was accorded a privileged position analogous to the role ascribed to mercury in Paracelsus' system. "Texts dealing with this topic," Radcliffe continues, "closely followed certain principles associated with the laws of nature and involved the generation of a mystical body that would be the vehicle to carry the soul to immortality" (Radcliffe).

One of the most acclaimed dramatizations of the principles of alchemy to be found in the history of anime as a whole is undoubtedly the series *Fullmetal Alchemist* (dir. Seiji Mizushima, 2003–2004). This chronicles the tragic fate of Edward and Alphonse Elric, two boys that roam the world in search of the Philosopher's Stone held capable of restoring the limbs lost by Edward and the entire body lost by Alphonse in their catastrophic effort to revive their deceased mother by alchemical means. While offering an original interpretation of Paracelsus' time-honored art, the show also functions as a powerful cautionary tale about the effects of the mishandling of magic by inexperienced practitioners. What Edward and Alphonse have overlooked is alchemy's primary principle — namely, the theory of equivalent trade, according to which people cannot gain anything without sacrificing something of comparable value in return. This view is also promulgated by the "Dimensional Witch" Yuuko in *Tsubasa: RESERVoir CHRoNiCLE* (briefly examined in Chapter 2) and *xxxHolic*, one of the main case studies offered in Chapter 5.

A magic nature veritably saturated by the principles of alchemy is proffered by *Aria*, the story of the aspiring gondolier Akari and her friends, set in the spellbindingly retrofuturistic world of Neo-Venezia. The TV series *Aria the Animation*, its sequels *Aria the Natural* and *Aria the Origination* and the OVA *Aria the OVA — Arietta —* (dir. Junichi Sato, 2005; 2006; 2008; 2007) dramatize the coalescence of magic and the natural world through their setting, Neo-Venezia: an imaginary realm pervaded by visual and symbolic echoes of the real city of Venice and, most importantly, by its proverbially bewitching atmosphere. Neo-Venezia itself is one of the small settlements built by humans in the parallel world provided by the planet "Aqua" at some unspecified point in the future, a terraformed Mars 90 percent of which is covered by oceans. (A cherished product unto itself, the anime has further extended its reputation by infiltrating the videogaming world in the form of two very popular visual novels by the Japanese company Alchemist: *Aria the Natural: Mirage of a Distant Dream* [2006] and *Aria the Origination: The Sky over the Blue Planet* [2008]). In the logic of Sato's show, the actual city of Venice is said to have sunk into its watery cradle several years prior to the story.

Aria explicitly invokes Paracelsus' doctrines in constellating its distinctive natural domain around the four "elementals" — namely, mystical entities presumed to reside within the spiritual essence of the fundamental elements.

These beings are life forces held to inform and influence the whole of nature. Neo-Venezia's gondoliers are appropriately dubbed "Undines," while "Salamanders" feature in Sato's anime in the guise of characters entrusted with the task of monitoring Aqua's climate. "Gnomes" are cast in the roles of people responsible for regulating the planet's gravity and "Sylphs," finally, provide the model for Neo-Venezia's airmail deliverers. It should also be noted that in *Aria*'s indigenous vocabulary, an Undine gains the title of "Prima" upon completing her apprenticeship. The term "Prima," it will be recalled, is used by Paracelsus to designate the three primary principles emanating from Mercury, Sulphur and Salt.

Aria chronicles the everyday experiences of its protagonist, the unremittingly generous, optimistic and resourceful Akari, and of her two closest friends: Aika, an exceptionally lively girl endowed with a sharp tongue and an often sarcastic sense of humor, and her dreamy and remote counterpart, Alice. Each of these heroines is an apprentice Undine to one of the gondolier firms based on Aqua: Aria Co., Himeya Co. and Orange Planet. The heads of the three firms at whose behest Akari, Aika and Alice are training — namely, the "Water Fairies" Alicia, Akira and Athena — complement the key personae at each turn with their enchantingly charismatic presence. The actual presidents of the organizations are not human beings of either terrestrial or Martian birth, however, but rather preternaturally intelligent blue-eyed cats. Revered throughout the Martian city as superior spiritual entities, these creatures are intensely redolent of Shinto's *kami*. Feline figures again assert themselves as major magical agencies as they were seen to do in *Da Capo* earlier in this chapter and in *Rental Magica* in Chapter 2.

Concentrating on unpretentious depictions of simple quotidian interactions in preference to spectacular entertainment, the anime stands out as a joyful celebration of the value of quotidian and even seemingly insignificant situations, inviting the viewer to acknowledge the incomparable importance of what the poet William Wordsworth has memorably described as the "little, nameless, unremembered acts / Of kindness and of love" ("Lines Composed a Few Miles Above Tintern Abbey," 1798). This world view consistently sustains the show's serene slice-of-life tenor, while investing it with an aura of intimacy capable of drawing viewers into Akari's and her friends' magical reality as far more active presences than mere onlookers. *Aria*'s markedly episodic character could, in principle, have caused it merely to yield an assortment of fragmentary vignettes. It is its unwavering devotion to the evocation of the feeling of warmth issuing from the simple beauty of contingent daily occurrences that enables it to forge a potent sense of dramatic continuity and thus avoid the danger of bittiness.

At the same time, *Aria* reinforces the magical force of gestures which might superficially come across as negligible by alluding to their enduring legacy through adventures that symbolically connect the present to the past (and even to the future), taking Akari back in time to Aqua's prehistory, when the oceans had not yet mantled the planet. While much of the time the anime focuses on the quotidian events and minor dramas unfolding through Neo-Venezia and its circumambient universe, it occasionally offers some genuinely spellbinding forays into fantastic territory. Hence, in one installment the protagonist might simply be engaged in guiding a honeymooning couple through the Neo-Venetian tracery of canals, and confronting no steeper a challenge than the down-to-earth problems presented by the unexpected appearance of a dead end. Yet, in the next, she might find herself transplanted, as though by sorcery, to her city's legendary past and have opportunity to interact with earlier generations and share both their dreams and their ordeals. Concomitantly, the natural magic of Neo-Venezia (and its planet at large) is elliptically thrown into relief by means of contrast, its aquatic constitution starkly at odds with the inhospitable and polluted reality of "Manhome" (Earth). For example, Akari especially enjoys swimming when taken on a short holiday with her friends by the three Water Fairies because the oceans on her original planet cannot be swum in. (The illustrations just cited come from the anime's first season.) Likewise pivotal to the anime's emphasis on simple moments is its respect for the here-and-now. As the main characters negotiate diurnally their desire, hopes, doubts and fears, the audience is urged to follow them moment by moment, savoring the magnitude of the fleeting instant irrespective of where the next adventure might take them tomorrow or the day after.

Furthermore, it is vital to appreciate that although *Aria*'s world is quintessentially magical in terms of both its philosophical underpinnings and its pervasive atmosphere, it also exhibits a pointedly pragmatic side. This consists of Neo-Venezia's commercial imperatives, a hard-nosed reality we are never quite allowed to ignore, which directly mirrors the history of the real city of Venice and its entanglement with money for time immemorial. Neo-Venezia is indeed a major tourist hub in which gondolas constitute a major attraction, and its gondoliers are highly esteemed throughout Aqua as tour guides. Any romantic tendency to idealize the city as a world of metaphysical purity would, therefore, be quite inapposite as it would fail to grasp the non-magical elements upon which the magic of *Aria* ironically depends for its cumulative effectiveness.

It is apposite to consider, on this point, that the historical city has been associated with conflicting images for centuries, and alternately portrayed as dreamy and materialistic, romantic and cynical, ghostly and corporeal, progressive and conservative, the vessel of high art at its most rapturously refined and a tawdry display of souvenirs and trinkets. The ancient city's hybrid nature is encapsulated by the somewhat monstrous character of its heraldic symbol: a lion consisting, like Frankenstein's creature, of pieces of diverse provenance more or less harmoniously assembled together. Furthermore, as Richard Goy points out, Venice is "half within and half out of the water, half eastern and half western, poised in that elusive zone between sea and sky" (Goy, p.14). The liminal character of Venice is further conveyed by its lagoon, as a physical boundary that is also, paradoxically, a denial of boundaries as a result of its hydric constitution. "Reaching Venice by boat rather than from the mainland," Elena Bianchi points out, "means capturing the city's genuine essence" (Bianchi, p. 39). The city's multiaccentuality, allied to its irreverent defiance of clear territorial demarcations, reflects the non-dualistic ethos pivotal to magical thinking as a discourse averse to strict categorization and binary logic.

As Sato's series progresses, the magic of the natural world per se incrementally coalesces with the magic of nature as represented by art. This issues from the anime itself, largely thanks to enthralling visuals reliant on subtly nuanced palettes abounding with luscious greens, vibrant blues and mellow pastels (especially baby pink, light blue, lavender, pale yellow, seafoam green, ivory). Simultaneously, *Aria*'s world derives palpable charm from a deft alternation of stylized backgrounds, aqueducts and gondola-strewn waterways, opulently textured aqueous expanses and bridges so delicate as to bring to mind the image of filigree, achieved through the conscientious synthesis of traditional and computer-assisted techniques. The magic of artistic representations of nature effected by the anime itself is further enhanced by the magic of the illustrious painters elliptically invoked by *Aria*'s visuals — Jacopo Tintoretto (1518–1594), Canaletto (1697–1768), Bernardo Bellotto (1720–1780) and, most resonantly, J. M. W. Turner (1775–1851). Furthermore, the art's integration with a well-modulated soundtrack combining soft jazz, piano pieces and Italian folk music greatly abets the overall magic of *Aria*'s nature. Artistically, *Aria* captures most faithfully the aesthetic trend described by Gombrich as a major aspect of Venetian architecture stemming from its imaginative absorption of a style previously established in Renaissance Florence. This lies with its ability to invest the austere forms favored by the initial model with "a new gaiety, splendour and warmth which evoke, perhaps more closely than any other buildings in modern times, the grandeur of the great merchant cities of the Hellenistic period." Furthermore, *Aria* evokes the very mood associated by the critic with Venetian painting — the unique "atmosphere of the lagoons, which seems to blur the sharp outlines of objects and to blur their colours in a radiant light, may have taught the painters of this city to use colour in a more deliberate and observant way than any other painters in Italy had done so far" (Gombrich, p. 325). It is from these stylistic preferences that much of the anime's magic ensues, as it fills its canvas with dancing balustrades, graceful sculptures and garlands that impart edifices with the semblance of tracery, while assiduously exploiting the interplay of light and color to balance forms and guide the viewer's eye without ever seeking to restrict a frame's visual exuberance.

A great deal of *Aria*'s natural magic (most pointedly in the second season) derives from deft cultural transitions. At one end of the spectrum, the action regales the eye with a bewitching phantasmagoria of iconic locations and monuments associated with the historical Venice. These include Piazza San Marco with its famous Basilica and Campanile, as well as the lore-encrusted Caffè Florian; and the quasi-magical cemetery of Isola di San Michele (a.k.a. the "Island of the Dead"). This particular setting is used by Sato in conjunction with a local ghost story regarding an executed Venetian woman reputed to have spirited away the gondoliers who rowed her to the place, stubbornly resisting burial. Numerous places directly modeled on real-life Venetian spots can also be seen in the course of the treasure hunt in which Aika, Akari and Alice engage in one episode — at the close of which it is intimated that the city's magic itself is the ultimate imaginable treasure. At the other end of the spectrum, the anime pays homage to specifically Japanese settings, as evinced by the episode where Alicia takes Akari to an island to visit a reproduction of a Japanese *inari* shrine — i.e., a Shinto shrine dedicated to the *kami* of foxes, fertility, agriculture, industry and worldly prosperity — and Akari even gets a chance to sample firsthand a wedding procession of fox spirits. Japanese lore is also touched upon in the installment where the main heroine falls asleep and dreams about the "spirit of the gondola" — i.e., a *tsukumogami*: a type of Japanese spirit or supernatural force emanating from objects that have reached their one-hundredth birthday and thus acquired aliveness and sentience. The third season again offers allusions to the historical Venice's topographical icons — such as the fifteenth-century Ca' d'Oro (the "golden house," a.k.a. Palazzo Santa Sofia), one of the most stunning mansions on the Grand Canal. Venetian customs also come to the fore, including the tradition of lace-making associated with the island of Burano. At the same time, explicitly Japanese elements are dominant in the episode where Akari introduces her friends to Japanese *tsukimi* rituals — the term *tsukimi* designating the Japanese custom, believed to have originated with the Japanese aristocracy in the Heian period, of holding parties to view the harvest moon.

Simultaneously, all manner of images and figures proverbially associated with Venice are either obliquely alluded to or overtly brought into play in several installments. A case in point is Casanova, appropriately cast in the role of the masked and charismatically enigmatic Master of Ceremonies for the no less renowned annual Carnival. The image of the mask here associated with Casanova (who turns out to be yet another magical cat) epitomizes the elusive and disquieting world of the carnival: a world where anything may happen, where designated identities and roles may be transgressed and where reality and fiction are free to meet and merge in mutual suffusion. Another famous custom linked with the historical Venice which the series gracefully invokes is the Festa del Redentore, a festival intended to mark the start of autumn. Furthermore, *Aria the Natural* makes reference to the *bucintoro* boat traditionally used for the "Marriage of the Sea," a ceremony meant to emblematize the maritime dominion of Venice, which in Neo-Venezia is said to be performed by the mayor instead of the Doge, as would have been the case in the old Venice.

Aria's sensitivity to the importance of culturally sanctioned events respected over time as a metaphorical guarantee of societal cohesion brings to mind Émile Durkheim's speculations on the subject of the "sacred," formulated in *The Elementary Forms of Religious Life*. Although Durkheim has little interest in magic as such, his perspective is nonetheless relevant to the current context insofar as his writings could be said to invest the sacred with magical undertones, albeit often in an oblique fashion. In Durkheim's view, the sacred is by no means synonymous with the divine. In fact, echoing the metaphysical perspective axial to Shinto, the philosopher contends that spirits and deities are not the sole candidates to the status of sacred entities since seemingly inanimate objects such as rocks and trees, or indeed practically anything which the human mind might be capable of ideating, could just as feasibly aspire to that position. What makes an object sacred, therefore, is not some intrinsic connection with the divine but its selection as somehow special, as worthy of separate attention and as subject to some prohibition that distinguishes it radically apart from something else, which is itself thereby labeled as "profane." Many of the time-honored sites and events in relation to which *Aria*'s plot is orchestrated owe their magical aura precisely to their differentiation as "sacred," at least in the metaphorical sense of the term, and hence deserving of particular notice or respect. Celebrating a traditional festival or visiting a revered location are ways of perpetuating their magic by retaining their separation from the prosaic and the quotidian. An especially powerful link between Durkheim's approach to the sacred and magical thought lies with the concept of contagion, here discussed in relation to sympathetic magic. For Durkheim, the sacred is incessantly capable of extending its sphere of influence because, "Far from remaining attached to the things it marks as its own," it "is endowed with a kind of fluidity" (Durkheim, p. 237). This property emanates from its sheer contagiousness, broadly understood as the power of transfer of a quality — positive or negative as the case may be — from one subject to another, and as the power to further such a transfer through repetitive and imitative rituals. Traditional festivities and public celebrations of the kind that punctuate *Aria* with arguably unmatched exuberance offer a paradigmatic illustration of such practices.

Magical locations of eminently crosscultural resonance also pepper the anime: the stairway to an alternate world where the characters are of the opposite sex is undoubtedly among the most entertaining instances of that modality. The magic of simple but deeply touching reflections, which aptly parallels *Aria*'s devotion to unostentatious "acts of kindness and of love" is beautifully encapsulated by the episode where Mr. Mailman explains that Neo-Venezia's people prefer to communicate by post rather than electronically because letters have the ineffable power to carry their senders' hearts and to touch those of their receivers, while creating ethereal bridges between the past and present. Akari equates letters to Neo-Venezia itself as a city likewise able to reach a person's soul, noting that her own being has been painted with "the color of Neo-Venezia." In the OVA, we learn about Akari's initial selection by Alicia as an apprentice, and *Aria*'s ubiquitous magic comes resplendently to the fore in the scenes where teacher and pupil experience Neo-Venezia's magic in the concurrently beguiling and eerie setting of the Campanile at night, well after visitors and tourists have left the scene. Akari herself is metaphorically emplaced as a magic agent as Alicia thanks the girl for being the special kind of student that does not merely expect to obtain knowledge to advance her personal aspirations but is, in fact, eager to show her teacher new wonders at each turn.

Aria portrays its aquatic city as a densely stratified palimpsest, resulting from the gradual accretion of historical, quasi-historical and altogether imaginary occurrences metaphorically connected with the actual Venice. Thus, even though Sato's city is posited as a futuristic reality, its essence is imbued with the magic of the past. Neo-Venezia, in this respect, brings to mind William Gibson's description of another often mythicized city, London: "the past ... seemed the very fabric of things, as if the city were a single growth of stone and brick, uncounted strata of message and meaning, age upon age, generated over the centuries to the dictates of some now all but unreadable DNA of commerce and empire" (Gibson 1995, pp. 11–12). In one of his later novels, *Idoru*, Gibson focuses on Venice itself, comparing the city's legendary mutability to the fluidity of cyberspace. Hence, Gibson's Venice is intimately connected with Sato's Neo-Venezia insofar as both versions of the original city are based on an inspired synthesis of the ancient and the ultramodern. In *Idoru*, Venice features in the guise of a virtual package that depicts the city as an esoteric space beyond its user's comprehension and yet, at the same time, as the very epitome of cyberspace. As the character of Chia virtually roams her simulated Venice, she feels as though the "stones of the Piazza flowed beneath her like silk," and as she darts into "the maze of bridges, water, arches, walls," she has "no idea what this place was meant to mean, the how or why of it." This description of Chia's virtual excursions vividly recalls Akari's and her friends' motion through Neo-Venezia, which likewise conveys a silky sense of flux at each turn, regardless of whether the girls are traveling by gondola along lustrous waterways or treading the cobbled alleys, *campi* and *campielli*.

Sato's city, like Gibson's virtual Venice, consistently evokes a magic tapestry woven from "water and stone slotting faultlessly into the mysterious whole" in a "default hour of gray and perpetual dawn" (Gibson 1997, p. 36). In this world, disparate elements coalesce in often unpredictable ways and the passing of time becomes hard to register or even irrelevant. In fact, it is capable of feeling uncannily real, unreal and surreal at one and the same time. What the characters — and, by extension, viewers or readers — perceive is quite real but they are frequently powerless to anchor it conclusively in a world they have ever empirically sampled. The fantastic images they encounter have their own intrinsic reality, yet much of the time they come across as akin to dreams, daytime reveries and trancelike states similar to those induced by magical incantation. The fluidity evinced by both the historical Venice and Neo-Venezia are beautifully captured by Jeanette Winterson's description of the Italian city in *The Passion*, where the character of Villanelle observes that Venice's spatial coordinates are so protean and flexible as to defy any conventional notions of linear progression or fixed destination. Venice, Villanelle avers, is "the city of mazes.... Although wherever you are going is always in front of you, there is no such thing as straight ahead" (Winterson, p. 49) "The city I come from," she subsequently observes, "is a changeable city. It is not always the same size. Streets appear and disappear overnight, new waterways force themselves over dry land. There are days when you cannot walk from one end to the other, so far is the journey, and there are days when a stroll will take you round your kingdom like a tin-pot Prince" (p. 97).

Neo-Venezia mirrors the actual Venice's aversion to mapping as depicted by Winterson. Incessantly planned and replanned since at least the Renaissance, the city has stubbornly resisted formalization: all the various projects designed to subject it to a rational urban grid have been either abortively executed or not undertaken at all. (The inconclusiveness of all efforts to restructure Venice is corroborated, alas, by the inadequacy of the plans which have been drawn for decades in the hope of rescuing the city from collapse.) One of the most radical attempts to remap Venice was made by Napoleon, who aimed to bring Venice "into the modern era by some drastic interventions," including the filling in of several canals and the clearing or demolition of several quarters to create "the Public Gardens which survive today " (Goy, p. 296). However, as Winterson's Villanelle ironically remarks, Bonaparte's efforts to rationalize and modernize Venice did not in the least erode the city's kinship with magical thinking and its defiance of binaries — its essential nature as a "Siamese" soul simultaneously "holding hands with the Devil and God" (Winterson, p. 57). With their incessant transformability and intoxicating sense of excess, both the real Venice and Neo-Venezia are capable of inducing an almost vertiginous sense of rapture. This is typified, to return to Gibson, by the feeling of total disorientation experienced by Chia in the space of her digital Venice, with "façades and colonnades springing up around her," "the prows of black gondolas" bobbing "like marks in some lost system of musical notation" and the rows of Carnival masks crowding around her with their "black, penis-nosed leather" and "empty eye-holes" (Gibson 1997, p. 186). Ultimately, it is a simple remark proffered by Akari herself that describes most tersely the magic of *Aria's* entire environment: "After all," the apprentice gondolier remarks, "humans are not the only beings out there who pursue encounters."

All of the anime explored in this chapter remind us that magic is, both as a word and as a practice, a moveable feast. As Michael D. Bailey remarks, "Scholars in many fields recognize magic as an important topic," and a large number of both lay people and experts in countless areas would agree that it holds the potential to provide "a system for comprehending the entire world." This can be attributed to the simple reason that it is "central to human culture" and that an investigation of the magic practices ratified or prohibited within a particular community is, therefore, integral to an adequate grasp thereof. However, in spite of this widespread acknowledgment of the ubiquitous value of magic, it remains "a profoundly unstable category." Official labels endorsed by various political or religious bodies have "varied dramatically across time and between cultures." Concurrently, not all practitioners will automatically regard their activities as facets of a unified "coherent system." Magic remains stubbornly elusive, moreover, insofar as "many people in various social and historical contexts have engaged in acts that their culture ... would categorize as magical without considering themselves to be performing magic. This seems especially true of simple spells or other common rites or superstitions" (Bailey, pp. 1–2). If magic is a fluctuating and polyaccented signifier in and by itself, its fluidity increases exponentially when it is brought into collusion with nature — another concept rendered proverbially unstable by its ongoing openness to conflicting interpretations and redefinitions. Magic natures, therefore, can take on a dizzying variety of forms, of which the titles here studied only offer a modest cross section. Whether we turn to the myth-encrusted cultures of feudal Japan or to the futuristically reimagined glory of Venice, for instance, magic and nature alike retain a phantasmagoric power to please and baffle us in equal measures.

Chapter 5

Magic Bildungsromans

Play reaches the habits most needed for intellectual growth. — Bruno Bettelheim

Travellers at least have a choice. Those who set sail know that things will not be the same as at home. Explorers are prepared. But for us, who travel along the blood vessels, who come to the cities of the interior by chance, there is no preparation. We who were fluent find life is a foreign language. — Jeanette Winterson

As a "novel of development," the bildungsroman typically deals with the formative stages of its protagonist's life, often culminating with maturity as a more or less reluctant acceptance of the adult sphere's rules and prohibitions. While magic bildungsromans likewise delineate a developmental trajectory, they tend to enlist the multifarious powers of fantasy to propose that genuine maturation should entail a recovery — or perhaps a rediscovery — of juvenile proclivities suppressed by the entry into the world of grown-ups: namely, a propensity to explore and experiment, a spontaneous capacity for play, and a willingness to dream. These tendencies translate into some of humanity's most deep-seated desires. Such desires, in turn, are caught in a double bind insofar as they constitute valuable points of departure for an individual's development and yet stand out as the psychic materials most likely to incur repression upon the individual's entry into the adult domain of language, laws and institutions famously dubbed by Jacques Lacan the "Symbolic Order" (Lacan). However, those inceptual desires are never totally elided. In fact, they retain a powerful, though abeyant, role in the psyche and find vibrant expression in dreams. Dreaming, here understood as a concurrently fantasizing and speculative drive, is the complex activity wherein atavistic longings are most frequently embedded. Dreams are experiences that play a unique part in most people's lives at one stage or another, and whose disappearance would feasibly signal the disappearance — or, at any rate, drastic attenuation — of sentient existence itself.

In its broadest sense, animation represents an unmatched means of capturing dreams and of transforming them, albeit fleetingly, into worlds that are seemingly real, credible, tangible and hence potentially inhabitable. As argued in Chapter 1, the topos of metamorphosis is pivotal to both thought and lore concerned with the operations and vicissitudes of magic. Thus, it could be argued that animation's transformative flair places it on a par with magical practice. This is especially applicable to thematically sophisticated anime eager to portray not merely drawn movements but also, and more importantly, moving drawings — i.e., images capable of enlisting an audience's affective powers and hence absorbing it into an act of creative interpretation: a magic act indeed. The protean, floating, spectral and gliding presences and pseudo- or mock-presences repeatedly summoned by magic-oriented anime have the capacity to infuse this process with a pervasive atmosphere of both enchantment and uncanniness.

If magic contracts, missions and natures exhibit remarkable diversity in their anime rendition, magic bildungsromans do not fail to live up to the "variety challenge," so to speak. In *Earl and Fairy*, it is the magic of old Europe that supplies the backdrop for the bildungsroman undergone by a seventeen-year-old English "fairy doctor." In *The Familiar of Zero*, the worlds of Oriental occultism and retrofuturistic fairy tale harmoniously coalesce to trace the protagonist's tragicomical bildungsroman from the moment she brings forth an unorthodox familiar, thereby blatantly confirming her proverbial inability to master any magical powers, to the revelation that she is actually a valiant mage. *Ponyo on the Cliff by the Sea* parallels *Earl and Fairy* in its election of a Western backdrop. The movie indeed invokes a well-known European narrative, enshrined in tradition as both a fascinating story in its own right and a wellhead of inspiration across various media: namely, the tale of "The Little Mermaid" commonly associated with Hans Christian Andersen upon which Hayao Miyazaki's film is loosely based. The bildungsroman traced by *Ponyo* is twofold. At one level, it concerns itself with the psychological development of a human boy as he discovers, names, befriends, loses and magically regains the object of his desire. At another level, the anime explores the titular heroine's own right of passage as, driven by a desperate yearning to become a human girl, she deploys powerful magic doomed to lead by turns to both dire and propitious outcomes. The bildungsroman delineated by *xxxHolic*, for its part, brings into play the theme of the magic contract as its protagonist enlists the abilities of a mighty witch to be rid of the visionary powers that torment him. While focusing on the protagonist's efforts to grow out of a most unwelcome ability, the anime throws into relief both the hurdles which the youth must confront on the scabrous path to self-realization and the unpalatable lessons he has to learn courtesy of his employer. (This developmental journey is prismatically elaborated over the course of two TV series and a movie.) In *The Girl Who Leapt Through Time*, finally, the magic bildungsroman mushrooms unexpectedly from an utterly prosaic everyday routine with profoundly defamiliarizing effects and potentially cosmic implications.

In all of the shows here examined, magic is deployed as a means of ideating, in an eminently metaphorical form, a pilgrimage of self-discovery and maturation that also functions, at least latently, as a metonym for macrocosmic phenomena of mutation and evolution. The processes of emotional and psychological development dramatized by the shows under scrutiny often gain pathos from their positioning in spatial contexts that combine starkly contrasting affects. Their urban settings, for example, frequently bring to mind John McCole's daunting depiction of the modern city: "The city's labyrinth of houses, by the light of day, is like consciousness; the arcades flow out unnoticed into the streets. But at night, beneath the dark masses of houses, their more compact darkness leaps out frighteningly; and the late passer-by hastens past them, unless we have encouraged him to take the journey down the narrow alley" (McCole, p. 243). Concomitantly, the anime repeatedly intimate that in spite of the current tendency to talk about space principally in terms of social practices, it would be absurd to equate it automatically to purely political and economic factors, for social space is also, inevitably, a geography of passions, emotions, longings and affects. As Henri Lefebvre observes, "Representational space is alive: it speaks. It has an affective kernel or centre: Ego, bed, bedroom, dwelling, house; or, square, church, graveyard. It embraces the loci of passion, of action and of lived situations" (Lefebvre, p. 42). Relatedly, "Space is liable to be eroticized and restored to ambiguity, to the common birthplace of needs and desires ... by means of differential systems and valorizations which overwhelm the strict localization of needs and desires in spaces specialized either physiologically (sexuality) or socially (places set aside, supposedly, for pleasure)" (p. 391).

In the realm of Japanese aesthetics, the affective qualities of space are enhanced in an utterly unique fashion by the valorization of the principle of *mu*—a sense of nothingness, inspired by Zen, that does not equate, as Andrew Juniper argues, to "nonexistence ... but rather the passing through to that which lies beyond the dualism of existence and nonexistence" (Juniper, p. 115). This notion finds visible expression in an approach that consciously and consistently upholds a distinctively Japanese "reverence for space and the feeling it can instill." This is most strikingly communicated by the "open expanses of the gardens," the "unused areas of monochrome painting," as well as the "complete lack of adornment in the tearoom." As the very spirit of space is thus allowed to "play an active role," practically all of the arts and crafts pursued on Japanese soil seek to open up not only "the space into which an object is placed, but also the space within it. There is a need to provide visual space so the nonmaterial aspect of the work can interact with and balance its material counterpart" (p. 116). This perspective is immediately pertinent to the discourse of magic insofar as the acknowledgement and cultivation of the invisible areas pervading reality in all its guises are primary aims for practitioners of the magical arts just as they are for painters, architects, sculptors, designers and, of course, animators eager to give magic metaphorical formulation.

The collusion of conflicting messages observed in relation to the anime's portrayal of urban settings finds an intriguing correlative in Japanese mythology, and specifically in its conception of space. In Buddhist cosmology, in particular, seemingly discordant philosophical perspectives often coalesce. This, as Michael Ahskenazi observes, is most patently borne out by the Buddhist attitude to the notion of Hell. On the one hand, this is depicted as a very concrete dimension wherein "the souls of those who have done evil in their life suffer torment until they expiate their sins or acknowledge the mercy of Buddha" (Ahskenazi, p. 101). However, while this description may seem to indicate that Buddhism accommodates a straightforward and unequivocal conception of Hell, this is not actually the case. In fact, there is also a sense in which the idea of Hell does not make a great deal of sense in the context of Buddhist thought at large insofar as "Punishment for sins in life should, in theory, occur in the process of rebirth" (p. 102). Damien Keown corroborates this point, maintaining that "Buddhism has no concept of Hell as a place of eternal punishment, and its notion of post-mortem retribution is closer to the Western notion of purgatory. The accumulation of bad *karma* can lead to rebirth in one of a number of Hells.... There are said to be both hot Hells and cold Hells, each with numerous subdivisions where evildoers are tormented by demons until their bad *karma* has run its course and they are reborn in a better state" (Keown). In this reading, Hell is a temporary — albeit possibly very prolonged — process or journey, not a permanent state.

Shinto space, by contrast, is mapped out in greater detail within Japanese mythology. Its most salient topographical features are the heavenly halls hosting a variety of deities, whence the "Floating Bridge" stretches towards the Earth; the Earth itself, which comprises the apparently limitless sea, an expanse of land in which the Japanese archipelago features prominently and, beyond the sea, the homeland of the wandering gods (the *marebito*, here referred to in Chapter 4). The subterranean "Land of Youmi," finally, consists of a lightless and colorless domain housing the halls of the dead. If Buddhism is ambivalent in its handling of the notion of Hell, Shinto is rather more upfront in eschewing the concept of eternal torment. Indeed, there is no evidence within its cosmology for any concept of punishment in the Western, Dante-inspired sense of the term, the sole affliction endured by the departed being their separation from their loved ones.

The underlying legend at the root of *Earl and Fairy* (TV series; dir. Kouichirou Sohtome, 2008) pivots on the mythical figure of "Blue Knight Earl," king of the "Fairy Nation"—a.k.a. the "Earl of Ibrazel." In Gaelic lore, it is proposed, "Ibrazel" is the designation for fairies reputed to live "beyond the oceans." The male lead, Edgar Ashenbert, claims to be the venerable knight's descendant and is determined to get hold of the "Noble Sword of the Merrow," a magical weapon and heirloom hidden three hundred years earlier. Edgar avers that the object is instrumental to his right to "assert his royal claim." In fact, the youth is a notorious larcenist suspected of myriad heinous crimes, known by the name of "John" among those who are aware of his shady background and current social standing. "Edgar" was indeed the character's "first name" but he lost it at the age of twelve when his father, an aristocrat suspected of treason, supposedly killed his family and then himself. Edgar renounced his lineage and now lives as though he were a mere "ghost" bwhat he self-deprecatingly describes as an entirely "fake" existence. Yet, he will stop at nothing to make the lie become the truth: hence, his desperate need for the Sword and for the heroine, an English fairy doctor named Lydia Carlton, as his sole hope of retrieving the portentous relic.

Shortly after being bereft of his aristocratic credentials, Edgar was sold to a man who required "white slaves," tortured and branded on the tongue. Although he eventually fled his tormentor, the "mark of a slave" inexorably follows him wherever he goes as an ever-present, dark shadow. In the course of the anime, we see Edgar being relentlessly pursued by "Gotham" (a name itself pregnant with fantastic connotations), a psychiatrist said to be addicted to brain experimentation and to be obsessed with appropriating Edgar's own brain as a proper test subject for research into criminal minds. Arrogant, vain and narcissistic, the hero nevertheless evinces a touchingly humane streak, especially in his protective attitude toward Raven, a fairy scorned and abhorred due to his non-human, ostensibly evil nature, whom Edgar has rescued and sheltered. As a result, Raven has become so totally devoted to his "master" as to be ready to kill for his sake. Indeed, the murders which Edgar is suspected to have committed have actually been perpetrated by his magical servant who, as a "bloodthirsty sprite," is driven to destroy instantly anything and anyone he perceives as a threat to his patron. By the time we meet him, however, Raven's malevolent magic does not hold sway since, even though his murderous instincts still obtain, he has gradually developed an understanding of the concept of conscience and a desire to be tamed (ideally by Lydia) into a more mindful being. Raven sports the same "peridot green" eyes as the heroine but whereas Lydia's expression invariably exudes infinite kindness and compassion, Raven's holds a malevolent light soaked with unspeakable sadness.

Daughter of an illustrious mineralogist, Lydia exhibits an unremittingly frank, independent and headstrong personality. Her most distinctive attribute is the rare ability to see fairies, a power she has inherited from her late mother. The girl avers that fairy doctors like her are not magicians but people that rely on their special "knowledge" and capacity to "communicate with fairies," namely, creatures in whom the prevalently secular mentality of late nineteenth-century England quite simply refuses to believe. In this respect, the anime recalls the works of Cicely Mary Barker, the English writer and artist active in the very epoch in which *Earl and Fairy* is set: a copious battery of volumes devoted to the characters of the "Flower Fairies"—wholly of Barker's own conception—and to the evaporation of the ability to perceive fairies as a sad concomitant of growing up and accepting the doxastic view that fairies simply *cannot* exist. The incredulous attitude informing Lydia's milieu entails that she does not habitually have much work (or cash, for that matter) and when we first meet her, she is indeed leading a quiet provincial existence on the outskirts of Edinburgh, Scotland. Her sole visible companion is a character destined to chaperon her throughout the adventure: the fairy Nico, who typically assumes the shape of a lazy cat but nonetheless comes equipped with the faculty of speech as well as a somewhat overindulgent passion for liquor. An especially felicitous touch, at the level of characterization, lies with the suggestion that even though it would be perfectly reasonable for Lydia to feel frustrated by her country's pervasive disbelief in magic, her good-humored resilience consistently keeps her bouncing, thus preventing her from declining into a downward spiral of despondency, for she knows in her own heart that fairies exist and that knowledge is the only thing that truly matters after all.

Fairy doctors are comparable to psychic investigators and in this respect, they are redolent of traditional figures such as itinerant medicine sellers and exorcists of the kind portrayed in the anime series *Mononoke* and *Mushi-Shi*, both of which are examined in detail in Chapter 4. Most importantly, fairy doctors act as "liaisons between humans and fairies," e.g., by creating paths for stray fairies that have inadvertently spilled into the human world in order to help them reenter safely their own magic lands. Edgar maintains that thanks to their knack of seeing creatures and hearing voices that most people cannot even vaguely sense, fairy doctors hold the power to "unravel the mysteries of the world." Lydia is drawn to the suave, handsome and chivalric Edgar even though she knows that he is mendacious and self-obsessed and, at one point, even has reason to suspect he might be guilty of mass murder, because her sixth sense tells her that he is not truly evil at root. It is for this reason, more than for lack of money, that she accepts the job required of her in the search for the Sword of the Merrow. However, Lydia suffers a wrenching emotional conflict when Edgar reveals his love for her, which she dismisses as just a manifestation of his usual, notoriously flirtatious, self in spite of the fact that deep down, she reciprocates her employer's feelings. Lydia's defensive attitude issues from an inveterate dislike of the idea of becoming romantically attached to anybody resulting from infantile traumas. Her bildungsroman is further complicated, on another plane, by her tortuous relationship with the rude and arrogant sprite Kelpie — a black water horse in his fairy incarnation but an attractive young man with enigmatic eyes in his human form — who is determined to make Lydia his bride at any price. Despite his blatant alterity and prepotent manners, Kelpie is rendered touchingly human by the indisputable authenticity of his feelings for Lydia and preparedness to comfort her in times of trouble or doubt.

Earl and Fairy makes reference to so bountiful a range of magical entities as to occasionally come across as a concise guide to the spirit world for newbies. This is not to say, however, that the creatures it brings into play as supporting characters or fleetingly touches upon as extras are simply thrown into the yarn for local color. In fact, they invariably serve a diegetic function and are therefore thoroughly integrated into the plot even when they are afforded only the briefest citation. The principal supernatural beings invoked by the series include brownies (frolicsome supercuties), pixies (Celtic fairies), spunkies (the anime's preferred term for "will-o'-the wisps"), silkies (shape-shifting marine fairies), phoukas (multiform demons often acquiring the form of glossy, dark horses with sulphurous yellow eyes and a long wild mane), banshees (female spirits from Irish mythology held to be messengers from the otherworld), leprechauns (mischievous fairies assuming the shape of elderly men clad in green), chulichauns (sprites fond of alcohol), coblynau (mining gnomes) and hobgoblins (troublesome but not generally malevolent creatures like Shakespeare's Puck), as well as various members of the Unseelie Court (Unseelie meaning "unholy" or "unblessed") such as Dullahan the Headless Fairy (a villain typically riding a horse and carrying its own head under one arm).

Besides, numerous magical objects such as talismans, heirlooms and mythological emblems pepper the action from start to finish, including an enchanted bow and a moonstone ring reputed to have belonged to the fairy queen Gwendolen, Blue Knight Earl's spouse. References to well-known fairy figures like Titania (another legendary fairy queen) also abound. Merfolk punctuate the visuals in tastefully restrained amounts. At one end of the spectrum, we meet the character of the classic pureblood mermaid, complete with streaming golden locks and exquisite features; at the other end, the more original figure of the hybrid, notably with the character of Edgar's kind butler Tomkins, whose status as a human-fish cross is just hinted at by the vague resemblance of his facial features to those of a fish, and by his proud assertion that he has a fin on his back.

On the cinematographical plane, one of the anime's most attractive — and indeed graphically magic — features is its use of frames representing fairy paintings dimly redolent of analogous works from the Victorian period, executed by the aspiring artist Paul Ferman. These are deftly juxtaposed with shots of actual characters from the show and elliptically encourage reflection on the animation-making system itself. The images focusing on actual characters encapsulate the final phase of the process insofar as they correspond to the finished drawings — which, though deliberately stylized in keeping with anime conventions, can be taken as cinematic equivalents of real people. The closeups of Paul's paintings, for their part, frankly expose their constructed status by laying bare both compositional devices and the material marks of brush, chalk or pastel, and thus call attention to the preliminary and intermediate stages of production.

One of *Earl and Fairy*'s principal strategies consists of its avoidance of too many explicit depictions of the spirits Lydia can perceive. In fact, with the exception of a few rollicking brownies, an evil giant hound and a sprinkling of meadow sprites, those otherworldly entities are left out of the screen altogether. Through this ruse, the anime elicits the audience's active contribution to the generation of meaning by requiring it to bridge the gap between the actual images appearing on the screen and the images perceived by the heroine's mind's eye through independent creative effort. The characters, events and situations portrayed in the anime could therefore be regarded not as a sealed product with a preordained message but rather as a potential or virtual narrative which it is ultimately up to the viewer to narrativize, i.e., constellate into an actual story.

In this regard, *Earl and Fairy* invites comparison with the *Natsume* series (discussed in Chapter 3), where the protagonist is likewise able to see and interact with supernatural agencies. Yet, in *Natsume*, many spirits are explicitly represented and allowed to throng the screen unimpeded. In this respect, the *Natsume* shows are actually closer to the reality of *Kamichu!* (TV series; dir. Koji Masunari, 2005), an anime teeming with hordes of spirits comparable to Shinto *kami* — not least among them the show's protagonist, Yurie Hitotsubashi, an ordinary middle-school student who suddenly discovers that she has, quite simply, become a deity with the power to perceive entities invisible to practically anyone else in her world. This does not mean that by regaling the eye with a plethora of spirits either *Natsume* or *Kamichu!* treat their audiences as passive recipients. In fact, they still aim to stimulate their imagination but by different means — i.e., by inviting them to ponder what it could conceivably be like to be an apparently unexceptional young person endowed with a magical capacity so special as the one harbored by the eponymous hero in *Natsume* and by Yurie in *Kamichu!* and yet have to harmonize that talent with human proclivities and desires in an effort to live like an ordinary kid.

Earl and Fairy dramatizes four interrelated bildungsromans. Lydia's own developmental trajectory encompasses two dimensions. On the one hand, the girl's journey carries public significance as a professional quest pivoting on her determination to grow into a full-fledged fairy doctor. This involves a commitment to interpersonal duties and responsibilities straddling the human and the magical dimensions. On the other hand, Lydia's buldungsroman is eminently private in documenting her struggle to overcome a deep-seated sense of inferiority. This is bred by the yearning to live up to the model set by her proverbially skilled and beautiful mother (while also striving to please her doting dad), as well as her reputation as a tomboy deemed unsuitable as an object of romantic attraction by her regular human peers, who feel intimidated by her preternatural abilities. (A parallel with the plight suffered by *Hell Girl*'s protagonist, examined in Chapter 2, is here observable.)

Edgar's own development witnesses his evolution from a privileged position as a pampered aristocratic kid; through severe dispossession and degradation to a practically subhuman status; subsequent indulgence in self-dramatizing ruses intended to establish his fame as a perfect knight, irresistible playboy and fashionable socialite; to the acceptance of his authentic self as a basically honest youth, capable of moving beyond his stunting solipsism and honor his true feelings. Raven's growth from a murderous sprite akin to a mindless killing machine to a reflective soul with a conscience and cognate sense of guilt is also noteworthy. Though less prominent on the diegetic plane than Lydia's and Edgar's respective bildungsromans, Raven's personal pilgrimage plays an even more axial part than either of those two in highlighting that without the desire to achieve self-understanding, the journey itself may never be embarked upon. Preparedness to embrace the task, in this instance, is posited as an even more significant developmental event than its undertaking. Paul's artistic evolution also deserves attention. Wishing to become a poet when he was a child, Paul had a change of heart when Edgar saw his juvenile sketches and opined that he had talent as a prospective painter. At the same time, the young man must learn to assess critically the repercussions not solely of his aesthetic aspirations but also of the alliances he strikes in his quest to avenge his father, and of the actual nature of the causes he implicitly embraces in so doing.

Earl and Fairy is not the kind of anime that asks to be taken seriously as a study in mimetic realism, and spectators approaching it in the hope of achieving that kind of satisfaction will almost certainly meet with disappointment. In fact, it is a show that glories in the magic of animation at its most honestly fictitious to evoke figurative analogies between the realm of fantasy and the realities of young people struggling to reach self-knowledge through their interactions with, and explorations of, other people and their circumstances. Thus, *Earl and Fairy* does have a realistic dimension but this consists of its psychological credibility, a virtue persistently abetted by the eschewal of character stereotypes and narrative clichés, rather than of a pursuit of representational verisimilitude. This also entails that nonsense is not shunned but affectionately fostered — as it is in the writings of authors more or less contemporaneous with the anime's pseudo-historical setting such as Lewis Carroll or Edward Lear. (Please see Chapter 3 for further reference to the former of these writers.) All in all, therefore, *Earl and Fairy* is best savored as a fairy tale, a narrative construct that does not hesitate to bend the rules of classical logic and even enjoys twisting its own internal rationale by capitalizing on codes and conventions that tend to generate and solve dilemmas as and when it considers it desirable, timely or expedient, yet in accordance with consistent narrative rhythms. Consistency, in fact, ironically stems from what might superficially appear to be a rampant lack of common sense.

While *Earl and Fairy* uses the magic of nineteenth-century England as the backdrop of its distinctive bildungsroman, *The Tale of Genji* (TV series; dir. Osamu Dezaki, 2009) depicts the magic-tinged developmental journey of a hero steeped in ancient lore through the adaptation of one of the greatest classics of Japanese literature, and putatively the world's first novel. The original work, created by Lady Shikibu Murasaki, offers a dispassionate anatomy of the decadent nobility of Heian Japan abetted by its author's direct insights into court life — as well as its innumerable rivalries and intrigues — resulting from years of service with the royal dynasty. Following quite closely Lady Murasaki's saga, the anime weaves an opulently embroidered magical tapestry of dense, at times even sublime, mythological complications. Dezaki's portrayal of the life and loves of a prince, the titular Genji, delivers an exotically colorful romance, energized at each turn by alternately vibrant and wistful poetry and by keen psychological observation.

The anime *The Familiar of Zero* comprises three series, the first of which was directed by Yoshiaki Iwasaki and originally aired in 2006. The sequels

The Familiar of Zero 2: The Knight of the Twin Moons and *The Familiar of Zero 3: The Princess's Rondo* were both directed by Yuu Kou and broadcast in 2007 and 2008 respectively. Louise de Vallière, the protagonist, is a second-year student at the acclaimed Academy of Magic situated in the Kingdom of Tristain. In calling forth her familiar, an assignment which all students in Louise's cohort are traditionally required to undertake, the inept mage fortuitously summons Hiragi Saito, a modern-day Japanese teenager powerless to comprehend the bizarre dimension to which he has so abruptly and mysteriously migrated just as he was going about his daily chores in Tokyo. This is barely surprising, given that the very landscape and architectonics of the alternate universe in which the boy has been dropped would be sufficient to puzzle even the most seasoned of time travelers — a swirling stylistic cocktail of motifs derived from disparate periods of European history, with special emphasis on Renaissance, Neoclassical, Rococo and Victorian elements. Saito's initial sense of disorientation is exponentially amplified by his realization that he cannot understand a word of the language spoken around him. Thankfully, Louise's ineptitude as a wizard at that stage in the story is such that upon casting a silence spell on Saito in order to render him utterly servile, the girl accidentally manages to endow him with the ability to communicate in his new environment as fluently as he could do in his native Japan.

In defying both orthodox practice and the dicta of officially recognized magic, the heroine's performance flusters both her tutors and her peers but does not altogether surprise them in consideration of her lamentable lack of wizardly abilities — a flaw that has indeed gained her the derogatory nickname of "Louise the Zero." In Louise's world, the dominant understanding of magic is redolent of both the Japanese doctrine of the Five Elements and Western alchemy: accordingly, magical power is measured in terms of a practitioner's ability to master any one or more of the four common elements. A "line mage" is a wizard or witch that can only control a single element, while a "square mage" can effortlessly manipulate all four. Louise, as her moniker makes incontrovertibly clear, has no authority whatsoever over any of nature's forces. What is not revealed until the climactic moments is that Louise is actually a magician of the "void" (the fifth element) and that her familiar is a "Gandalfr," a person able to use any weapon with preternaturally sophisticated skillfulness. This ability is accompanied by physical augmentation, resulting in monumentally increased strength, agility, speed and resistance to injury. The special combination of magical factors projected by Louise and Saito's partnership situates the heroine as the most powerful and rarest of all recorded sorcerous types. The unusual familiar, for his part, little by little displays astounding abilities of his own. Saito's standing is visibly confirmed by the appearance of runes on his hand, there inscribed by the force of his bond with Louise, that glow whenever his magic skills activate.

As a result of both her aristocratic upbringing as a member of a dynasty in the upper strata of the nobility and a defensive bitterness bred by her sense of inferiority as a grossly incompetent mage, Louise initially treats Saito like the lowliest of mutts. As the adventure unfolds, however, she gradually comes to appreciate not only her familiar's magic worth — which proves especially advantageous when he protects her while she casts her formidable void-oriented spells — but also, and even more importantly, his value as a flexible, equanimous, sensitive and long-suffering kid blessed by a refreshing sense of humor and disarming resilience. By the end of the first season, Louise has already grown so attached to Saito as to fear the prospect of his return to his world when the boy chances upon a Japanese aircraft used in World War II capable of abetting the task, which his magic powers enable him to operate in spite of the vehicle's derelict condition and Saito's lack of any prior knowledge of its functionings. In the course of the second season, Louise's fondness for Saito develops into genuine love.

Louise's bildungsroman entails radical shifts in her initial attitude toward not only her familiar but also her privileged social status. This momentous maturation reaches its apotheosis when, in the third season, the girls casts off her noble title and rights to save fellow student Tabitha. It is at this point that the anime's fairy-tale flavor asserts itself most exuberantly, as the Queen of Tristain rewards Louise's selflessness by making her second in line to the throne. Predominantly jocular in tone throughout the earlier segments of the drama, *The Familiar of Zero* grows progressively somber as the dark phantom of war gains an increasingly palpable presence while the relationship between Louise and Saito simultaneously acquires complexity not only as a magical partnership but also as a frankly and painfully human romantic liaison. The early portion of the third season marks some especially tense moments in the story, as the magical runes on Saito's hand inexplicably vanish, and the familiar's status as a Gandalfr is thereby called into question. Saito reappropriates his supernatural markings upon being resummoned by Louise, at which juncture he also receives a knighthood from the queen for his valiant service to the country and elevated to the ranks of a true hero by the Academy's members.

One of the most cherished coming-of-age tales underpinned by magical lore, and specifically by the figure of the teenage witch, is offered by the film *Kiki's Delivery Service* (dir. Hayao Miyazaki, 1989) — a work that could be regarded as *The Familiar of Zero*'s predecessor in its prioritization of a heroine striving to prove her otherworldly worth against all odds. In dramatizing its protagonist's efforts to become a full-fledged witch despite her lack of any obvious magical skills, and her difficulty even mastering a broom to boot, Miyazaki's movie yields an alternately touching and hilarious celebration of the values of perseverance, self-reliance and humility — traits which Louise initially appears quite devoid of — and, most crucially, of the importance of selfless commitment to the welfare of others as the catalyst without which even those cardinal virtues would ultimately amount to precious little.

In comparison with Miyazaki's previous masterpieces, most notably *Princess Mononoke* (1997), *Spirited Away* (2001) and *Howl's Moving Castle* (2004),[1] *Ponyo on the Cliff by the Sea* (2008) comes across as a gentler, less populous or theatrical and, on the whole, more pointedly fairytalish film, smoothly gliding between rolling waves of innocent delight and peaks of ecstatic frisson through magisterially timed directorial sleights of hand. *Ponyo's* mellow atmosphere, enthusiastically acclaimed at the 65th Venice Film Festival (September 2008) upon its first Western exhibition, matches its dedication to the portrayal of an intimate bildungsroman centered on one of Miyazaki's youngest protagonists to date. As Andrew Pulver amusingly points out, the wizardly director's "version of the handsome prince" pivotal to Andersen's tale is a five-year-old kid named Sousuke who lives on a cliff by the sea, "one of those adorable anime moppets with large round eyes" amid "many a winsome tummy-poke and nose-wiggle" (Pulver).

Sousuke's developmental journey begins with his rescue of a plucky little goldfish that has run away from her underwater home and is desperately keen on becoming human (presumably unaware that such a status is by no means unproblematically advantageous), whom the boy calls Ponyo, vowing to protect her at any price. At the same time, the anime's intimate mood is reinforced by its close focus on domestic life and the little boy's relationship with his mother Lisa. The bildungsroman dramatized in *Ponyo* concentrates concurrently on two interrelated journeys. One of these addresses the human protagonist's emotional and intellectual development as he negotiates the various complications attendant on his relationships not only with the heroine and the marine domain she comes from but also his caring mother and often absent father. The other focuses on Ponyo's evolution from the moment she decides to abandon her father's protected abode and explore the outside world with all its unforeseeable wonders and perils.

A lurking sense of menace redolent of the atmosphere prevalent in *Princess Mononoke*, *Spirited Away* and *Howl's Moving Castle* emanates from the character of Fujimoto, Ponyo's father. However, the forest *kami* depicted in *Princess Mononoke* are surrounded by an alarming aura even when their actions are charitable, *Spirited Away's* bathhouse spirits are invariably invested with sinister iconographic connotations despite their often comical traits, and the mutants deployed as military machinery in *Howl's Moving Castle* are even more explicitly baleful, lacking any concessions to humor in their alternately repugnant and horrific constitutions. Ponyo's father, by contrast, comes across more as a solipsistic patriarch with a peculiar sense of fashion than as a consummate villain. Nor is he utterly devoid of benevolent intentions. A sorcerer intent on the concoction of life-giving elixir that could purge the mess humanity has unleashed into the ocean, Fujimoto is determined to confine his daughter to his watery lair. There is every chance that the wizard's objection to his daughter's desires has a lot to do with its stark contravention of the role model he has set. He indeed describes himself as an "ex-human"—a type ostensibly issuing from some sea-change intervention — and, like most fresh converts, is driven by the manic fervor of a zealot. Thus, *Ponyo* only echoes the epic scope of *Princess Mononoke*, *Spirited Away* and *Howl's Moving Castle* insofar as Fujimoto's efforts to restrain Ponyo evince the tone of a figurative mini-crusade.

While Fujimoto appears relatively harmless by comparison with either the malicious Yubaba or *Howl's* warmongering despots, he is initially successful in tearing Ponyo away from her beloved Sousuke. If Sousuke, palpably heartbroken, is powerless to intervene, Miyazaki's version of the Little Mermaid will stop at nothing to see her wish to be human and to live with her savior fulfilled. In the course of a fierce confrontation with Fujimoto, she rejects the name the sorcerer has imposed upon her, "Brünnhilde," and declares her name to be Ponyo (the allusion to Norse mythology is worthy of notice). With the help of her sisters, she then manages to flee the paternal prison once more and turns herself into a human by recourse to Fujimoto's own magic. Regrettably, by releasing into the sea the wizard's entire supply of elixir, Ponyo also triggers a massive environmental imbalance, which in turn causes the seas to boil, mammoth prehistoric fish from the Devonian era to invade the flooded land, the Moon to stray outside its customary orbit and satellites to race across the sky like frantic shooting stars. In this respect, the movie stands out as a subtle parable about the precariousness of ecological equilibrium. Miyazaki's preoccupation with environmental issues, a crucial aspect of both his political perspective and his cinematic signature, obliquely permeates the marine habitat depicted in the film even though the recurrent images of dolphins and whales swimming about unmolested bear scarce resemblance to the reality of Japan's notorious fishing ventures. Most importantly, as Richard Corliss maintains, "Miyazaki also creates a tsunami that, however fantastical and benign he portrays it, can't help recall the fatal force of nature" (Corliss).

Both *The Familiar of Zero* and *Earl and Fairy* rely on the magical powers of the visual image itself to evoke their enchanted worlds with, by and large, a preference for decorous restraint. In *Ponyo*, the magic of the image is allowed free rein, occasionally reaching such peaks of effervescence and dynamic glee as to convey a sense of intoxication. As Wendy Ide observes, this aesthetic facet of the movie matches its approach to the diegesis itself: "All of Miyazaki's films have their own blithe disregard for narrative logic, but *Ponyo* is as chaotic and exuberant as a story told by a hyperactive toddler who has just been mainlining Fruit Shoots (...and then a whale did come and it did turn into a wave. And then they did eat noodles...)" (Ide). The power of Miyazaki's wand to animate *Ponyo*'s characters and watery setting with gentle undulations and daunting buoyancy by turns comes to the fore right from the start with the sequence where the titular heroine emerges under the shade of a jellyfish umbrella and gets trapped in a jar, is pulled out by Sousuke and, upon licking the blood that flows from his finger when he gets cut in breaking the container, begins to acquire rudimentary human features while also magically healing the kid's wound. Ponyo rapidly develops an appetite for all things human and this gives Miyazaki plenty of opportunities to dwell on some exquisite vignettes — as delightfully evinced by the scene in which Ponyo samples honeyed tea: few facial expressions in live-action cinema equal the wordless charm of the creature's mien in this particular moment. Miyazaki and his team have demonstrated unflinching dedication to the convincing and heartwarming portrayal of children for decades and "by now," as the *Twitch* review of *Ponyo* stresses, "they know perfectly well how to transfer their exclusive little world onto the big screen. The way Ponyo and Sousuke move, react, look around and think, play around and enjoy the simplest of things, Miyazaki has it covered and turns it into pure magic. But even the simplified fish form of Ponyo's character is beyond cute. The magic is often hidden away in little details, how she jumps up, runs into things or looks at the wonders of instant noodles" ("Hayao Miyazaki's *Ponyo* review").

The lifelike motion evinced by Miyazaki's young characters despite their obviously simplified shapes and watercolor nuances nourishes the visual spell at each turn. David Gritten corroborates this point: "Miyazaki's ability to express extremes of emotion in his child characters without resorting to sentimentality or treacly music is remarkable" (Gritten). Any audience familiar with the director's anime magic will recognize his hand in *Ponyo*'s jaw-dropping visuals. What is most striking, in an age when Western animation of the kind routinely produced by the likes of Pixar, Disney and Dream-Works relies massively on CGI, is Miyazaki's cultivation of the two-dimensional cartoon style associated with the medium's salad days. Ironically, the hand-drawn effects evoked by the studio behind Miyazaki's movies, the legendary Studio Ghibli, are often invisibly abetted by digital tools. Their manufactured flavor, therefore, derives not from the company's resistance to state-of-the-art technology but rather from its both tenacious and astute exploration of pioneering styles in which traditional and novel techniques can be successfully harmonized, so as to bring into existence something that is new and yet captures the timeless beauty of the old. The aesthetic perfection evinced by its images is therefore anachronistic and up-to-date at once. *Ponyo* itself, however, is entirely handmade. In a press release held in Venice at the time of the 2008 Film Festival, Miyazaki explained the rationale underlying his use of this particular method as follows: "I think animation is something that needs the pencil, needs man's drawing hand, and that is why I decided to do this work in this way" (cited in Corliss). The visuals' simplicity, paradoxical as this may sound, add to the pellicule's sophistication insofar as it helps the complexity and vitality of the animation per se to assert themselves. This is most evident in Miyazaki's representation of the ubiquitous waves, where photorealism is shunned in favor of minimalistic lines rendered in tastefully modulated tints. Though almost childishly basic, when the lines start zipping and whishing across the screen, they exude a dynamism unmatched by more mimetically accurate depictions of water. The immensity of the director's accomplishment is thrown into relief by the opening sequence, where the sheer profusion of unique fantastical creatures and the multilayered animation elicit nothing short of awe. As Fionnuala Halligan remarks, in this matter, "The opening sequences feel like a trip through the type of rainbow paintings you might see in a kindergarten, so keenly does Miyazaki capture the spirit of his five-year-old protagonist" (Halligan).

Ponyo's cinematographical enchantment also benefits from the judicious use of "pillow shots." As Roger Ebert explains, these consist of visual correlatives of the so-called pillow words utilized in Japanese poetry. A pillow word, according to the critic, "represents almost a musical beat between what went before and what comes after." Its filmic counterpart is the pillow shot — a frequent trait of Japanese cinema paradigmatically epitomized by the works of Yasujiro Ozu. This is a transitional and often quite prosaic image located at the close of a "phase" before the next portion of the action begins. It thus operates as a system of "punctuation," as well as "a form of silence," which is essentially a way of suggesting "let's not rush headlong from each scene to the next scene." When they are deployed specifically in the field of animation, pillow shots impart the medium with an aura of "thoughtfulness." In addition, since the frames on which they rely are often "inconsequential" in diegetic terms, the fact that anime producers should be "willing to go to the trouble" of devoting no less attention to these moments than to focal sequences eloquently testifies to their artistic passion and integrity (Ebert). Especially notable in *Ponyo* are the pillow shots that focus on crashing waves and storm effects.

Adopting a decidedly utopian take on the original story that echoes Disney more closely than it does Andersen, Miyazaki's film proposes that as long as Ponyo and Sousuke can pass a test, the fish-girl will be allowed to go on living as a human and the world's balance will be reinstated. Replete with the classic visual symbols characteristically deployed by fairy tales to mark the decisive stages of a journey of maturation and self-discovery, such as the tunnel and the submarine alcove, the movie's finale candidly enthrones selfless love as a supreme virtue bound to be ultimately rewarded by human and magical dispensations alike. This finale suggests that the crux of *Ponyo*'s magic, both as a pictorial feat and as a dexterously choreographed narrative ensemble, consists principally of its take on the concept of the hybrid. Sousuke's climactic stance commodiously welcomes the hybrid into the human world. His declaration that he will always love Ponyo, regardless of whether she evinces a human or a piscine physique, is instrumental in guaranteeing a happy ending as a rejection of conventional prejudices and hence an indictment, metaphorically speaking, of racial discrimination. Nevertheless, the film never loses sight of the latently menacing undertones borne by hybridity in various civilizations and in their distinctive mythological heritages. Throughout history, hybrid creatures have functioned as remarkably versatile vehicles for the expression of abiding cultural anxieties. On many occasions, they have been rendered just about tolerable by the sublimation of their uncanny anatomies into so-called "curiosities." Yet, this has frequently led to a paradoxical situation, insofar as our attraction to those beings' intractable alterity is never conclusively anesthetized: much as we may seek to domesticate the threatening connotations they are held to carry, by relegating them to the province of the abnormal or the repulsive, the sense of menace abides as a vital component of their bizarre, monstrous and fearful beauty. In other words, hybrids' attractiveness is inextricable from their intimidating power.

When hybrid creatures are incorporated into the context of magic-inflected fantasy adventures, their bodies may take a considerable variety of appearances. Among countless popular specimens, we encounter angels, centaurs, chimeras, devils, garudas, gryphons, hydras, maenads, merfolk, satyrs, sirens, sphinxes, termagants and tritons. Moreover, the moods evoked by magical hybrids are vertiginously varied, with ethereally delicate winged fairies at one end of the gamut, and grotesque or downright disturbing monsters, at the other end.[2] Some of the entities referred to in *Earl and Fairy* exemplify the former category, whereas the demons persecuting *xxxHolic*'s protagonist tend to veer toward the latter. Many of the familiars in *The Familiar of Zero*—

in fact, practically all of them with the blatant exception of the heroine's own personal associate — are configured as deliberately weird admixtures of disparate life forms. Yet, while *xxxHolic*'s spirits feel predominantly baneful, the otherworldly actors cast in *The Familiar of Zero* are so extravagantly caricatured as to come across as amusing or even, at times, outrageously hilarious. All of the magical hybrids that feature in the anime here examined, however, share one basic philosophical message. That is to say, they remind their human viewers of the radical instability of their own physical boundaries by intimating that the human body is always vulnerable to fantastical misrepresentation, and hence to metaphorical invasion by bizarre and outlandish entities. In blending disparate and even logically incompatible elements, hybridity drastically subverts the myth of corporeal unity doggedly fostered by Western humanism. In so doing, it also violates the dividing-line between human beings and other animals and thus subverts the supposed superiority of the rational civilized subject, compelling us to reassess what being human really means.

On the one hand, hybrids tersely show that the inherent nature of the human species in unstable and that any attempt to measure unequivocally its similarities with, and differences from, other breeds is inexorably conducive to insoluble dilemmas. On the other hand, they implicitly suggest that affirming our separateness from non-human species supplies no reliable evidence for our superiority for it may well spawn, in fact, disabling feelings of estrangement and loneliness. By contrast, an understanding and acceptance of the interconnections that obtain among disparate beings, and relate them to one another within a continuous flow, can release an uplifting sensation of at-homeness on Earth. This grasp of underlying bonds between seemingly incompatible entities is gloriously asserted, as Meri Lao points out, by Picasso's art and especially by its desire "to explore all the intermediate stages between man and horse in the search for a more complete harmony" (Lao, p. 13). It could further be argued that hybrids both alert us to our inevitable incompleteness and help us keep it at bay by investing the inchoate Other with visible and potentially playful, albeit deviant, forms. It is by communing, at least in fantasy and play, with alien creatures that we may gain access to a world in which partial and contradictory identities can be cherished rather than perceived as sources of raw fear, and a cosmic scenario of ongoing birth, death and rebirth can be likewise enjoyed.

The hybrid figure around which *Ponyo*'s narrative source revolves — namely, the mermaid — is also, as we have seen, central to *Earl and Fairy*. Traditionally, mermaids have been used (and abused) as metaphors for a dark feminine lure. As Lao observes, as "feminine divinities who are also part of the animal order," sirens and their close relations posit the threat of "a double nature" holding "prerogatives of both their components; irrational entities, eternally provocative and disturbing" (p. 11). Homer's account of their drawing Ulysses toward certain death by means of their irresistible song has reverberated over the centuries in the works not only of Andersen but also of writers and painter as diverse as William Shakespeare, Friedrich de la Motte-Fouqué, W. B. Yeats, T. S. Eliot, James Joyce, Oscar Wilde, Hieronimus Bosch, Peter Paul Rubens, David Delamare, Arnold Bocklin, J. W. Waterhouse, Lord Leighton, Aubrey Beardsley, Edvard Munch and René Magritte, as well as in Hollywood movies such as *Million Dollar Mermaid* (dir. Mervyn LeRoy, 1952) and *Splash* (dir. Ron Howard, 1984). By adopting a positive perspective on the figure of the mermaid, both *Ponyo* and *Earl and Fairy* challenge the stereotypical attitude that demonizes her as an insidious and predatory agent, inviting us to admire her dual makeup rather than fear or distrust it. In *Earl and Fairy*, the inclination to regard merfolk in all its gradations as a respectable life form is epitomized by the portrayal of the aforementioned character of the amiable majordomo Tomkins, as well as by the magnanimous conduct of the regal mermaid rewarding Lydia's quest in her underwater dreamland. In *Ponyo*, that same proclivity is most patently borne out by Miyazaki's treatment of the ecological theme referred to earlier. The dramatization of the riotous uprising of the marine world does not posit it as a rebellion against the human species but rather as a considerate warning, articulated in metaphorical form, about the potentially cataclysmic repercussions of humanity's attempts to tamper with the natural environment. If the oceans are not afforded the respect they deserve, *Ponyo* advocates, disaster will strike — and not always in a fairy-tale style, as the victims of Hurricane Katrina and the Indonesian Tsunami know only too well.

The *xxxHolic* anime, a classy blend of fantasy, horror, irony and dark surrealism indebted to the unparalleled talent of the manga artists CLAMP, comprises the film *xxxHolic the Movie: A Midsummer Night's Dream* (2005), the two TV series *xxxHolic* (2006) and *xxxHolic: Kei* (2008) and the two-part OVA *xxxHolic: Shunmuki* (2009), all four of which have been helmed by Tsutomu Mizushima. The narrative pivots on the character of Kimihiro Watanuki: a young man haunted by ghouls (which nobody else can see) in the most literal sense of the word "haunt" one could possibly imagine, insofar as he attracts them magnetically despite his best intentions. Watanuki turns for help to the charismatic sorceress Yuuko Ichihara the day he finds himself inexplicably drawn into a shop by an invisible force. Yuuko, whose job is to assist people struggling to overcome supernaturally induced woes at a price equivalent to the value of the wish, is prepared to help Watanuki overcome his affliction in exchange for his services as her cook, cleaner and shop assistant — chores which the youth conscientiously strives to undertake, while desperately dodging the magical objects and creatures that infest the witch's dwelling and seem addicted to latching onto him.

Yuuko is highly unpredictable and arbitrary, in harmony with the capricious rhythms followed by magic phenomena at large, coming across as grave and trenchantly sarcastic one moment and cheerfully girlish the next. She always seems to have loads of tricks up her sleeve which she has not yet disclosed to either her associates or the audience but there is little doubt that at base, she cares deeply for the hapless Watanuki. As intimated in Chapter 1, Yuuko lives according to the principle of *hitsuzen*, which advocates that there are no such things as coincidences or accidents in life but there is only, ever, inevitability. Like *The Familiar of Zero*, *xxxHolic* grows darker and darker as Watanuki begins to participate in various jobs with his employer and it gradually transpires that under these missions, there lies a malign plot which Yuuko is endeavoring to stop by using Watanuki's powers unbeknownst to him, while the boy's tragic past concurrently comes to light. Watanuki's destiny turns out to be far more intimately intertwined with the magic world than he ever suspected prior to meeting Yuuko. It is mainly through this theme that the first *xxxHolic* show focuses increasingly on its protagonist's development and change as he works with the enchantress.

xxxHolic's more somber connotations are further thrown into relief in the second TV series, where Watanuki falls prey to the wrathful Spider Spirit, whose anger he has inadvertently triggered, and loses an eye as a result. (CLAMP's passion for ocular impairment as a concurrently dramatic and symbolic ruse parallels the use of the same theme in *Tsubasa: RESERVoir CHRoNiCLE*, here discussed in Chapter 2, where Syaoran is presented as its victim.) Furthermore, throughout *xxxHolic*'s unfolding, emphasis is incrementally placed on the concept of *hitsuzen* and on its ultimate inextricability from the male lead's accomplishment of an onerous bildungsroman. The sequel also underscores an important formal aspect of the franchise as a whole, which Diane Tiu aptly describes as follows: "all events are interconnected and ... one good turn deserves another, while grudge and sins come back to haunt. Rewards are never reaped immediately, and audiences are always treated to a pleasant surprise when Watanuki is later remembered for the good deeds he had performed in the past and is reciprocated" (Tiu).

Across the prismatic adventure cumulatively chronicled by the film, the two TV series and the OVA, disparate cases are investigated and — more or less conclusively — solved by Yuuko and her assistant. Each installment carries a poignant ethical lesson, highlighting the price to be paid for indulging in habits so addictive as to have degenerated into veritable diseases. Throughout the franchise, these obsessions are seen to pollute their victims via the supernatural dimension, which thus serves as a metaphor for real-world societies. Yuuko functions as a mystic therapist of sorts, striving to help her clients overcome their problems, yet also stressing that people must learn, most importantly, how to help themselves. Alongside Watanuki and Yuuko, a major cast member is Shizuka Doumeki, Kimihiro's classmate, who has a flair for dispelling otherworldly presences as skillfully as the hero can see them. Watanuki resents Doumeki even as he slowly befriends him, largely because he sees him as a rival in the quest to win the heart of the girl with whom he is infatuated, Himawari Kunogi. Yet, Watanuki cannot deny that he is only truly safe in the presence of the calm, self-possessed and generally laconic Doumeki thanks to the latter's exorcistic abilities. Doumeki proves indeed capable of saving the protagonist's life on more than one occasion in the course of the story. The childlike Marudashi ("Streaking") and Morodashi ("Flashing") — a.k.a. Maru and Moro — also feature regularly throughout the anime. Created by the witch, they are tied to her store and are responsible for beckoning people requiring Yuuko's assistance. Unless Maru and Moro intervene as mediating agents capable of liaising between the ordinary world and the magical dimension of Yuuko's business, the outfit remains shrouded in invisibility.

The mission dramatized in the movie takes as its point of inception the day when a girl powerless to enter her home seeks Yuuko's aid and extends a magical-looking key as payment. The girl's request coincides with Yuuko's invitation to an auction to be held within a peculiar mansion which, it gradually transpires, is the very location her new client is so desperate to access. Even though the witch knows full well that the invitation is being deployed as a bait by some as yet unspecified villain, she faces up to the challenge, keen on ascertaining her prospective host's identity and goals. Seven additional bidders initially feature at the auction venue — all of them avid collectors of peculiar objects — but evaporate in rapid succession even before the auctioneer has made his appearance. Equipped with doors that open and close of their own accord and strewn with snaky corridors, passageways and galleries, the eerie mansion in which the Gothic murder mystery is set oozes with creepy noises evocative at once of buried secrets, inchoate dimensions, forbidden dreams and dormant memories that lurk just beneath the surface of the visible. Eventually, the reason behind Yuuko's invitation to the peculiar auction and the uncanny events taking place in the mansion in its wake turns out to be an old promise made by its owner, respected for a long time and then slowly consigned to oblivion. The girl seeking Yuuko's assistance at the beginning reappears as the person to whom the host is bound by his promise in a twofold incarnation: i.e., both as the aged lady she now really is and as the little girl she was at the time the vow was sealed, the latter being also the shape in which the man sees her in the present. On the aesthetic plane, the movie owes much to the unsettling beauty of the haunted house, the visuals' spellbinding power issuing principally from the sheer wealth of architectural and decorative details.

The most striking aspect of the style adopted by the *xxxHolic* franchise in its entirety consists of its character design. The principal personae evince overly elongated physiques, with spindly limbs and almost absurdly extended necks. While this penchant for deliberate overexaggeration may initially prove jarring for viewers as yet unfamiliar with CLAMP's work, it will almost certainly contribute, in the space of just a few episodes, to draw the audience intimately into the anime's distinctive world by virtue of its visual uniqueness. All of the main and supporting characters are, in any case, meticulously individuated at the levels of both somatic attributes and vestimentary details. Peripheral actors and extras, conversely, are blank and almost amorphous, being given merely a basic outline devoid of color and detail. This technique serves to increase the principal actors' prominence throughout. Simultaneously, it reminds us that invisibility is not merely an attribute of the magical domain since it actually inhabits the here-and-now at all times — most harrowingly, in the shape of depersonalized masses of humans so busy living their own quotidian lives and, whenever possible, pursuing their self-interest as to become blind to one another. The vacuity and meaninglessness of the material world are thus succinctly communicated. At the stylistic level, *xxxHolic*'s recurrent visual effects are likewise noteworthy: the plumes of smoke billowing around Yuuko, hypnotically enhancing her enigmatic aura, are undoubtedly one of the most memorable notes in CLAMP's cachet. Additionally, CLAMP's art makes bounteous use of lacelike ornamentation reminiscent of filigree. This is harmoniously synthesized with many of the aesthetic elements characteristically favored by Art Nouveau, with its delicately sinuous and whiplash lines often based on stylized organic shapes, alongside starker graphics typical of Art Deco such as sweeping curves, prismatic patterns and trapezoidal or zigzagged patterns.

xxxHolic abounds with references to indigenous mysticism and folklore, allied to frequent and detailed allusions to feudal Japan and to the country's intriguing spiritual history in the design of most of its paranormal actors — so much so that it could be regarded as an ideal companion to those subjects for the novice keen on exploring the traditional roots of Nipponic culture. Creatures already encountered in Chapter 4, such as fox spirits (*kitsune*) and house specters (*zashiki-warashi*), make their appearance beside rain sprites (*ame-warashi*), phantoms of various kinds, diviners, supernatural occurrences (such as the sprouting of wings out of a human's back), magic lanterns and haunting photographs. *xxxHolic*'s cornucopian profusion of culinary references, moreover, abets at each turn the anime's cultural significance. Furthermore, despite its reliance on supernatural motifs enshrined in the most ancient legends and superstitions, *xxxHolic* consistently strikes timelessly relevant chords. It does so, primarily, by presenting its protagonist's predicament as a literalization of a feeling most people have at some point experienced in real life — namely, the sensation that someone or something is watching them: an absent presence they cannot pinpoint and feel intimidated by against both reason and logic. This element, compounded with *xxxHolic*'s emphasis on moral dilemmas and related rites of passage, delivers a narrative that cannot be summarily dismissed as "just an anime about a wacky, over-stimulated teen with physic powers. The true charm of *xxxHolic* is its complex nature as an entertaining and emotional drama laced with moral lessons and the paranormal" ("*xxxHolic*, Season One Review").

While capitalizing to unique effect on the concurrently pictorial and narrative magic of indigenous lore, *xxxHolic* also makes memorable use of the symbol of the butterfly — an image traditionally deployed as the repository of rich metaphorical associations in literature and the visual arts alike. Butterflies have been deployed as symbols of metamorphosis and rebirth the world over for centuries or possibly even millennia. At the same time, the motif has frequently been brought into play to convey the transience of beauty and happiness — a theme, as noted in Chapter 1, that is absolutely axial to Japan's perception of the phenomenal world and finds paradigmatic expression in the aesthetic tenet of *mono no aware*. In Japanese poetry, particularly, the butterfly trope features insistently as a compact metaphor for irretrievable bliss. As Chris Eisenbraun points out in the entry devoted by his online dictionary of symbols to the ubiquitous image of the butterfly, "There is a line of Japanese poetry expressing sorrow over the lost pleasures of the past, a response to the maxim, 'The fallen blossom never returns to the branch'; 'I thought that the blossom had returned to the branch — alas, it was only a butterfly'" (Eisenbraun). It is here also worth noting that another recurrent symbol of endless transformation assiduously employed in Japanese literature and art, the phoenix, also features as a favorite in CLAMP's graphic repertoire as the inspiration for legion decorative motifs and chromatic combinations. Unlike the butterfly, whose metamorphosis typifies the ephemerality of the fleeting moment, the successive phases of death and resurrection associated with the figure of the phoenix are typically conceived of as interminable processes.

Referred to in ancient Greek with the term also used for "soul" (*psyche*), the butterfly can also emblematize the transformations experienced by the spiritual cores of both human beings and other both animal and vegetative breeds. Lepidopteral transitoriness can also be linked with the inscrutable domain of magic entities, as evinced by the fact that the likes of fairies, elves, pixies and other supernatural beings (e.g., the character of Hypnos, the Greek god of Sleep) are often endowed with iridescent butterfly wings. In Aztec mythology, moreover, the butterfly was associated both with the power of the Sun and with starlight. These ideas are reflected in *xxxHolic*'s utilization of the butterfly motif as a means of buttressing the themes of metamorphosis and evolution, and of alluding at once to the spiritual, psychological and physical undertones of the transmutations undergone by its characters in the course of the composite adventure. The insect's traditional connection with both the magic realm and dazzling light is likewise echoed. The anime also pays homage to the meaning attached to the butterfly in the specific context of Japan, where the creature as a single specimen has often typified young womanhood, while couples of dancing butterflies have been adopted as metaphors for marital harmony. The image also plays a pivotal part in one of Japan's most cherished fairy tales, "The White Butterfly." This pivots on the character of an ancient and dying man named Takahama, who has devoted his life to honoring the memory of his erstwhile betrothed Akiko, the victim of a fatally consumptive disease who died shortly before the date fixed for their wedding. As Takahama nears his final breath, Akiko returns to him in the shape of a white butterfly symbolizing her unflinchingly faithful spirit.

An earlier instance of a magic-saturated anime (and manga) issuing from CLAMP's prolific pens and pencils is *Cardcaptor Sakura* (TV series; dir. Morio Asaka, 1998–2000), one of the longest series ever aired to date. *Cardcaptor Sakura* focuses on ten-year-old Sakura Kinomoto, a typical elementary schoolgirl whose life takes an astronomical leap into the supernatural universe following her discovery, in her father's library, of the ancient magical "Book of Clow," containing a pack of likewise magical cards. Magic and textuality are once again twinned in this anime as they are in a few other titles peppering this book—in particular, *Kagihime* and the two *Natsume* series, here examined in Chapter 3, as well as *Mushi-Shi*, discussed in Chapter 4, in some of its most striking episodes. The cards are accidentally dispersed when Sakura utters the word "windy," the name that one of them bears, and thus brings about a preternatural wind whence a cute yellow beastie called Cerberus (a.k.a. Kerberos or Kero-chan) materializes. Introducing himself as the "Guardian of the Clow Cards," the beanie-like critter informs the protagonist that it is now incumbent upon her to retrieve the scattered cards as the sole hope of warding off the momentous disaster which the errant esoteric entities are capable of triggering. Sakura thus embarks on a journey to gather the cards in the company of Kero-chan himself and of her best friend Tomoyo Daidouji — who enthusiastically designs the heroine's Magical-Girl costumes at each stage in the adventure while also videotaping Sakura's exploits for future enjoyment. One of the series' most interesting relationships is the one developing between Sakura and Syaoran: a boy initially presented as her antagonist who gradually turns into a friend and ally.

Punctuated by frequent encounters with many new friends, foes and attendant challenges, Sakura's voyage soon rises to the level of an elaborate bildungsroman. As Carlos Ross and Christina Carpenter comment, *Cardcaptor Sakura* abides as a memorable landmark in the recent history of anime by accomplishing a truly wizardly feat: "a fresh spin on the concept of magical girls. It borrows a little from every show of its kind before it, including *Sailor Moon* [please see Chapter 3], but manages to come up with something unique." For one thing, although Sakura takes her duty seriously and grows increasingly competent and forceful as the series progresses, she also makes sure she takes pleasure from the quest at every conceivable opportunity. So does Tomoyo who, though not endowed with magical attributes herself, is so unreservedly fond and protective of her friend as to partake vicariously in each and every one of Sakura's achievements. Most importantly, where characterization is concerned, Kero-chan "has a more fleshed-out personality than previous familiars. He doesn't exist to nag Sakura, for he feels gathering the Clow is as much his responsibility as it is hers, an attribute sorely lacking in most magical girl familiars" (Ross and Carpenter). It is also noteworthy that while Sakura, Syaoran and Tomoyo are younger-looking versions of the characters bearing the same names in *Tsubasa: RESERVoir CHRoNiCLE* (here discussed in Chapter 2), they exhibit quite distinct personalities and fulfill different roles. Sakura and Syaoran, as noted, are at first portrayed as rivals — even though the boy lends the heroine his support when it really counts — whereas in *Tsubasa*, their mutual love provides the very core of the multidimensional saga. Infused with the unmatched magic of CLAMP's graphic verve, compounded with an intelligent, thought-provoking and impeccably paced yarn, *Cardcaptor Sakura* chronicles a bildungsroman in which the ordeals that young people have to endure on the path to adulthood are depicted with both genuine sensitivity and an uplifting sense of irony.

The bildungsroman dramatized in *Oh My Goddess!* (OVA series; dir. Hiroaki Gouda, 1993), another unequivocally unique interpretation of the Magical-Girl formula invoking diverse mythical motifs of both Eastern and Western provenance, takes as its point of departure a hilarious yet life-transforming incident. When Keiichi Morisato — an amiable but hapless youth that is often bullied by his senior dorm mates into carrying out all sorts of menial chores and taking phone messages on their behalf— accidentally contacts the "Goddess Technical Help Line" and the gorgeous "Goddess" Belldandy thereby appears in his room, he is rewarded with the quintessentially magical gift: the chance to have one special wish instantly granted. Suspecting that he is at the receiving end of an especially convoluted prank, Keiichi expresses the desire to have Belldandy at his side forever — with which, to his utter astonishment, she immediately complies. Since the freshman's dormitory is strictly intended for the exclusive use of male guests, the new couple has no choice but to venture into the night in search of alternative accommodation and eventually find shelter in an ancient Buddhist temple. The young monk in charge grants them permission to stay on a temporary basis as long as they maintain the venerable edifice and its grounds. Although the monk is initially fearful that Belldandy might be a pernicious imp, her punctilious devotion to the temple's upkeep and commitment to immaculate meditation soon win him over to her and Keiichi's side. When the monk goes on a pilgrimage to India, the couple are allowed to make the temple their home for an unlimited period of time. It is at this point that Keiichi's unusual bildungsroman begins.

While this diegetic premise prioritizes indigenous traditions, consolidating their authority through the painstaking rendition of the religious premises and accessories, the anime's magic universe as a whole is fashioned mainly around Norse mythology. This accommodates three apparent worlds alongside numerous invisible dimensions embedded therein: Heaven, the domain of the "Lord" and "Goddesses" like Belldandy; Hell, the realm of "Demons" and their supreme avatar, Daimakaicho; and Earth, the province of humans: an area that has supposedly remained relatively unexposed to the existence of beings from either Heaven or Hell until recently insofar as these forces hold the potential for upsetting drastically its overall equilibrium. The anime's reality as a whole is ostensibly governed by a monumental and unthinkably sophisticated computer apparatus dubbed Yggdrasil after the "World Tree" or "Tree of Fate" of Norse mythology, upon which the entire universe depends. The coupling of magic and technology, discussed in detail in Chapter 3, again plays an important role in this context. [3]

Goddesses' magical powers vary considerably in both nature and magnitude — hence, each has a particular designation based on "Class," which indicates the creature's power and precision levels; "Category," which refers to the range of actions she is allowed to perform; and "License," which sanctions the limits set upon those actions. Belldandy, for instance, is described as a "Goddess First Class, Second Category, Unlimited License." Since Goddesses' faculties are so great that they could annihilate the Earth quite effortlessly were they to be indiscriminately unleashed, they are equipped with apposite power limiters. Should a Goddess neglect her duties, her license would be suspended for a period of time that might be as short as a single week or as protracted as half a century or even more — though it should be noted that the human concept of time is scarcely relevant to the anime's magical universe, whose temporal scale entails that time flows much more sluggishly in Heaven than it does on Earth and obtaining absolute measurements is therefore impossible.

As shown in Chapter 4, natural substances and atmospheric phenomena play a pivotal part in numerous esoteric traditions, including the branch of Japanese thought dedicated to the investigation of the Five Elements and the Chinese *I Ching. Oh My Goddess!* brings natural factors explicitly into play in its portrayal of the Goddesses' magical skills. Each Goddess specializes in a discrete area associated with a specific phenomenon or form of matter: Belldandy relies on wind magic; Urd, Belldandy's older half sister and a hybrid of Goddess and Demon, uses fire magic; and Skuld, Belldandy's younger sister and a technowizard with astounding electronic and engineering skills, masters water magic. In addition, both Belldandy and Urd are proficient in the highly sophisticated art of lightning magic. Mature Goddesses normally have "Angels," born as fully grown and sentient beings reputed to reflect the Goddesses' inner selves, and distinctive magical means of transport: mirrors in Belldandy's case, TV screens in Urd's and water in Skuld's. The most intriguing esoteric quality ascribed to the Goddesses is a psychometric talent that enables them to perceive the aura of other creatures of their ilk that have previously been in contact with certain objects, and reconstruct the events occurring at that point in time by focusing their energies on the extrasensory perception. Most importantly, in the disarmingly optimistic ethics of the anime, the Goddesses' supreme objective is to bring happiness to everyone around them.

All of the titles here studied eloquently confirm the contention, proposed in Chapter 1, that magical thinking is inextricably intertwined with the tradition of the fairy tale. Their distinctive imagery often echoes the formulae and symbols favored by that art form: Yuuko's magical store, for instance, could be regarded as a latter-day version of the traditional marzipan cottages, wish-granting caves or enchanted castles associated with various sorceresses and mages; *Earl and Fairy* and *The Familiar of Zero* varyingly exude a fairy-tale atmosphere in their rendition of old Europe, in the case of the former, and of a synthesis of disparate quasi-magical settings, in that of the latter; as to *Ponyo*, one of the most cherished fairy tales ever recorded lies at the root of its very story. The connection between the fairy tale and the magical domain is especially important, in the present context, insofar as the fairy tale as a genre has been traditionally imbricated with the process of enculturement of the young and is hence closely associated with magic's metaphorical role in the advancement of various bildungsroman adventures. In spite of their more or less overtly outlandish themes and metaphors, fairy tales have been assiduously employed as a means of consolidating the status quo by prescribing standards of exemplary behavior for both children themselves and, by implication, for the grown-ups into which those kids are meant to develop. Early writings on this topic were eager to emphasize the positive implications carried by the employment of fairy tales as an educational tool, and did not have any apparent qualms about the disciplinary or even constraining effects which that practice might entail.

A true classic in the field is Laura Kready's *A Study of Fairy Tales* (1916), where it is confidently proposed that since fairy tales have the power to "contain" the child's "interests," they can also be regarded as a valid "means for the expression of his instincts and for his development in purpose, in initiative, in judgment, in organization of ideas, and in the creative return possible to him." Kready would feasibly have doubted the usefulness of fairy tales delivered by the popular art of animation, insofar as she appears to consider any form other than the literary as questionable in value or impact. This is because she aims principally "to show what fairy tales must possess as classics, as literature and composition, and as short-stories; to trace their history, to classify the types, and to supply the sources of material" in order to ascertain the quality of the "creative return" one might feasibly expect of a young reader or listener. "The fairy tale," Kready sunnily advocates in the climactic passage of the preface to her monograph, "is also related to life standards, for it presents to the child a criticism of life. By bringing forward in high light the character of the fairy, the fairy tale furnishes a unique contribution to life. Through its repeated impression of the idea of fairy-hood it may implant in the child a desire which may fructify into that pure, generous, disinterested kindness and love of the grown-up, which aims to play fairy to another, with sincere altruism to make appear before his eyes his heart's desire, or in a twinkling to cause what hitherto seemed impossible. Fairy tales thus are harbingers of that helpfulness which would make a new earth, and as such afford a contribution to the religion of life" (Kready).

More recent criticism has tended to embrace a less utopian approach to the subject of the fairy tale's potential function as an edifying instrument. It has thus sought to demonstrate that fairy tales do not unproblematically supply the young with ennobling models and lessons in a pleasurable form, thereby helping them develop into generous and tolerant adults. In fact, they have been gradually adapted and divulged from one generation to the next as a means of regimenting children's lives through the regulation of their moral values, relationships and both private and public conduct. Jack Zipes has persuasively promulgated this idea, arguing that although the tales themselves have come to be enthroned in cultural history as "universal, ageless, therapeutic, miraculous, and beautiful" (Zipes, p. 1), they are actually entangled with contingent ideological priorities. Relying on varyingly elaborate metaphors, those narratives have proved immensely resilient in adapting themselves to the expectations of particular sociopolitical contexts and their ethical, ideological and aesthetic agendas. The momentous potential held by fairy tales as socializing devices first proclaimed itself in seventeenth-century France, a culture in which both the traditional aristocracy and the rising bourgeoisie had a vested interest in inhibiting young people's natural instincts and in inculcating the imperative of self-control as a paramount rule of conduct. In aiming to educate children, fairy tales have progressively endeavored to tame the murkier elements of the traditional stories from which they tend to derive. This has often involved a translation of old peasant tales considered crude and uncouth into a supposedly civilized literary form.

Such a trend is paradigmatically typified by Charles Perrault's *Histoires ou contes du temps passé avec des moralités* (*Stories or Tales of Past Times, with Morals*, 1697). In this instance, folk materials have been edited not only through the elimination or edulcoration of their darker aspects but also through the celebration of a notion of self-discipline couched in overtly gender-inflected terms: "Gone are the blood, gore and rape of the traditional folk tales.... Gone as well are all semblances to a strong and resourceful female character. In the perfect universe constructed by Perrault's pen, the women are inevitably beautiful, industrious, obedient, passive, meek, dependent, silent and nameless" ("Female roles in the fairy tales of Charles Perrault"). Relatedly, fairy tales have often prescribed starkly differentiated roles for boys and girls — for example, by setting up the character type of the female locked in a tower or slumbering in a bower for hundreds of years against that of the male unremittingly eager to battle dragons or trick his way into the upper echelons. Such roles are time and again problematized by the fairy tale's reliance on double-bind mentalities. In numerous narratives based on the Beauty-and-the-Beast topos, for example, the Beast functions as a metaphor both for the feral urges to be expunged from children and for the forces of male reason to which Beauty must submit if she is to overcome her own yearning for physical pleasure. However, as Joseph Campbell emphasizes, fairy tales ultimately operate for both sexes as "initiation ceremonies" or rites of passage aimed at "killing the infantile ego" (Campbell, J., p. 168). As L. C. Seifert maintains, boys and girls alike are caught up in the ideological imperative to guarantee "the harmonious existence of family and society at large" (Seifert, p. 109).

Despite the often harsh domesticating and purging measures to which fairy tales subject their young protagonists in order to advance socially regulating programs, many of those characters preserve an ability to live with the unnamable while adults fumble through life in their vain struggle to understand and curb it. Kids remain capable of challenging rules and undermining exemplary authority figures because they instinctively know, as Suzie Mackenzie emphasizes, that "the nightmare is real" (Mackenzie, p. 16). In James Joyce's unforgettable words, "Children may just as well play as not. The ogre will come in any case" (Joyce, III, p. 144). This is unambiguously confirmed by several anime using fairy-tale magic to depict their journeys of maturation and self-discovery: no matter how severely their freedom may be curtailed, the protagonists retain a salubrious connection with the play instinct. Disciplinary strategies, as a corollary, are only peripherally effective. Play, regardless of its own acculturing function, defies definitive control by means of irony, which enables it to bracket pleasure and fear together. According to Marina Warner, this is demonstrated by children's inclination to "make fun of intimidation, and turn its threats hollow," fueled by an apparently spontaneous tendency "to play the bogeyman and scare themselves into fits. The pretence appears to match the observed pleasure in fright that children take: it defies fear at the very same moment as conjuring it. It exemplifies a defensive response that is frequently adopted in real experience: internalizing the aggressor in order to stave off the terror he brings" (Warner 2000, pp. 168–9).

This instinctive fascination with the ludic commingling of pleasure and dread, and the related, albeit sporadic, proclivity to retain this value in the transition from childhood to adulthood implies that an acceptance of the grown-up world and its rules does not automatically entail the relinquishment of the ability to apply alternative or even transgressive ideas to the game, no matter how serious and menacing it might be. In *The Familiar of Zero*, Louise must bow to the imperatives of the adult domain, grow out of her initial snooty-kid mode and deploy her magic in the service of her country. Yet, Louise's unique wizardly talent also provides her with a ludic tool of sorts through which she could reconfigure reality as though it were a magnificently enhanced Lego or plasticine town. In *Earl and Fairy*, the heroine must accept that communing with fairies and mediating between their world and the human dimension is not an activity that can be unequivocally approached as a game insofar as it is conducive to the assumption of onerous responsibilities and exposure to grave dangers. Nonetheless, Lydia's flexibility, generousness, creativity and unshakeable independence of mind (despite her inner insecurities) ultimately enable her to continue deriving innocent pleasure from her job even when potentially lethal threats close in on her. *xxxHolic*'s protagonist, for his part, is forced to bow to the adult world's demands as he realizes that he cannot obtain magical help from his employer unless he is prepared to put his heart and soul into the job. In *Ponyo*, likewise, Sousuke is forced to mature through the endurance of separation and loss, and related obligation to confront the clash between potentially irreconcilable levels of existence: the human and the marine, the natural and the supernatural, the prosaic and the magical. At the same time, however, both Watanuki and Sousuke are never rendered so disillusioned or bitter by their experiences as to lose conclusively their endearing aura of playfulness and hence the power to take us onto exploratory voyages that go on feeling new and exciting every time we sample their adventures.

A couple of anime with a pronouncedly fairytalish tone can be used to illustrate further the propositions expounded above: namely, the TV shows *Scrapped Princess* (dir. Soichi Masui, 2003) and *Petite Princess Yucie* (dir. Masahiko Otsuka, 2002–2003). In both of these productions, the inseparability of fear and delight is consistently communicated. At the same time, while both of their protagonists have no choice but to bow to the requirements of the adult sphere as a result of their magically determined duties, they nonetheless manage to retain a modicum of playfulness and creativity in the face of adversity that enables them to bend the rules and — whenever possible — reconfigure reality in a sportive spirit.

Scrapped Princess revolves around the character of fifteen-year-old Pacifica Casull, the girl in a set of twins born to the family that rules the "Kingdom of Leinwand" and thrown off a cliff as a baby due to the "5111th Grendel Prophecy," which deems her fated to destroy the world upon reaching the age of sixteen. Saved by a royal mage and fostered by the humble Casull family, Pacifica grows up with two very special adoptive siblings: the magic user Raquel and the swordsman Shannon. Throughout the peregrinations around which the bulk of the anime is orchestrated, Raquel and Shannon take it upon themselves to protect the "scrapped princess" from countless foes, and especially from the godlike "Peacemakers," who are fearful of her predicted future actions. Seemingly cheerful and relaxed even under duress, the heroine is innerly tormented by self-doubt and subliminally haunted by apprehension regarding the prophecy and its possible veracity. As the adventure progresses,

Pacifica must increasingly resist the future divined on her behalf by tradition and perpetuated by superstition and fear, and fathom her true hidden fate. By recourse to a classic fairy-tale reversal, *Scrapped Princess* proposes that Pacifica is actually humanity's last hope. This disclosure crowns a series of revelations concerning the protagonist's present world. We thus discover that the Peacemakers were originally created by humans as weapons to be deployed against aliens prior to the so-called "Genesis Wars," held to have taken place five-thousand years earlier, but sided with the enemy in imprisoning the human survivors in an artificial environment, regressing their advanced civilization to the Middle Ages, and periodically exterminating large portions of the population to prevent humans from grasping their predicament and rebelling. This state of affairs is redolent of the sci-fi situations dramatized in the anime *Megazone 23* and *Zegapain* (as well as the *Matrix* movies and their videogaming spin-offs), here discussed in Chapter 3. The Peacemakers themselves have served as the fulcrum of a pseudo-religion intended to discipline humanity into docile subservience: so powerful is the creatures' influence that no human can oppose their will or remain immune to their overbearing gaze. Pacifica is the only person unaffected by this force, which in itself would be sufficient to make her inconvenient to the status quo. More worrying still, from the oppressors' point of view, is her dormant ability to communicate her unique power to others, which is destined to blossom upon her sixteenth birthday.

Petite Princess Yucie, for its part, charts the adventures of an endearingly scatterbrained yet resolute seventeen-year-old girl who, due to a curse that impedes her physical development, looks as though she were only about ten. Glorying in the classic symbolism and iconography of the fairy-tale tradition, *Petite Princess Yucie* regales the eye with a genuinely enchanting multiturreted castle, assorted dragons, jewels and picturesque medieval towns. The story focuses on Yucie's intrepid efforts to become the "Platinum Princess" through exacting training at the "Princess Academy," where ruthless antagonist for that treasured position abound, and reassemble the "Eternal Tiara" whose pieces are scattered throughout the Human, Demon, Heaven, Spirit, and Fairy realities. Deemed able to fulfill any wish, the jeweled headdress holds the power to allow Yucie to develop into an adult at last. *Petite Princess Yucie* is rendered memorable, above all else, by its tonal range. Although Otsuka's series at first appears solidly rooted in the domain of undiluted fantasy, its mood darkens as it emerges that the heroine's attainment of her target comes with a very steep price: the erasure of all of the other contenders in the tournament, whom Yucie has rapidly come to regard as loyal friends. If the candidate picked by the Eternal Tiara to become the Platinum Princess rejected the appointment, her world would be destroyed. Yucie is at first protected from this ominous truth as the judge of the Magic World compassionately obliterates her memories of her former companions. Nonetheless, these gradually reemerge in the guise of a haunting feeling of loss, which causes the protagonist to sense that a crucial part of her identity is missing, yet remain powerless to identify its significance. Eventually, Yucie pulls off the ultimate magical feat, relying not solely on magic but also on sheer human guts, imagination and ludic verve, and returns the lost girls to their world.

An apposite exit point for this chapter is supplied by *The Girl Who Leapt Through Time* (dir. Mamoru Hosoda, 2006), a movie in which the play instinct is generously upheld. Moreover, the five principal themes examined in this study are here deftly blended with the adoption of the bildungsroman topos as a narrative leading thread. The film hence proposes that the development of its protagonist, Makoto Konno, is indisseverable from her sense of duty to others: an ethical principle so potent as to acquire the binding authority of a contractual obligation even though, ironically, the people supposed to benefit from it are quite oblivious to Makoto's intent. Concurrently, the girl's earnestness raises her actions to the level of history-altering missions even though their immediate objectives are often relatively trivial. As these deeds are performed, the natural environment itself is progressively reconfigured in more or less drastic ways. In braiding together these narrative strands with both elegance and verve, the adventure's overarching thrust points in the direction of a thoughtful, engaging and wistful coming-of-age scenario replete with sensitive references to the themes of alienation and isolation. The main actor's characterization plays a crucial role in sustaining the narrative from beginning to end. What makes Makoto most appealing, in the context of a yarn that could easily have developed according to fossilized sci-fi formulae, is her refreshing portrayal not as a conventional superheroine but rather as an ordinary, self-absorbed and clumsy teenager prone to impulsive behavior. The key supporting characters, the clever and reliable Kousuke and the fun-loving Chiaki, offer a pair of complementary personalities that allow disparate aspects of Makoto's own mentality to emerge through quotidian interaction in a natural, unforced fashion.

The film's early segment makes bountiful use of comedy, especially in the depiction of a day initially expected to unfold according to a familiar pattern but incrementally degenerating into an accumulation of at first just irritating and then downright calamitous occurrences. Its climax is a poignantly suspenseful sequence blighted by Makoto's apparent "death" when the brakes on her bike suddenly cease to work and she rides straight into an oncoming train. The magic starts when Makoto realizes that she has not died in the seemingly fateful crash and, in fact, never even reached the level-crossing but came to a halt a few yards away from the spot and a few seconds earlier. Her charismatic aunt, a character that is repeatedly compared to a "witch" as the story progresses, nonchalantly explains that Makoto has time-slipped. The girl indeed finds that she possesses the power to control time by taking flying leaps of increasingly daring magnitude. What she does not yet know is that her skill issues from a walnut-shaped device from the future brought into her era by Chiaki, who has been tenaciously searching for a painting of bewitching beauty: a work, as it happens, which Makoto's aunt has been intent on restoring for public exhibition at the museum where she is employed. The device, despite its futuristic affiliations, exudes a venerable aura of magic through its very design and could be said to encapsulate (literally *in nuce*) the entire feature's wizardly feel.

Initially, Makoto exploits her power to alter relatively menial occurrences — e.g., to oversleep in the morning without being late for school, to jump back to the beginning of a karaoke session when the allocated time runs out, to improve her grades by taking a test again once she knows the correct answers, and to fix up friends harboring hopeless crushes. The jocular tone established by the scenes preceding Makoto's first accidental time-leap is buoyantly heightened once the protagonist deliberately begins to deploy her talent. As she blithely storms from one scene to the next, her time-leaps repeatedly result in collisions, dives, smashups, stumbles, flips, plummeting falls and random chains of mishaps worthy of a Buster-Keaton film at its most flamboyant. Yet, the overall mood emanates a heartwarming sense of spontaneity and never smacks of stagy clownishness. In fact, it conveys a realistic sense of awkwardness that is fully consonant with the maturation strand of the story, and unobtrusively flows from the physical realm to the emotional and psychological dimensions of the characters' lives and intermingled destinies. From a formal point of view, *The Girl Who Leapt Through Time* is most commendable in virtue of its knack of matching its dramatic tempo and generic mood to the pace of its heroine's own evolution. Thus, as Makoto's quest progressively accrues gravity and momentum, the show's rhythm accordingly acquires a greater sense of urgency. Playful at first, the film's tone gradually darkens as the murkier tinges of its protagonist's powers transpire. In the process, Makoto understands that changing the past can have serious and unexpected consequences and might ultimately have to be used to change not merely the past but the future, too. This shift of mood is so subtly effected as to appear to creep up on the audience in an almost deceptive fashion. It is also noteworthy that in spite of the movie's deliberate atmospheric shift and the disruptions triggered by Makoto's time-jumping ruses, the action conveys a potent impression of dramatic unity. This owes much to the movie's exceptionally smooth animation, with its impeccable handling of space, weight and gravity, and by the use of recurrent locations punctuating the action and marking its most emotionally intense moments. These include the local baseball field, the winding roads of suburban Tokyo, a river bank bathed in dusky light, and long vistas stretching towards a remote horizon allusive to the transience of youth and innocence.

Chapter 6

Magic Destinies

*That's the thing with magic. You've got to know it's still here,
all around us, or it just stays invisible for you.* — Charles de Lint

*The metaphor is perhaps one of man's most fruitful potentialities.
Its efficacy verges on magic.* — José Ortega y Gasset

As foreshadowed, all of the principal themes addressed in this study collude in the anime's treatment of both personal and collective destinies traversed by magically oriented conjectures, attitudes and imperatives. On the one hand, the chosen titles aim to weave tapestries of intersubjective obligations invested with magically binding authority. On the other hand, they give narrative shape to elaborate missions endeavoring to equip the questors with fresh identities and help them rediscover forgotten or repressed histories. These enterprises variously enjoin the protagonists to engage with the natural habitat and its dizzying profusion of both visible and hidden forces, while concurrently propelling them into meandering voyages of development informed by the bildungsroman tradition. In the process, the chosen anime deliver varyingly elaborate metaphorical formations that figuratively underscore the inextricability of magical thinking from the often laborious processes through which humans struggle to define themselves and both their natural surroundings and their societal contexts.

It should also be noted that while the concepts of destiny and fate are often used interchangeably in the anime under investigation, subtle differences between them are also alluded to with varying degrees of explicitness. It is thus suggested that fate refers to the cosmic power or agency capable of preordaining the course of future events and of endowing them with a semblance of finality or ineluctability. In numerous mythological systems the world over, fate is said to be the product of the indefatigable spinning of threads representing individual human destinies by mystical or divine entities. Within a tradition which, like Buddhism and Shinto, preaches the interconnectedness of all life forms, the universe as a whole can be thought of as a gigantic network akin to a magic spiderweb. While fate is supposed to be immune to human intervention, destiny allows for an element of autonomous, willful involvement on the part of singular beings. Thus, although destiny may also be shaped by external or transcendental forces, humans have the freedom to participate in the achievement of particular outcomes. In their articulation of narratives wherein the unfolding of both individual and collective destinies is influenced by supernatural powers (or accidents), the shows here discussed play simultaneously with diverse interpretations of the idea of destiny.

Overall, the anime appear to work on the assumption that destiny is fixed and inevitable. Humanity's spiritual journeys. in this reading, are no less extrinsically ordained than the mechanical functionings of the material world probed by physics or biology. Sometimes, this position veers toward fatalism, the philosophical view according to which no human action can affect the future for good or ill irrespective of its intentions. Any choice or deliberation on the part of an individual is, in this world picture, simply idle. (Fatalism is based on the approach to the concept of fate outlined earlier.) Alternatively, strict fatalism may be superseded by determinism, the doctrine that claims, like fatalism, that the future is anchored to necessity, yet also advocates that our present actions will affect how that future comes about. Whereas in a fatalistic perspective, people's ordeals are arranged occurrences in which they have no decisive part, in a deterministic one, they stem from those individuals' essential dispositions. In some cases, libertarianism is asserted instead, and it is therefore proposed that the future can never be considered settled insofar as humans are fundamentally free.

In a world ruled by formal logic, the approaches outlined above would be deemed incompatible with one another, and a world view presuming to foster their coexistence, relatedly, would be dismissed as inconsistent, unreliable or even downright absurd. However, as repeatedly indicated in the course of this study, magical thinking is not constrained by the dicta of formal (let alone binary) logic, and it is hence at liberty to propose that humans might well be both captives and creators of their destinies at one and the same time. Thus, even when a character's — or group of characters' — destiny seems to be so inexorably sealed as to foreclose any chances of reorientation, it often proves possible to tamper with the world's spatial and temporal coordinates in order to suggest fresh ways of looking at reality. Such moves, it must be stressed, are indeed ways of formulating alternative *perspectives* and not alternative *realities* as such. If by manipulating space and time through magic the actors were to bring about new worlds from scratch, their actions might result in happiness but this would only be the vaporous beatitude notoriously provided by utopias: an escapist flight into a pseudo-reality from which no lessons can be gleaned and no self-understanding, therefore, is likely to be achieved. By interfering with space and time just enough to tilt their axes and engineer shifts in perspective, conversely, the characters create novel angles from which the world can be inspected — and, when practical intervention becomes necessary, accessed and interacted with. This move can help them to look at themselves and their situations differently and, ideally, to learn something from the experience. Relatedly, while characters may be cognizant of their preternatural powers and attendant magic destinies from the start, they nonetheless have to recognize the actual onus entailed by being a magic practitioner though arduous journeys of self-exploration. The individual analyses offered below will hopefully illustrate this hypothesis, insofar as all of their protagonists initially appear trapped in destinies they cannot hope to transcend or elude, yet gradually develop and express an ability to break through those cages with courage, enthusiasm and, at best, a modicum of humor to boot. In these circumstances, magic functions as an adaptable metaphor for the creative drive at its most vibrant and adventurous.

At times, magic joins forces with generous contingents of humor and romance in the cherished format of school-based drama of the kind many Western audiences would tend to associate with the *Harry Potter* saga: the *Negima* franchise is a resplendent case in point. Quite a different type of magic destiny is traced by anime inspired by venerable literary sources wherein wizardly components already play a role, and eager to enhance those facets through imaginative interpretation of their sources. A notable instance is offered by *Romeo x Juliet*, where the appetite for metamorphic flourishes seen to pervade the magical universe in practically all of its guises asserts itself in the form of a daring reconceptualization of the famous Shakespearean tale. Adopting a pointedly antiquarian take on Europe with a focus on the revered art of doll-making, *Rozen Maiden* and *Rozen Maiden: Träumend* invoke a cognate tradition but resolutely embrace a Japanese world view in their treatment of the doll figure as the repository of symbolic powers capable of defying the boundary between the animate and the inanimate, the human and the non-human. In all of the productions here examined, however, a distinctively Nipponic approach to myth can be observed. Japanese culture hosts a panoply of mythological traditions combining indigenous and imported elements. The foreign ingredients emanate principally from China and India (though Western elements, as noted, also come into play) and reveal an inveterate desire to reinterpret the available source materials rather than absorb them wholesale. The sheer élan with which this task is undertaken makes it comparable to a process of magical transmutation. Hence, while both the Chinese pantheon and its Indian counterpart have influenced Japanese mythology, this has never unquestioningly embraced either the complex and strict hierarchy inherent in the former nor the comparably regimented caste system associated with the latter.

Some myths consist of folktales rooted in the indigenous oral tradition, some intersect with ghost stories imbricated with Buddhist beliefs about the afterlife, and some encapsulate particular political agendas laid out by powerful personages. Furthermore, a number of mythical formations encompass a narrative dimension, which makes them overtly appealing as forms of entertainment, whereas others depict in non-narrative form — and often by recourse to the visual rather than verbal arts — the most salient attributes of various legendary figures and related cosmological principles. Moreover, certain myths reflect local beliefs and customs characteristic of relatively small communities or regions, while others seek to codify and glorify broad national trends. These constructs aspire to engender ideological cohesion by inducing people to grasp their inscription in a specific world order with reference to the elaborate processes though which such an arrangement has evolved from the hazy past to the present. As Michael Ashkenazi persuasively argues, "For many modern Japanese, the relationship between myth and life is a complex one. Myth consists of stories about nebulous and concrete beings and items. It also consists of beliefs about origins ... which are unquestioned, often unquestionable. And few Japanese will admit to 'believing' in these myths. They simply act as if they do. ... religion and ritual, household practices and national ones blend in subtle and unpredictable ways" (Ashkenazi, p. 1).

As persistently argued throughout the preceding chapters, the concept of space plays a very significant part in the metaphorical adaptation of supernatural themes and imagery for the purpose of exploring magically determined pacts, quests, natural habitats and evolutionary trajectories. The treatment of the theme of magic destinies once more enthrones space as a protagonist. In this instance, attention is consistently drawn to baffling locations that pointedly bring to mind Michel Foucault's concept of "heterotopia." Foucault's earliest assessment of this idea occurs in "Of Other Spaces," where heterotopias are described as "something like counter-sites, a kind of effectively enacted utopia in which the real sites, all the other real sites that can be found within the culture, are simultaneously represented, contested, and inverted." While utopias are nowhere lands, heterotopias are real, albeit hidden, places: they are "outside of all places, even though it may be possible to indicate their location in reality" and are capable of juxtaposing several incompatible spaces in a "single real place" (Foucault 1986, p. 24). According to Benjamin Genocchio, they "constitute a discontinuous but socially defined spatiality, both material and immaterial at the same time" (Genocchio, p. 38). Heterotopias may be obscured from view for a variety of reasons. At times, as Edward Soja notes, they consist of "privileged, sacred, or forbidden spaces"; at others, of spaces of "deviation" (Soja, p. 15). Their functions and meanings, moreover, alter over time as a result of numerous geographical and historical remappings. The concept of heterotopia is examined further by Foucault in *The Order of Things*. Here, the notion that radically heterogeneous elements may coexist within one single space is regarded primarily as an assault on discursive ordering: "[Heterotopias] make it impossible to name this and that ... because they shatter or tangle common names, because they destroy syntax in advance, and not only the syntax with which we construct sentences but also that less apparent syntax which causes words and things ... to 'hold together.' ... they dissolve our myths, sterilize the lyricism of sentences" (Foucault 1994, p. xviii).

As highly equivocal levels of reality averse to rigid compartmentalization and to the dictates of causality, heterotopias parallel the workings of magic as a discourse that operates both within and beyond reality at once, all the time promoting ongoing metamorphoses unfettered by the strictures of classical logic. Magic enjoins us to engage with heterotopias as fecund spaces for imaginative reflection, yet also warns us against the danger of attempting to grasp heterotopias so conclusively as to deprive them of the otherness that makes them what they are. At one level, magic's geography places various heterotopias on an atlas of emblematic analogies, correspondences and interweavings that may seem to rob them of their incommensurable difference. Yet, magic concurrently undermines this domesticating move by intimating that even though all sorts of heterotopias (however bizarre or monstrous) may be situated in an all-encompassing symbolic cartography, and thus rendered readable, what remains unthinkable is the tabulating system itself. What is ultimately impossible to imagine is the very existence of a cohesive space within which the spatial configurations encompassed by magic's geography could durably coexist. The heterotopia's subversive function therefore persists, since any illusion of order may only be entertained within a purely suppositious abstract scheme.

The meeting of multiple destinies in an elaborate tapestry of intersubjective alliances and conflicts is the principal animating force at the core of the *Negima* franchise. This comprises an extensive manga, the TV series *Negima!* (dir. Nagisa Miyazaki, 2005) based upon it, the direct-to-video releases *Negima!—Spring* and *Negima!—Summer* (2006), the alternate retelling of the manga in the TV series *Negima!?* (2006–2007) and the OVAs *Negima!—The White Wing* (2008–2009) and *Negima!—Another World* (2009), all of which were directed by Akiyuki Shinbou. The individual destinies of *Negima*'s vast array of actors orbit around an unusual protagonist: the ten-year-old

Welsh wizard Negi Springfield, who aims to become a powerful mage both to assist ordinary humans in their everyday misfortunes and to find his father Nagi, a wizard of legendary repute known as the "Thousand Master" and believed to be dead. Yet to complete his training, Negi is required to pass one last test before he can become a qualified practitioner and obtain the prized title of "*Magister Magi*"—i.e., "Master Mage" or "Magic Master." This consists of taking up a job in the real world—which, bizarrely, turns out to be that of English teacher at the all-female Mahora Academy in Japan. Soon surrounded by a gaggle of older girls consisting of no less than thirty-one students—and including a ninja, a time-traveling Martian, a ghost, a robot, an internet idol, a half-demon and a sprinkling of alarmingly proficient martial artists—Negi is henceforth fated to confront a twofold trial. On the one hand, he must deal with the succession of magical incidents and threats which his training can be expected to entail. On the other hand, he has no choice but to put his heart and soul into earning the trust and respect of his class while adjusting to the distinctive personalities and quirks of some very special young women.

Little by little, each of them is drawn into the magic world, its operators, spirits, traditions and rituals, in a tantalizing whirlwind of fantasy, comedy and romance. Central to the diegesis is Negi's relationship with Asuna Kagurazaka, a student that initially claims to detest the new appointment insofar as he has putatively replaced the older tutor she has a crush on but gradually becomes his closest mate. As the relationship develops, Asuna and Negi join forces in negotiating their respective magic destinies. In the process, Asuna helps Negi garner clues about his missing dad, while the boy wizard, in turn, endeavors to release her from the ten-year contract that binds her to the "Demon King" and is bound to culminate in the girl's death on her fourteenth birthday. Eventually, Asuna and Negi's lives turn out to be more intimately connected than either of them could ever have imagined as it transpires that the girl's ominous fate is indirectly connected with Nagi Springfield's mysterious past. Asuna's pact with the aforementioned Demon King is said to have endowed her with magic-canceling abilities intended to suppress her initial ability to summon demons: a capacity doomed to cause devastation and chaos wherever she went. The girl's accidental erasure of Nagi's own magic barrier during a fight with a demon supposedly triggered his disappearance.

The first series follows the original manga quite closely but develops independently in the course of the climactic installments to supply the adventure with a satisfying closure—something which the parent text could not then be expected to offer having not yet reached that stage in the narrative. The Spring OVA released after the first TV show adopts a predominantly comedic approach, focusing on a trip to a gorgeous island undertaken by Negi and his class during their Spring break and on the protagonist's quasi-romantic attritions with Asuna. The Summer OVA, for its part, preserves the jocular tone established by its Spring antecedent while dramatizing the abortive attempts made by the characters of Yue and Nodoka to cast a spell known as the "red string of fate." The topos of magic destinies is central to this mini-adventure since the spell, when properly performed, is meant to reveal a person's future partner. The OVA is also notable as an instance of magic-based parody in that the bathhouse therein portrayed consists of a comical adaptation of the analogous edifice central to Hayao Miyazaki's *Spirited Away* (2001)—here discussed in some detail in Chapter 3 and briefly alluded to again in Chapter 5. The supernatural beings inhabiting the venue, in this case, are rendered even more pointedly absurd than their Miyazakian models by the fact that they work on treadmills. The 2008–2009 OVAs also evince a predominantly jocular mood. *White Wing*, in particular, indulges in comedy of the kind most likely to be appreciated by fans of the parent manga, insofar as it spans an arc of the saga not overtly connected with the events chronicled in either the first TV series or the *Negima!?* adaptation. The plot takes as its basic premise the discovery that Negi's father is still alive and that Negi might be able to meet him if he were to return to Wales, where a door to the magic realm would be more likely to open. This revelation fills the young wizard's class with renewed enthusiasm, leading to the establishment of a club wherein the girls may undergo thorough training and hence develop the skills necessary to abet their tutor's quest. The sheer sense of verve, cooperativeness and determination conveyed by these scenes is enough to make the OVA a treat even for viewers not conversant with the source and its specific narrative complications.

The second TV series offers a radical retelling of the original story starring the same basic characters but adopting new character designs and placing greater emphasis on humor and action. At the same time, however, the tenser moments in the second *Negima* series bear many of the distinctive traits evinced by Shinbou's handling of supernatural themes in other shows of a magical stamp helmed by the same director: most notably, the TV series *MoonPhase* (2004–2005), here discussed in Chapter 3, the TV series *Soul Taker* (2001) and the OVA series *Petite Cossette* (2004). *Soul Taker*'s protagonist, Kyosuke Date, is capable of morphing into a formidable mutant, the titular figure, as a result of an unusual DNA caused by a disease said to have annihilated the lunar colony whence he has escaped, and uses his power to combat other mutants and a band of corporate assassins. *Soul Taker* gravitates toward the action-adventure pole, with generic concessions to science fiction along the way, thereby yielding a gritty anatomy of human greed, exploitativeness and iniquity. *Petite Cossette*, for its part, carries the flavor of an inverted fairy tale with Gothic nuances. The OVA revolves around the spectral figure of the eponymous heroine: the daughter of an eighteenth-century nobleman murdered by her fiancé, the artist Marcelo Orlando, and cursed ever since to live on within the prison of an antique glass. The coprotagonist is Eiri Kurahashi, an art student who feels attracted to the hapless spirit and wishes to set her free. Unfortunately, as Cossette informs him, only a man willing to accept punishment on the criminal artist's behalf might accomplish that magical task. (Shinbou, it should be noted, has also left his signature in the magical-anime arena with the direction of the TV series *Magical Girl Lyrical Nanoha* [2004], here addressed in Chapter 3.)

Set a year after Negi's arrival at Mahora Academy, the reconfigured yarn provided by the second TV show revolves around the disappearance of a magical object known as the "Star Crystal," and its subsequent effects — malevolent and unpredictable in equal doses — on Negi and his pupils. As the story unfolds, the protagonist becomes increasingly absorbed in speculations regarding his lost father while many of the girls around him strive to abet the young wizard in his efforts to face up to a taxing, albeit noble, destiny. *Negima!?* is faithful to the source manga in its delineation of the basic story's premises: namely, Negi's efforts to adjust to Mahora Academy and its position as a sort of school-centered city state, while striving to find an apposite partner, in a world where magic is still very much a secret and keeping a low profile is therefore a high priority for any fledgling mage worth his salt. Much of the comedy issues precisely from the fact that the hero's endeavor to conceal his true nature and magical connections proves repeatedly inadequate. As a result, he accidentally reveals himself to several of his students, all of whom tend to find him attractive for one reason or another and are hence unlikely to let his actions go by unnoticed. This urges Negi to strike up successive alliances with all of the girls who have unveiled his secret to commit them to protective silence while he, in return, grants them magic abilities.

The second series initially focuses on the character of Evangeline, the aforementioned vampire in the hero's class. Evangeline's destiny is entangled with Negi's own history, insofar as the boy's dad is supposed to have been tangentially responsible for the curse locking the centuries-old undead within her current girlish body. The dramatization of this particular story arc in the show's early episodes thus serves to establish from the start some important connections between the past and the future, while also shedding light onto key structural elements of the magic world and its peculiar laws. In interweaving scenes from Evangeline's present life, with its bloodcurdling nocturnal hunts and uneasy collusion of bestial rapaciousness and sensitivity, and flashbacks to her past, *Negima!?* eloquently proclaims its caliber as a stylish animation. Its most memorable aspects, in this regard, are intelligent character designs, a dexterous juxtaposition of bright and somber hues that endow both the actors and the settings with a sense of presence, solidity and depth, and markedly fluid motion for action sequences and meditative moments alike. The Mahora scholastic *polis* stands out as a character in its own right thanks to thoroughly individuated locations exuding a palpable sense of history and sumptuous architectural components replete with carpets, stained-glass windows, woodwork and wrought-iron structures. The library is especially striking since it consists of a distinct island reaching down into inscrutable levels of the Academy, asserting itself as a profusive celebration of the poetic lure of magic space per se. These artistic traits abide as defining attributes of the series as a whole, gaining novel resonance as it progresses toward its satisfyingly reparative finale. An important shift of locale occurs in the second show's latter segment, where Negi (who has been morphed into a cute *chupacabra*, a mythical cryptid), his students and his colleague Takahata get stranded in the "Illusory World": a magical domain containing no obvious opportunities for escape. At one point, the young wizard and his companions believe they have successfully managed to make their way home but soon find themselves in an alternate, deserted version of the Mahora compound, with the once grand Academy itself in a decrepit state. With this incident, the series provides one of the most felicitous instances of experimentation with the metamorphic magic of space to be witnessed in recent anime.

The second anime's comic mood reaches its apotheosis in this part of the story, as the protagonist and his metaphorical harem tumble along from one crazy and deliberately chaotic adventure to the next, dealing by turns with magical threats of variable magnitude and assorted personality clashes, hobbyhorses and misunderstandings. In the closing installments, the show accrues intensity in both kinetic energy and drama, as the team accomplishes the task of collecting the "fairy shards" needed to return home, the Star Crystal is released, and the true villain behind Negi's and his students' mishaps is exposed. Importantly this disclosure is not presented as an ebullient coup de théâtre, which could logically be expected of an anime prioritizing playful dynamics at each available option. In fact, it is sensitively handled as the acme of a long-standing emotional crisis surrounding the character of Anya, Negi's childhood friend and erstwhile classmate prior to the boy's departure for Mahora Academy. Anya is said to have traveled to Japan to urge Negi to go back to his native country and to have been shocked to find that the boy had not only overtaken her in the area of magic skills but also made lots of new friends — an impossible feat for Anya due to her pathological difficulties in socializing. Driven by the self-imposed imperative not to "lose to Negi," she has putatively stolen the Star Crystal, thereby triggering all sorts of preternatural troubles. However, Anya's own soul has been incrementally consumed by the malevolent artifact's dark agency and it is now up to Negi and his loyal retinue to save the girl from being swallowed by the Star Crystal altogether. Although Negi does his best to discourage his students from getting involved in this mission, his fate is by now far too dear to their hearts for them to withdraw from the fray. The girls' collective will thus proves instrumental in their defiance of destiny and irreverent disregard for the fatalistic messages which the sinister forces closing in upon them seek to assert. Some genuine gems of animation at its most vibrantly, yet considerately, spectacular are yielded by the climactic sequences in which the hero himself is gobbled up by the Star Crystal and his students must do everything in their power to save him from the direst of destinies: irreversible descent into the Netherworld.

The concept of a magically fueled will capable of challenging fate, so pivotal to *Negima!?*'s climax, finds one of its most notable formulations in *Magic Knight Rayearth* (TV series; dir. Toshihiro Hirano, 1994–1995). This is another fruit of CLAMP's endlessly prosperous graphic harvest, alongside *Tsubasa: RESERVoir CHRoNiCLE* (please see Chapter 2), *Cardcaptor Sakura* and *xxxHolic* (both of which are here addressed in Chapter 5). In this instance, the power of the will is enthroned as the foundational principle of an entire magic land of spiritual forces and creatures, Cephiro. The three protagonists, junior high-school students Hikaru Shidou, Umi Ryuuzaki and Fuu Hououji, are transported to this world in the course of an ordinary school trip and survive its challenges thanks to abilities they already possess despite their seemingly unexceptional standing. Their appointed destiny is to rise to the rank of "Magic Knights," release Princess Emeraude from the clutches of the Dark Priest Zagato and, in so doing, guarantee the survival of the Cephiro reality itself. (The character of Princess Emeraude, incidentally, also appears in *Tsubasa: RESERVoir CHRoNiCLE* in quite a different role, as the pivot of a tale of hauntings and child abductions rendered with unique antiquarian flair.) Like *Negima* in all its multifarious incarnations, *Magic Knight Rayearth* is a paean to solidarity, devoting close attention to the three heroines' growing commitment to one another in the confrontation of myriad unexpected obstacles — as well as equally fickle villains and allies — as they learn from their mistakes, managing to remain confident when all seems lost.

Negima! emplaces magical iconography as a mainstay of its occult register by recourse to a system indigenous solely to the world of the franchise, the "*Pactio.*" The ensuing segment of the discussion assesses this symbolic system and then proceeds to delineate its links with the Tarot tradition — i.e., one of the oldest and most popular vehicles of magic signification. Thereafter, the use of the Tarot in an earlier and likewise prolific anime franchise, *Vision of Escaflowne*, will also be evaluated for contextualing purposes. The word "*Pactio*" comes from Latin and designates the establishment of a "*pactum,*" an "agreement." The topos of the contract, analyzed in depth in Chapter 2, therefore comes into play in the *Negima* universe at large as an important theme. The agreements dramatized in the series involve magic practitioners and their companions, each of whom is endowed with supernatural powers inspired by their intrinsic natures. The practitioner goes by the name of "*Magister Magi*" (the title, as noted, aspired to by Negi) if male and "*Magistra Magi*" if female, whereas the companion is known as "*Minister Magi*" or "*Ministra Magi*" (namely, "Magic Servant" or "Mage Servant"). Upon sealing a pact with a companion, the practitioner transmits some of his or her power to the other party by means of a spell, thereby enhancing the latter's own abilities and resistance to harm, while also supplying him or her with an "Artifact"— a magically charged object of talismanic significance. The companion, in return, vows to protect the master from assaults and chanting charms.

Echoing *Fate/stay Night*, here examined in Chapter 2, the *Negima* franchise proposes that if a master dies, the contract with his or her companion can be considered void. Additionally, a bargain struck in a fashion other than the magically sanctioned one — that is to say, with both parties entering a magic circle drawn with chalk by the mediating character of Chamo, Negi's ermine familiar, and exchanging a mouth-to-mouth kiss — will be deemed invalid and branded as "Mistake *Pactio*." An agreement intended to have unlimited duration is known as "Permanent *Pactio*," while a temporary one (of the kind that is sometimes advisable for underage participants) goes by the name of "Probationary *Pactio*." An especially important Probationary *Pactio* is formed by Negi in the climax of the first anime with the whole of his class — which he has inadvertently taken along while traveling back in time to learn about Asuna's preternatural powers — in order to break the contract that binds his best friend to the Demon King and fates her to certain death.

It is in order to validate the establishment of a magical agreement in emblematic form that a card ("*Charta Ministralis*" — i.e., "*Minister*'s/*Ministra*'s Card") is created. In the set of cards closely inspired by the manga, each image displays the character of the *Minister* or *Ministra* with its full name in the company of diverse esoteric motifs and ritual items, as well as a number and assorted captions highlighting his or her "*tonus*" ("color tone"), "*astrali-*

tas" ("star affinity"), "*virtus*" ("virtue" or "quality"), "*directio*" ("direction" or "cardinal point"), and professional designation in Latin. For instance, the character of Asuna is symbolically associated with the color red, the planet Mars, the virtue of "*audacia*" ("courage"), the East, and the title of "*Bellatrix Sauciata*" ("Wounded Girl Warrior"). Nodoka Miyazaki is linked to the same basic quality but in conjunction with the color blue, the planet Mercury, the West, and the tag "*Pudica Bibliothecaria*" ("Modest Librarian"). Both Kazumi Asakura, in her capacity as "*Reportatrix Denudans*" or "Reporter who Discloses Facts," and Yue Ayase, in hers as "*Philosophastra Illustrans*" or "Elucidative Philosophaster," symbolize "*sapientia*" ("wisdom") but as distinct or even contrasting personalities — the former being associated with blue, Neptune and the East, and the latter with black, Mercury and the West. When a bond is forged, the master retains possession of the original card, which enables him or her to communicate telepathically with the magical assistant, while the latter can make use of the card to summon his or her Artifact.

The *Negima!?* anime utilizes a marginally different kind of *Pactio* in accordance with its alternate take on the original story as recounted in the parent manga. Dubbed "Neo-*Pactio*," this does not require a hand-drawn circle since Chamo is now capable of simply conjuring up the hermetic diagram. When a bond is forged, three cards are created: the "Dud," where servants are portrayed in a superdeformed style and don animal costumes (hints at the shamanic tradition can here be detected); the "Cosplay," where servants acquire special costumes and minor skills; and the "Armor," where servants again obtain special accoutrements, in this case matched by superior abilities enhancing their martial prowess. Depending on which of the three available cards is drawn (through entirely random selection), the magician's associate will undergo a specific type of physical and mental metamorphosis. The show handles this motif very proficiently through a delicate synthesis of ceremonial solemnity and comedy. Thus, while the invocation itself bears the traits of an awe-inspiring ritual, the effects of a transformation are often portrayed in a jocular vein: for instance, since the powers deployed by a *Minister* or *Ministra* during a mission are fueled by the food in his or her tummy, once the task is over, he or she will tend to be ravenous. Also amusing are the situations in which a magical companion loses energy excessively fast due to emotional distress or nervousness.

All of *Negima*'s *Pactio* cards recall the Tarot system at a number of parallel levels. In purely pictorial terms, they bring to mind the Tarot deck's sixteen Court Cards (which constitute the Minor Arcana alongside the forty cards numbered one to ten in each of four suits). The younger and bouncier-looking characters equate to Knaves, the more martial or athletic to Knights, and the older and sterner to Kings and Queens. In iconological terms, they mimic the Tarot's dense and multilayered symbolism by recourse to their own remarkable range of cryptic signs (at times, meaningful in relation to particular narrative developments; at others, playfully and self-consciously nonsensical). The *Negima* cards also pay tangential homage to an intricate symbolic network that has accrued to the Tarot tradition over the centuries, and has resulted in the gradual establishment of correspondences among the Tarot suits, the elements and related alchemical spirits, and the signs of the Zodiac, thus bringing together some of the most deep-rooted esoteric systems ever recorded. (Please note that the alchemical elementals are discussed in Chapter 4.) The most salient connections are outlined below.

1. *Tarot Suit:* *Wand*

Element:	**Elemental:**	**Star Signs:**	**Cardinal Point:**	**Meaning:**
Fire	Salamander	Leo, Aries Sagittarius	South	Animation Growth Energy

2. *Tarot Suit:* *Cup*

Element:	**Elemental:**	**Star Signs:**	**Cardinal Point:**	**Meaning:**
Water	Undine	Pisces Cancer Scorpio	West	Feeling Unconscious Femininity

3. *Tarot Suit:* *Sword*

Element:	**Elemental:**	**Star Signs:**	**Cardinal Point:**	**Meaning:**
Air	Sylph	Gemini Libra Aquarius	North	Strife Aggression Courage

4. *Tarot Suit:* *Pentacle*

Element:	**Elemental:**	**Star Signs:**	**Cardinal Point:**	**Meaning:**
Earth	Gnome	Taurus Virgo Capricorn	East	Wealth Business Enterprise

Most importantly, *Negima*'s cards echo the Tarot's Major Arcana: the twenty-two allegorical pictures held to portray the incessant flow of protean forces — both physical and spiritual — that shape life and direct human destinies. Traditionally, different Tarot packs varying in size and design have shared one essential feature: their emblematic standing as visual processions of various phases of human existence encompassing not only the past as it was actually experienced and the present as it is being experienced in the here-and-now but also all the possible pasts and presents one could have lived or be living. More crucially still, where the topos of destiny is concerned, the Tarot is believed capable of housing an archetypal, unconscious understanding of the future and hence of the legion potential experiences which that dimension always entails. The connection between *Negima*'s cards and the Major Arcana are not, by and large, explicit. Nor are they acknowledged or alluded to in the franchise as such. In fact, they are the product of speculations regarding the anime's commitment to the delineation of interwoven magic destinies — conjectures entertained in the light of the *Pactio* and Neo-*Pactio* as emblematic repertoires formally redolent of the Tarot tradition and language. A few examples of elliptical affinities between *Negima*'s cards and the Tarot are worth considering for illustrative purposes.

Symbolic of the beginning of a new journey, and hence of fresh openings and choices, the Major Arcanum 0, the Fool, normally features the figure of a wanderer — a character type, as seen in Chapter 4, pivotal to Japan's mythical and magical heritage. In some decks, the Fool is accompanied by the emblem of domestic loyalty par excellence, the dog, and set against a mountainous background: a facet of the natural world to which Japanese lore, specifically, attaches special significance insofar as mountains are often thought of as the repositories of the mightiest *kami*. *Negima* signals oblique deference to the Tarot's Fool with the card associated with the character of Konoka Konoe who, though not portrayed overtly as an itinerant magic agent, recalls Japan's shamanic tradition (and hence the Shinto-inspired nomadic healers of old) in the use of the classic *miko* costume complete with propitiatory accessories. (It is worth pointing out, incidentally, that Konoka is the most traditionally garbed of the anime's female personae, while the character of the legendary fighter Jack Rakan, with his *hakama* and *furoshiki*, holds the same position among the male members of the cast.) The sense of commodiousness of spirit enshrined in the Fool as a symbol of openness to the new and the unforeseeable finds a parallel in the concept of "*caritas*" — i.e. "charity" — with which Konoka is linked. The card devoted by *Negima* to the character of Yue (and hence, as seen, to "*sapientia*," or "wisdom") and the one centered on Rakan (another "*audacia*" character like Asuna and Nodoka) recall the Major Arcanum IX, the Hermit, in their use of somber clothing and a pervasive mood of solemnity denotative of the characters' unwavering commitment to their tasks. As proposed in Chapter 4, when darkness is associated with voyages into the unknown blessed with generosity of heart and latitude of mind, it does not equate to either concealment or menace but rather to a necessary stage in the transition to maturity, and hence to an enlightened preparedness to accept one's destiny whatever it might deliver. In the Tarot system, the Hermit is supposed to stand for a tireless pursuit of knowledge against prejudice, superstition and self-interest — though the reversed reading (i.e., the alternative interpretation to which all Tarot cards are susceptible) actually alludes to intolerance, dogmatism and impetuousness.

The Major Arcanum XII, the Hanged Man, typically emblematizes the triumph of the spirit over the flesh (or selfish escapism in the reverse reading) and displays a figure hanging upside down in a curiously relaxed demeanor, often conveyed by the detail of the casually folded arms. Moreover, the Hanged Man is often connected with mighty trees symbolic of nature at its most exuberantly alive. In *Negima*'s system, this Arcanum is echoed by the image representing Albireo Imma (one of Nagi's former companions). Although the character, one more version of "*sapientia*," appears trapped in a double helix formed by strings of tokens of wisdom and study, he exudes a tremendous aura of poise, calm and self-control with no hint at either constraint or discomfort. To cite one final example, the Major Arcanum representing Temperance, card number XIV, signifies self-possession and restraint in the upright reading but extremes of dynamism or passion in the reversed reading. The positive interpretation of the Temperance Arcanum is mirrored by the *Negima* card dedicated to Setsuna Sakurazaki (which is linked with "*justitia*," or "fairness"), where sweeping wings frame the character with remarkable vigor. As for the Setsuna card's connection with the Tarot's own version of Justice, card number XI, this consists of its use of a compositional rhythm redolent of the image of the scales with which that Major Arcanum is habitually associated. The negative interpretation of Temperance resonates in two of *Negima*'s cards that are, in fact, associated with "*temperantia*" ("self-control," or "moderation")—namely, the ones centered on the characters of Haruna Saotome and Chisame Hasegawa—where hints at wing-based imagery also appear and an overall mood of bursting exuberance asserts itself triumphantly.

The TV series *Vision of Escaflowne* (dirs. Kazuki Akane and Shouji Kawamori, 1996) and its alternate retelling in the theatrical feature *Escaflowne: The Movie* (dir. Kazuki Akane, 2000) will feasibly abide in the memory not only of seasoned anime aficionados but also of any lover of fantasy adventure in any medium as an epoch-making blend of magic and science fiction. The anime revolves around the sprightly and athletic—but otherwise initially ordinary—high-school student Hiromi Kanzaki, chronicling her spectacular transposition from Earth to the magical world of Gaea, where she encounters the young monarch of Fanelia, Van Fanel, is drawn into his epic quest to unite that world's various countries against the portentous Zaibach empire, and gradually discovers her dormant abilities—not least among them, her mystical connection with a legendary *mecha* that goes by the name of "Escaflowne." In the present context, Akane and Kawamori's anime is particularly notable in virtue of its implication with the tradition of the Tarot. As seen, this time-honored divination tool is indirectly alluded to by the *Negima* franchise in the design of its *Pactio* cards. *Escaflowne* has likewise been accompanied by greatly cherished Tarot-card collections, while also attaching great narrative significance to that tradition by positing its heroine's talent as a Tarot reader (a skill she has been taught by her grandmother) as integral to the shaping of her magic destiny and as inextricable from the development of the adventure as a whole. The anime refrains from conclusive explanations of the exact nature and scope of Hitomi's power, leaving it to individual viewers to decide whether the heroine's readings are actually influencing the course of events or simply mirroring predetermined outcomes. Concomitantly, *Escaflowne* posits the Tarot as a storytelling experience connecting past, present and future by bringing into play disparate aspects of the Questioner's psychological and affective baggage. Such a narrative is never shown to be utterly predetermined by destiny, since free will, courage and determination always retain their hold. When Hitomi tries to employ the Tarot to steer the course of destiny, she only succeeds, ironically, in making things more problematic. Conversely, even though she and Van Fanel are the two characters most grievously assaulted by fate, they are also the only ones that prove capable of taking it into their hands and mastering their future.

Each of Escaflowne's twenty-six installments opens with a Tarot card, progressively covering all twenty-two of the Majora Arcana and four Minor Arcana, in the following order: XVI, the Tower; Ace of Dragons; XIII, Death; XII, the Hanged Man; XX, Judgement; XI, Justice; VII, the Chariot; XIV, Temperance; Ace of Birds; Knight of Beasts; XV, the Devil; II, the High Priestess; IV, the Emperor; I, the Magician; XVII, the Star; X, the Wheel; III, the Empress; XXI, the World; 0, The Fool; XVIII, The Moon; V, The Hierophant; XIX, The Sun; IX, The Hermit; VIII, Strength; VI, The Lovers. As Monica Ho notes, the pack used by Hitomi is supposed to be "based on the Merlin Tarot. However, this is only partially correct. ... the Merlin Tarot is much different from generic tarots ... and instead of the usual four suits of the tarot ... it uses the more occult animal suits (bird, dragon, fish, and beast.) Other than this similarity in suits, the Merlin Deck does not resemble Hitomi's tarot. In my opinion, the art design of Hitomi's tarot is much prettier" (Ho). Although it is not hard to share Ho's aesthetic judgment in this matter, it would be preposterous to assume that the Tarot as used in *Escaflowne* serves a purely — or indeed primarily — decorative purpose. In fact, as a tortured struggle to bridge the gap between the natural and the supernatural, the everyday and the ultramundane, the visible and the invisible, the anime insistently revisits one core theme: how to reconcile the dictates of destiny with those of free will. As Ho maintains, this focal preoccupation takes the form of two interconnected questions of existential significance: "do certain events happen by twist of fate or does the past influence future events? Furthermore, how much of the future is determined by past and present actions? These questions cannot be easily answered upon initial inspection" (Ho). [1]

A scholastic milieu populated by a bevy of barmy characters akin to *Negima*'s is likewise central to the TV series *Magician's Academy* (dir. Takaomi Kanzaki, 2008–2009). The anime is based on a popular manga whose protagonist, Takuto Hasegawa, attends both a regular school and a magic academy unmarked on any known human map, and inadvertently brings into being a girl named Tanarotte in the course of a spell-invoking test. The creature, who is eventually revealed to be a part of the boy's own soul, readily declares unflinching loyalty to her summoner — which is just as well, given her potential to release a power so great as to cause the entire country's annihilation. Like several other magic-oriented anime, *Magician's Academy* features a multidimensional universe wherein the human world is supposed to coexist with the heavenly realm of "Gods" and the spirit province of "Demons." Neither Gods nor Demons are too keen on advertising their existence to humans, even though the latter are a source of unmatched amusement for both of those otherworldly breeds, and human artifacts are deemed worthy of clandestine transfer from Earth to the heavenly and spirit domains as entertaining toys. A reasonable youth staunchly opposed to the use of violence, Takuto must juggle the often onerous duties imposed by his sense of responsibility toward Tanarotte, whose antics give rise to all manner of incidents, his commitment to multifarious magic missions, and his innate ability to create both Gods and Demons, which causes the two races to want him dead lest he should upset the balance of power between them. This yarn bears affinities to *Negima*'s own plot in its dramatization of the destiny of a young man torn between the dictates of human and supernatural laws.

It must also be noted that the *Negima* franchise finds an illustrious antecedent in the tradition of magic anime with concurrently romantic and comedic leanings in *Fushigi Yuugi* (TV series; dir. Hajime Kamegaki, 1995–1996). When junior high-school students Miyaka and Yui accidentally venture into a restricted part of the library and chance upon an ancient tome titled "The Universe of the Four Gods," Miyaka is thrust into an alternate world and enjoined to write the story which the book is meant to contain: the tale of the "Priestess of Suzaku" and her efforts to muster a band of seven holy warriors in ancient China so as to bring to an end an age of strife and bloodshed. While Miyaka comes across as pointedly unheroic despite her attempts to live up to her magically appointed destiny, Yui, when her turn to enter the narrative arrives, stands out as dramatically striking and endowed with a degree of depth one would not automatically expect of this kind of show in both her role as a lethal villain and her genuine expressions of sympathy and benevolence. In its employment of a venerable volume as a major diegetic trigger, *Fushigi Yuugi* also anticipates the *Natsume* shows and *Kagihime* (here explored in Chapter 3) as an instance of anime drawn to the collusion of magic and textuality.

The narrative strategy of transposition so central to *Fushigi Yuugi* is common in magic-driven anime, and especially adaptable to the chronicling of destinies influenced by supernatural agencies. This is epitomized by a TV series cherished the world over since its first airing, *InuYasha* (dirs. Masashi Ikeda and Yasunao Aoki, 2000–2004), in which the present-day protagonist, Kagome Higurashi, is pulled into feudal Japan by a demon via a well and there discovers that a legendary jewel has been reborn inside her very body. When the jewel accidentally shatters and its fragments are scattered, the girl must forge an uneasy alliance with the eponymous hero, a half-demon drawn to the jewel's power, whom she first spots, asleep, sealed to the "Sacred Tree" with a magical arrow. Another illustration of the same basic topos is the TV series *Haruka: Beyond the Stream of Time—A Tale of the Eight Guardians* (dir. Aki Tsunaki, 2004–2005). Its heroine, Akane Motomiya, is torn away from her everyday life in contemporary Japan and transposed to a fantasy version of the Heian era (794–1192). She is here informed that she has inherited the powers of the "Priestess of the Dragon God," and instructed to restrain the "Demons" from gaining dominance over the entire planet by deploying supernatural abilities to which she has thus far been utterly oblivious. In pursuing this mission, the heroine is assisted by the "Eight Guardians." What imparts *Haruka* with an original flavor despite its utilization of an otherwise quite formulaic narrative mold is its reformulation of the protagonist's mission. Although Akane is meant to engage in a fundamentally cosmic quest, she chooses to prioritize a goal of her own choice: namely, looking for her friends Tenma and Shimon who have also been wrenched away from their ordinary routine and gone missing. The emphasis on selfless solidarity so crucial to *Haruka*'s diegesis links it directly to the ethical principles assiduously fostered by *Negima* even at its most outrageously funny.

As foreshadowed in this chapter's introductory segment, the TV series *Rozen Maiden* (dir. Kou Matsuo, 2004) and *Rozen Maiden: Träumend* (dir. Kou Matsuo, 2005–2006) thrive on an antiquarian fascination with the revered art of doll-making. The anime's take on magic destinies is tastefully suffused throughout by this distinctive aesthetic. A reclusive youth ("*hikikomori*") [2] unable to attend school due to psychologically traumatic experiences he associates with that environment, Jun Sakurada spends most of his day purchasing goods online and returning them before the payment is due. When Jun receives a letter informing him that he has won a prize, instructing him to choose between "yes" and "no" and then place the letter into his desk drawer, at which point it will putatively be conveyed to the spirit world, the boy follows the request even though he skeptically dismisses it as a convoluted prank. However, the chain of events thereby unleashed is bound to reorient Jun's whole destiny in utterly unpredictable directions. An exquisitely executed wooden case containing a gorgeous antique doll garbed in French aristocratic attire materializes out of the blue in his room. The entity, named Shinku, gains a life of its own the moment it is appropriately wound up, and tersely rebukes the boy for handling her in a fashion she considers disrespectful. No less disturbingly, for the solitary and largely unsocialized Jun, the doll immediately proceeds to treat him as though he were a servant. Shinku introduces herself as "the fifth doll of the Rozen Maiden," a unique collection of likewise animate dolls manufactured by an artist whom the creatures refer to as "Father," and entrusts Jun with the duty of protecting her "Rosa Mystica" as she engages in an age-old tournament — the "Alice Games" — involving all of the Rozen Maiden and intended to culminate in the victor's assumption of the title of "Alice." (Please note the tangential connection with *Kagihime*'s local terminology, as described in Chapter 3.)

The youth's life comes to be punctuated by fierce battles that retain a potent sense of menace throughout despite the generous dose of humor instilled into Shinku's and her sisters' capers, the contestants' cute appearance, and the fact that the dolls seem happy to spend much of their time indulging in decidedly nonbelligerent pursuits, such as drinking tea, drawing with crayons on floors or, at worst, breaking windows. The anime's structure is dictated by a simple diegetic principle in that it sequentially explores the distinctive characteristics, habits and guardian spirits of each of the seven dolls that enter the lives of Jun and his sister Nori as the story progresses. While this narrative premise may seem to hold little promise for viewers eager to engage with a dramatically challenging anime experience, *Rozen Maiden* gradually yields a satisfying sense of affective density and psychological sophistication as Shinku helps Jun recover from his depression and attendant dread of human contact. It could therefore be argued that the first season concentrates on its protagonist's emotional rehabilitation, turning the classic trope of the magic tournament (also pivotal, incidentally, to the aforementioned *Fate/stay Night*) into a metaphor for the dramatization of an existential tale eager to fathom the extent to which individuals might ultimately be held responsible for shaping their destinies — magic or otherwise. As Stig Høgset comments, in this matter, even though *Rozen Maiden* "does predictably culminate in a huge battle amongst the dolls, the show itself isn't as much about fighting as it is about different people's personalities and psychological situations. Not only are we being taken on a tour of Jun's own pandemonium of a mind, but some of the other dolls are also taken in by masters with personal baggage of their own. This is the part of the show where metaphors are taken in use, though it never gets ... heavy-handed" (Høgset).

In the sequel, the anime's graver connotations become more overt right from the start. While Jun, no longer the victim of self-imposed domestic confinement, is busy catching up on his studies, Shinku is tormented by troubling memories of earlier exploits which tend to manifest themselves in the form of terrifying nightmares. As the story unfolds over the anime's two seasons, the full import of the Alice Games is revealed. We thus learn that a doll's prime source of power is a "medium," or human host, whose bond to the doll is emblematized by a magic ring. Each game comprises a number of duels in which the dolls confront one another deploying their distinctive guardian spirits and preternatural skills. The losing doll must surrender her respective Rosa Mystica and hence the ability to move, at which point all of her memories and feelings will be retrieved and incorporated by the victor. In order to gain the title of Alice, a doll must collect each of the seven Rosa Mysticas on the scene. One of Shinku's most remarkable attributes consists of her somewhat idiosyncratic ethical stance: though willing to take part in duels, she strives to win the game without killing her sister dolls. Upon obtaining the prized designation, the winner of the Alice Games will become entitled to meet "Father" and gain a human incarnation as a young woman of unparalleled beauty and virtue whose soul is supposed to reside within the artist himself. Two concepts of crucial weight within *Rozen Maiden*'s individual vocabulary and pseudoscientific framework are the "N-Field" and the "Sea of Unconsciousness." As the *Crunchyroll* analysis of the series' main themes elucidates, the former refers to "a world in between worlds" that may be accessed "through any reflecting or 'living' surface"—even though "it seems a doorway can be forcefully created on other objects too." This parallel dimension hosts "small dream-worlds" that may be unveiled in the course of their subject's slumber by recourse to a "Renpika or Amethyst Dream." The Sea of Unconsciousness, for its part, constitutes the uncanny location wherein "all the unconscious minds of the world are pulled in together and form a sea of memories" ("Rozen Maiden Field of N").

Rozen Maiden alludes, with varying degrees of explicitness, to a wide variety of doll-related arts and rituals (embedded in both indigenous and European cultures) that are concurrently relevant to traditional and contemporary contexts. It should first be noted that the figure of the doll is intimately linked with that of the mascot, as borne out by the utilization within countless societies, cults and magical practices of emblematic artifacts with human or humanoid physiques conceived of as harbingers of good fortune. The term "mascot" derives from the old Provençal word "*mascotto,*" the diminutive form of the feminine noun "*masco,*" namely, "witch." Dolls and mascots have been involved in a reciprocally supporting partnership for time immemorial, since dolls can be deployed as mascots and mascots, in turn, often take the guise of dolls. While the relationship between dolls and witchcraft is overtly pertinent to the topic at hand, likewise noteworthy is the additional connection of the word "*masco*" with the Medieval Latin term "*masca,*" i.e., "ghost." By using the internet as the channel through which the protagonist is first ushered into the magical world of Shinku and her sisters, *Rozen Maiden* also intimates that at the same time as doll-like figures permeate traditional cultures as virtually omnipresent ghosts, new spectral forms unrelentingly develop in conjunction with evolving technologies and media. Both old and cutting-edge channels of communication and information are permeated by ghostly icons and cryptopresences. The internet itself could be regarded, in the logic of Matsuo's anime series, as the generator and propagator of phantasmic creatures comparable to techno-ectoplasms.

The *Rozen Maiden* anime are evidently informed by the arcane lure of the past, and their magic destinies are accordingly tinged by that aesthetic preference. By contrast, the TV series *Someday's Dreamers* (dir. Masami Shimoda, 2003) and *Someday's Dreamers: Summer Skies* (dir. Osamu Kobayashi, 2008) situate magic in a resolutely mundane contemporary world to trace the protagonists' efforts to fulfill their own supernaturally oriented destinies. *Someday's Dreamers* focuses on Yume Kikuchi, a young girl training to become a mage who moves to Tokyo to undertake her apprenticeship under the supervision of an experienced magician — the charismatic Masami Oyamada — in preparation for her certificate exam. Upon leaving her rural hometown to travel to the big city, Yume harbors an unrealistic view of the beneficent power of magic to solve all imaginable problems and must gradually accept that matters are not quite so straightforward. In the process, Yume must also overcome the daunting phantoms of insecurity and self-doubt, the petty vicissitudes of daily life, the challenges posed by new encounters and relationships, the dawning of hitherto unknown feelings and, last but not least, the discovery that her preternatural capacities far exceed those of most mages in town.

One of the anime's most endearing traits lies with its seamless synthesis of overtly fantastic elements and honest verisimilitude. Thus, viewers are strongly encouraged to embrace a willing suspension of disbelief— if they are not normally inclined to believe in the existence of people endowed with magical abilities — in order to enjoy the drama for what it essentially is. Yet, the show makes so many imaginative concessions to the requirements of realism as to enable even the most incredulous of spectators to engage spontaneously with its world. This atmosphere of disarming authenticity owes much to the consistency with which the anime's society is portrayed. Notably, there are strict rules determining the circumstances in which magic users may legitimately deploy their skills, and all requests to do so must be monitored by a special government agency to ensure the probity of the prospective users' intentions. Furthermore, magic in this world is supposed to traverse the fabric of regular human existence on a quotidian basis, not merely to inhabit a transcendental realm populated by spirits or deities, and users who are allowed to perform by the relevant body tend to carry out familiar social tasks as doctors, firefighters, policemen or rescue workers, for example.

Characterized by astonishingly realistic animation, solidly and subtly individualized character designs and touching sensitivity to the magic of the seasons, *Someday's Dreamers: Summer Skies* offers an alternate version of the same basic story presented in Shimoda's original anime crowned by a more pointedly mystical climax. Having promised to her father that she would grow up to be a mage, Sora Suzuki moves to Tokyo from the remote village of Bie in Hokkaido to train at a specialist school. The institution abides by a punctiliously detailed modus operandi, whereby each student is allocated to a personal tutor, and student and tutor then go out together into the world in response to appeals eliciting the deployment of their supernatural abilities in a wide range of varyingly serious situations. As in the world depicted in the earlier series, so in Sora's society, the activities of magic users are regulated by very precise restrictions and codes of practice. *Summer Skies* also conveys quite explicitly the vulnerability to discrimination, prejudice and ostracism afflicting magicians in a world where many lay citizens consider such creatures to be inherently malign. Although the romantic element already played an important part in the original *Someday's Dreamers* anime, it acquires novel complexity in the second series with the dramatization of a slowly evolving liaison between the heroine and Gouta Midorikawa — a youth she meets at the academy who hates magic, and is therefore reluctant to nourish his embryonic powers, due to a tangle of personal and familial reasons. As Sora gradually enables Gouta to overcome his aversion, face up to his magic lot and let his potential flourish, the two characters' destinies become more and more interlocked with each passing day, while they learn both to accept what appears to have been preordained for them by fate and to act upon the unfolding events in accordance with their own free will.

While virtually all of the titles here explored tend to interweave the concept of destiny with those of the contract, the mission, nature and the bildungsroman, this is most pointedly the case with the anime *Romeo x Juliet* (TV series; dir. Fumitoshi Oizaki, 2007). The series indeed articulates all of the principal themes addressed in this book, wreathing them together through a remarkably imaginative deployment of the metaphorical potentialities of magic. The protagonists' duties toward both their respective families and their fellow citizens are akin to contractual obligations and rapidly draw them into missions of veritably epic proportions. These feature, in a particularly prominent position, the quest to protect an endangered natural environment traversed by potent magical energies. At the same time, the two characters are engaged in painful bildungsromans in the course of which they must learn concurrently to nourish their private emotions in the face of adversity and to embrace their political and social roles. Their destinies are incrementally steered by the confluence of the contracts and missions to which they are committed, by the forces of nature among which those unfold, and by the developmental trajectories thereby traced by their psyches. Given the series' centrality not solely to the specific topos examined in the present chapter but also to the entire scope of this study, it seems fitting to grant it especially detailed analysis both as a cogent case study in its own right and as an apposite exit point for the book as a whole. The show's wry, intelligent and unremittingly atmospheric flavor seems further to justify its crucially climactic positioning.

As noted earlier, the magic destiny chronicled in *Romeo x Juliet* is inspired by a famous literary source in which magical elements already feature conspicuously but is keen on maximizing the original's supernatural affiliations in order to advance its own autonomous narrative. Oizaki thus interprets Shakespeare's original story in a decidedly magical vein, setting the adventure in the aerial city of "Neo-Verona," sustained by an arcane technology, and dotting its skies with winged horses sporting dragon tails named "*ryuuba*" (a.k.a. "dragonsteeds") that serve not solely as handy means of transport but also as esteemed status symbols. Both the image of an airborne world and that of the peculiar technology underpinning its functionings are redolent of Hayao Miyazaki's film *Laputa: Castle in the Sky* (1986), whereas Neo-Verona's structure brings to mind both that work and another magic-suffused movie issuing from the hands of the same director, *Howl's Moving Castle* (2004). If the *ryuuba*, with their balletic gracefulness and awe-inspiring solemnity connote the positive end of the anime's magic spectrum, at the opposite end stand scenes of apocalyptic ruination unleashed by the darkest of spells. Age-old curses, metamorphoses, golden rain showers, charms and invocations spice up the series' bewitching brew from start to finish.

Director Oizaki has usefully elucidated the rationale underpinning his decision to instill the original tale with markedly fantastic connotations in an interview released at the time of his anime's launch. Wishing to retain the original play's basis "structure," and therefore not "to stray from the straight-forward love story," the director and his team were nonetheless aware that "if all you're doing is a love story, it's definitely more compelling as a live-action drama than as an anime." Hence, they sought to capitalize on qualities that are unique to the art of animation, and would be capable of imparting the source with a distinctive power that could not be expected of a live-action drama. It was on the basis of this vision that the "fantasy element" was brought into play as a major agent of *Romeo x Juliet* since this is "the part that you can do only in anime." In this medium, Oizaki maintains, "it's easy to do things that humans couldn't actually do in real life" (Oizaki). Thus, instead of try-ing to use animation as a mere surrogate for live action cinema and approx-imate to that medium's capacities, the Gonzo crew aimed to maximize those aspects of the story — only available in embryonic guise in the Shakespearean original — that would both warrant its translation into an anime and turn it into something that could honestly celebrate that art form's specificity.

A number of traditional magic symbols also come into play. Among them, the iris is especially notable as the catalyst bringing the protagonists together and progressively consolidating their bond. The flower is famously revered as an emblem of faith, wisdom, friendship, hope, chivalry, courage and, most vitally in this context, promise in love. The iris limpidly reflects the anime's visual mood in all its facets by capturing the colors of the rain-bow within the purest white, and the gentle motion of butterfly wings with its fluttering petals stirred by gentle summer breezes. The aforementioned *ryuuba*, for their part, resonate with the esoteric qualities attached to winged horses across disparate cultures as symbols of light, spiritual illumination, and the triumph of good over evil. In Buddhism, the creatures are frequently portrayed bearing the sacred Book of Law. In Shakespeare, the most explicit reference to magic comes with the famous "Queen Mab" speech delivered by the character of Mercutio. The mythical figure is described by the nobleman as "the fairies' midwife" who "gallops night by night / Through lovers' brains" and "plaits the manes of horses in the night." With this portrayal, the speech offers an irreverent assessment of love as the quintessential nightmare and of its harbinger, a magical being, as a fundamentally pernicious agent. Thus, love and magic are yoked together as negative forces by the ever pragmatic Mercutio, the voice of disillusioned reason par excellence.

Although *Romeo x Juliet* might be thought of as a magical romance piv-oting on the kind of love one might expect to find only in fairy tales and hence bearing tenuous links with the harsh realities of history and politics, the drama actually stands out as a dispassionate anatomy of the iniquities of despotism from its inceptive stages. The show indeed opens with epic-scale moments of premeditated cruelty and bloodshed worthy of Akira Kurosawa's cinema at its most heroic. These scenes dramatize the extermination of the entire Capulet family by the Montague usurpers fourteen years prior to the present-day adventure. The sole survivor of the slaughter is the deposed ruler's daughter, Juliet Fiammata De Capulet, who thereafter lives hidden with a few surviving retainers of her dynasty, adopting a male disguise whenever she leaves her humble chamber. It is not until she reaches the age of sixteen that the beleaguered Capulet henchmen who have been lurking in the shadows since the bloody coup reveal to Juliet the full truth about her lineage and her intended destiny as the leader of a rebellion meant to depose the illegitimate Montague ruler. Breathtakingly staged in a ruinous cemetery at night, with a thunderstorm to complete the scene's Gothic mood, this revelation is proffered by Conrad — the Captain of the Capulet Guards responsible for rescuing the heroine at the time of the mutiny, and now the primary instigator of her assumption of the role of leader somewhat regardless of her personal happiness — in the presence of all the surviving Capulet supporters, who convene for the great occasion to bow to their new head. Although Juliet is so shocked as to lose consciousness the moment her father's sword is presented to her and, catching her own reflection in the gleaming metal, suddenly remembers her parents' slaughter, there can be little doubt that the heart of the naive maiden discovering the bittersweet pleasures of first love coexists with the spirit of a brave heroine bound to ascend to the very peak of epic valor.

Juliet's obliviousness to her heritage prior to her sixteenth birthday does not entail that up until that crucial moment the girl has led a pampered existence of comfortable innocence. For one thing, Juliet has come to silently resent her enforced disguise as the boy "Odin." This is made clear at an early stage in the saga. Indeed, few scenes in the history of anime at large communicate as uplifting a sense of elan as the one from the opening installment in which the heroine temporarily relinquishes her male pseudo-identity in preparation for the "Rose Ball" held at the Montague Keep to which she has fortuitously gained admission, and swirls around her dwelling delighted with the simple feeling of donning a gown. (Please note that in the source, the diegetically vital opening ball is hosted by the Capulets instead, with the young Montague heir as an interloper eager to see Rosaline, the girl he initially claims to love.) The Rose Ball is also cleverly used as a means of conveying the idea that even though Juliet appears to have completely forgotten her infancy, the sight of the castle's grandiose interior causes her to experience a flashback in which her childhood self features for an instant as a ghostly presence on the gallery whence the usurper inspects the scene below with self-congratulatory pride.

Being a fiery, intelligent and resourceful young woman, unlike her timid and submissive Shakespearean antecedent, Juliet has taken fate into her capable hands and deployed the crossdressing ruse to splendid advantage by acting as a Robin-Hood champion of justice reminiscent of the Scarlet Pimpernel, endowed with astonishing martial skills and dubbed the "Red Whirlwind," on behalf of the oppressed Neo-Veronese in defiance of the despot's draconian rule. In this role, the lionhearted Juliet has thus far represented the only glimmer of hope in the city's future. This proposition is trenchantly validated by the heroic actions performed by Lancelot, the doctor that loyally assists Juliet whenever she receives an injury in he course of her crusade. Leaving behind a wife (who knows Juliet's secret and does not blame her for its dire repercussions on the destiny of her own family) and two little daughters, Lancelot poses as the Red Whirlwind and perishes by self-immolation to free a cageful of captives accused of being the crimson-clad outlaw, in a desperate effort to abet the heroine's cause. This sequence unquestionably stands out as one of the entire anime's most pathos-laden moments.

The immensity of the Montagues' nefariousness is ominously conveyed right from the start, not only through the flashbacks to the mutiny and attendant massacre of the Capulet family but also with the sequence dramatizing the public harassment of a girl deemed to be a descendant of the deposed rulers, threatened with the prospect of summary execution just as the Red Whirlwind swoops to her aid from the turrety heights of Neo-Verona. It is thereafter revealed that the Montague government thrives on unbridled exploitation and abuse, doing nothing to ameliorate the living conditions of the indigent and the invalid — whom the Capulets, by contrast, were wont to sustain even though Prince Montague has rewritten history by painting them as oppressors. In addition, the illegitimate ruler is only too keen on condoning the rogues eager to take advantage of the situation by abducting and trading commoner girls for the delectation of lascivious noblemen. Although this hardly renders the tyrant's actions pardonable, it is suggested that Prince Montague's ferocious hunger for power is rooted in his murky background. An illegitimate issue of the Capulet line mothered by a lowly prostitute and raised as a pauper, the man has never forgiven the Capulets for his misfortune and will stop at nothing to exact his vengeance.

Juliet's first encounter with Romeo Candore De Montague, a kindly youth who sternly disapproves of his father's monomaniacal pursuit of power, occurs while she is dressed up as the Red Whirlwind and he comes to her rescue on his dragonsteed. On this occasion, both characters appear spontaneously drawn to each other, and to go on feeling inexplicably affected at a visceral level by their fleeting contact with each other's hand well after their parting. However, while Romeo does not conceal his interest in the mysterious figure he has saved from her ruthless pursuers, the crossdresser is quite unwilling to express her gratitude to a "nobleman" and shields behind a protective wall of rudeness. If Juliet instantly rises to the status of the drama's main star in Oizaki's version of the classic tale, Romeo, for his part, at first comes across as rather more melancholy and sedate than his Shakespearean predecessor. The vital meeting, where the quintessence of love at first sight is wordlessly captured by the visuals, coincides with the aforementioned Rose-Ball escapade. From this point onward, the protagonists are indissolubly bound in a race against fate unfurling in the midst of civil unrest and dynastic strife. While Juliet is tormented by the awareness that her private feelings for a Montague are incompatible with her political obligations as a Capulet, Romeo struggles to resist his father's insane resolve to mold him into what he considers a worthy successor — which entails, among other restrictions, an unwanted engagement to the meek aristocrat Lady Hermione. (In the source, it is Juliet that is portrayed as the victim of forced betrothal to a young aristocrat, Paris.) Even the most unromantic of viewers would feasibly concede that the early scenes laying the foundations of Romeo and Juliet's time-defying love are sufficient unto themselves to instill the drama with oodles of magic.

Pivotal to the adventure's supernatural fabric is the image of the "Great Tree Escalus," a massive enchanted tree of truly mesmerizing beauty located within the Montague stronghold held to be one of the two surviving trees responsible for sustaining the foundations of the floating Neo-Verona world. Its guardian, a spooky hooded woman named Ophelia, maintains that Escalus has the power to bless and protect the humans in its proximity but is destined to wither and fail to yield its radiant pomes when people's hearts harden and hate reigns supreme. Given the Montague autocrat's truculent disposition, the Great Tree has unsurprisingly begun to weaken and it gradually emerges that only an apposite sacrifice might save it from perishing altogether. Concomitantly, an underlying connection between Escalus and the Capulets comes to light. (In Shakespeare, Escalus is the name of the Prince of Neo-Verona, who is said to despise the rival families for their petty bellicosity.)

While *Romeo x Juliet* rewrites the Shakespearean source by imbuing it with magic energy as a metaphor for the shaping of both individual and collective destinies, it also takes audacious textual liberties with the Bard's opus as a whole. Thus, the script juggles with both fairly literal transcriptions of famous lines from *Romeo and Juliet*, as well as other Shakespeare plays, and cryptic allusions to less well-known passages and related situations. Among the all-time favorites, we find "Keep up your bright swords, for the dew will rust them" (spoken by the Red Whirlwind and taken from *Othello*) and "So far in blood that sin will pluck on sin" (a line from *Richard III* actually cited by Ariel, William's mother, as a quotation from one of her son's plays the title of which she cannot recall). The English-language dub released by FUNimation pays homage to the original through its dialogue's decidedly Shakespearean tenor and credible adaptation of various portions of the parent script. The Anglophone rendition actually plays even more adventurously with the Shakespearean source than the Japanese original by weaving a greater range of the Bard's lines and rhetorical tropes into the dialogue.

An especially felicitous touch on Oizaki's part is the inclusion of Shakespeare himself into the cast as William: a prolific and insightful playwright whose genuine talent is often neglected by the public, oscillating between truly inspired flourishes of genius and juvenile clownishness. Addressed as "Willy" by several of his associates (including Juliet in her Odin semblance), the dramatist occasionally peppers his ordinary discourse with lines from the "real" Shakespeare (whoever such a creature might truly be). In the second installment, for example, *As You Like It* is explicitly cited: the link between that comedy and Juliet's experiences as a crossdresser awakening to love's mysteries can hardly go unheeded at this juncture. (Notably, Juliet and her protectors reside in an edifice financed by William's formidable mother and safeguarded by the façade of a popular playhouse which not many respectable members of the upper classes would even dream of entering.) The intertextual relationship between Oizaki's anime and Shakespeare's output is most proficiently — and touchingly — conveyed by the sequence in which William reveals that he has known Juliet's secret for a long time, and observed her predicament in search of a yarn capable of rising to legendary status. Following the girl's quotidian moves "with an eye to the tale" he "could glean," the playwright admits to having "expected bloody tragedy" all along. Yet, witnessing Juliet's current "struggle forward," William now senses that "the love story that has so long eluded" him "has at last graced" his "quill." Hence, he urges the girl to "surrender" to her true feelings so that he "may cut it into little stars and adorn the heavens for time eternal." Juliet, however, does not submit to her intended status as an acquiescent narrative tool or theatrical stereotype but pithily states: "Forgive me, Willy. I cannot play your hero."

A major marker of the anime's creative manipulation of its source materials lies with its use of characters named after people found not only in the original play but also in Shakespearean works other than *Romeo and Juliet* itself. Although Oizaki's personae are not cast in roles identical to those of their ancient namesakes, their designations are cleverly chosen, insofar as the personalities of the anime characters latently bear traits inherent in those of their forerunners. Thus, the Montague despot's given name is said to be Leontes — the appellation employed by Shakespeare in *The Winter's Tale* to designate another likewise blind and solipsistic patriarch. Romeo's betrothed shares with her namesake from the same play a stoical resignation to the vagaries of fate. Romeo's mother, Lady Portia, echoes both the heroine of *The Merchant of Venice* bearing the same name in her unshakeable sense of justice (resulting in the dereliction of her place in the Montague family and self-relocation to a convent) and the Portia cast in *Julius Caesar* as a paragon of womanly strength and virtue. On other occasions, Oizaki's reasons for selecting particular denominations for his characters are far from transparent. For instance, the choice of Ophelia for the Great Tree's keeper is somewhat puzzling, given this character appears to have precious little in common with *Hamlet*'s hapless maiden except, perhaps, a volatile emotive makeup. The aforementioned Ariel, current head of the prestigious Farnese family as well as William's mother, is named after the spirit from *The Tempest*, and indeed operates, metaphorically, as a magical agent in both allowing Juliet and her immediate followers to shelter in the theater and secretly hosting Juliet and her closest associates in her Mantua estate following the heroine's capture by Prince Montague.

Juliet's childhood friend, acting as the heroine's maid, confidant and elder sister, is named after the youngest daughter in *King Lear*, Cordelia, and echoes the latter's personality with her unflinching sense of loyalty. Lear's second daughter, Regan, supplies the source name for the plucky granddaughter of Ariel's butler Balthazar who, in turn, is named after Romeo's manservant from the original *Romeo and Juliet*. The aforementioned Conrad shares his designation with the totally different character of a villain from *Much Ado About Nothing*. Possibly so designated after two personae from *Hamlet* and *The Tempest*, the suavely refined Francisco is cast in the role of one of Juliet's most faithful comrades: he is the one who openly advocates the legitimacy of the protagonists' mutual love. Francisco's closest mate, who also acts as Juliet's fencing teacher, is the laconic and surly Curio: a character that somewhat ironically shares his denomination with a gentleman attending Duke Orsino in *Twelfth Night*. The name Antonio, here associated with Conrad's grandson, may hark back to a number of disparate Shakespearean personae, including the hero from *The Merchant of Venice*. In Oizaki's anime, the kid is distinguished by a flair for pyrotechnics and spying. The actress Emilia, who is besotted with Odin unaware of "his" true identity, is named after Shakespearean characters appearing in *Othello* and *The Winter's Tale*. The character of Tybalt, who features in the parent play as Juliet's maternal cousin, is here recast as Romeo's half-brother and said to seek revenge for his mother's violation by Leontes Montague. Tybalt is instrumental in mediating between the protagonists at times of extreme peril.

Benvolio, Romeo's best friend, plays a role akin to that of the analogously named character from *Romeo and Juliet* (Romeo's cousin, in that case) by functioning as the voice of reason and moderation when the male lead appears inclined to give in to impetuousness. Benvolio's father, incidentally, is worth mentioning in this context even though he does not have any obvious Shakespearean predecessors insofar as he plays an important part as the head of the House of Frescobaldi and as Neo-Verona's humane mayor. His leniency toward the dispossessed and their claims to fairer treatment by and by renders his presence within the Montague government detestable to the implacable Prince and leads to the rescinding of his title and to his exile alongside his wife and son — who are thereafter sheltered by Conrad and Juliet's friends. Of all the people drawn from the source play, one of the most intriguing is indubitably Mercutio. A hot-blooded free spirit endowed with a wry sense of humor and a penchant for dark irony in Shakespeare, Mercutio is reimagined in Oizaki's adaptation as a likewise disrespectful youth. However, in the show, Mercutio acquires more sinister tones from his portrayal as a sly and ambitious nobleman keen on stepping into Romeo's place as Prince Montague's descendant. Among other supporting actors with latent Shakespearean connections, we find Mercutio's alcoholic father Titus, somewhat bafflingly designated with reference to the titular hero in *Titus Andronicus*; Conrad's treacherous friend Camillo, who shares his denomination with a member of Leontes' retinue from *The Winter's Tale*; and Petruchio, a boy met by Romeo at the Gradisca mines, where he is at one point sent as a punishment for abetting Juliet's escape from the despot's clutches, whose name would appear to be a nod to that of the male lead in *The Taming of the Shrew*. Even though intertextual linkages such as the ones mentioned above are fun to spot (particularly for fans of the Bard's corpus), it is vital to bear in mind that far more significant than any game of quasi-scholarly "I spy" is the autonomous standing of *Romeo x Juliet*'s ample and magnetic cast as a gallery of well-rounded and steadily evolving personalities disposed not only to maturation but also to some wily shifts, switches and reorientations.

Oizaki's imaginative take on the original story is principally attested to by its heightened political significance, whereby the topos of revolution and the related tropes of martial rule, anarchy, civil turmoil and sub-rosa resistance, gain unprecedented centrality. This owes much to the show's redefinition of the power balance presented in Shakespeare's play, where the Capulets and the Montagues stand as rivals of equal authority ("Two households, both alike in dignity"), in favor of a starkly polarized tension between a usurper family and a persecuted one. Accordingly, while the original drama opens with a brawl between representatives of the warring factions, Oizaki's anime, as seen, finds inception with the brutal record of one family's complete overthrow by the other. In addition, *Romeo x Juliet* flaunts a distinctively individualized villain of the piece with Prince Montague himself— a sinister presence looming over the whole adventure that is simply absent from the source. The show deftly integrates these broad ideological themes with an ever-lingering sense of the inseparability of joy and pain at the heart of its protagonists' tragedy. Hence, Romeo and Juliet's ordeal is portrayed at once as a piece in a much broader political puzzle and a very personal effort to reconcile private emotions and public duties in the face of destinies wherein reality and magic smoothly intertwine. In the process, both protagonists grow as complex individuals enjoined by fate to take decisions that affect both the political reality around them and their personal relationship. This evolution is fraught with burdens that occasionally feel so ponderous as to become downright unbearable.

In Juliet's case, this is sorrowfully conveyed by the episode where, following the insurgents' betrayal by Camillo, she is rescued by Tybalt, who ungallantly informs her that the only reason for which he has come to her assistance is that he has promised Francisco to do so, since he actually regards the girl as a spoilt child unlikely to abet any valid cause. Feeling personally responsible for the blood spilled by her comrades as a result of the traitor's devastating snare, and convinced that she is now a hopeless failure, the heroine is found unconscious in the streets of the red-light district to which Tybalt has taken her to ensure her utter anonymity, and sheltered by a kindly woman that turns out to be none other than Romeo's estranged mother. From this point onward, Juliet not only regains her former enthusiasm but also begins to buttress the shaky edifice of her resolve as a mature young woman, constantly keeping a vigilant eye on the as yet unpredictable but inevitable outcomes of her actions. However, even once Juliet has endured and bravely overcome the most tormenting phase of her rite of passage, her development is portrayed as a very gradual process, still beset by uncertainty in the face of a destiny for which she feels inadequately equipped or indeed prepared. This aspect of the story contributes vitally to its cumulative psychological realism by eschewing grandiose coups de théâtre in favor of laboriously unfolding emotional discoveries.

Romeo, for his part, vainly endeavors to oppose the evil Prince Montague by stirring change from within the government in the name of equanimity and peace. While the youth's political struggle may seem less sensational than Juliet's, it nonetheless leads to analogous results for Romeo, too, as he learns the truth about his father from Portia, realizes that he can no longer lead the life of a privileged young nobleman and must embrace an unforeseen and very possibly adverse destiny. It is at this stage in the drama, importantly, that Romeo understands that pursuing his relationship with Juliet amounts to much more than merely indulging an adolescent passion ruled by personal desire and, in fact, carries grave ideological implications. A major turning point, in Romeo's evolution, lies with the boy's direct exposure to the appalling conditions of the people working in the Gradisca mines, which leads him to commit himself wholeheartedly to their betterment during his own time as a captive therein and, when he returns to the capital, to the future of his oppressed fellow citizens at large. As the protagonists' developmental trajectories pick up momentum, while their ethical and civil aspirations accordingly soar to unprecedented heights, so do the actions of several of the supporting actors around them. This serves to add fresh layers of depth and intricacy to both personal and communal goals and thus enables the anime to assert itself incontrovertibly as a stunning display of imagination and creativity.

In the dramatization of the quieter, more meditative and sentiment-laden moments, the series intentionally refrains from standard anime cuteness (the aesthetic model described as "*kawaii*" in Japanese) in order to foreground the story's intrinsic gravity. Concomitantly, even iconic scenes such as the one in which the young lovers exchange their first kiss evince a magical aura abetted by carefully handled theatrics, yet manage to communicate a strong sense of realism through the acting — especially, in that specific instance, with the transition from Juliet's initial resistance to her reluctant admission of her true desire. The ideal equilibrium of the fantastical and the realistic dimensions in scenes such as this imparts the series as a whole with a commendable atmosphere of conviction, while also intimating that those dimensions are never quite as mutually exclusive as common sense would have us believe in day-to-day life. The action sequences are more congruous with typical anime fare, regaling the eye with dashing swirls, out-of-this-world feats of leaping and gravity-defying descents. Yet, even in these ebullient shots, drama never relinquishes its central place in the service of spectacle.

A case in point is the memorable sequence where, in very rapid succession, the Red Whirlwind rescues Lancelot from the dungeon wherein the "Carabinieri" are busy torturing the valiant physician — having sensationally come crashing through a glass ceiling — and Romeo joins the fray just as the masked rebel and her charge are about to be cornered. Upon detecting the scent of irises with which he instinctively associates his beloved, Romeo pretends to engage in a duel with the Red Whirlwind on the pretext that he wishes to be personally responsible for the outlaw's capture and then engineers their fall into a canal beneath the tower, thus consigning both the rescuer and the doctor to safety. The sequence itself is nothing short of adrenaline-pumping but sheer sensationalism is never allowed to detract from the dramatic richness of the characters' interactions. Moreover, the show's emphasis on complex emotions in preference to action per se is tersely confirmed, in the sequence's immediate aftermath, by the heartrending scene in which Juliet finally learns that Romeo is the tyrant's son and that her love for him is therefore doomed. It is also worth observing, in this respect, that *Romeo x Juliet*'s action sequences are rendered unremittingly captivating by their knack of building up to climaxes that cannot be easily anticipated by even the most seasoned of viewers. Concurrently, they are so judiciously juxtaposed with the romantic and introspective moments as to prevent the series from indulging in pedestrian melodrama even when it approximates most closely the depths of emotionalism.

The artistic quality quite unanimously recognized in the studio behind *Romeo x Juliet*, the aforecited Gonzo, shines forth in this series at several levels and most notably in the depiction of the sumptuous interior design used for the aristocratic settings and of Neo-Verona's multilayered architecture. Seemingly resulting from the superimposition of at least three medieval or Renaissance conglomerates, this blends classic stonework and ruins with countless bridges, waterways and cobbled alleys that cumulatively exude a palpable sense of history despite the city's fictitious standing. Thus, the magical elements do not in the least deprive the setting of the lush period feel, redolent of Shakespeare's own version of old Verona, communicated by the more naturalistic facets of the urbanscape but actually enhance it in marvelously unexpected ways. The coalescence of realism and magic observed in relation to the romantic scenes is therefore no less pronounced in the case of the anime's locations. Especially memorable sites are the lakeside hut where the protagonists at one point find shelter from the pelting rain, and Romeo spectacularly discovers that the boy he has befriended is actually Juliet in disguise. Likewise noteworthy are the iris-strewn grounds atop a vertiginous Neo-Veronese tower and amid a crumbling graveyard exuding the spirit of the Sublime at its purest.

Beyond the city's walls, Romeo and Juliet encounter all manner of enchanting landscapes, ranging from the magical forest where Romeo's *ryuuba*, Cielo, is set free so that he may be with the one he cherishes unfettered by human laws, the abandoned country church (felicitously placed within yet another field of irises) where the protagonists privately exchange their vows, the river along which they travel by boat toward an illusory glimmer of safety and the cottage they briefly elect as their home in their doomed idyll. Finally, the scenes set in the hidden caves where Escalus and its rapidly deteriorating roots are located ooze with the most refined sense of spatial magic one could ever hope to encounter in anime — or indeed in any imaginable art form. The visuals' magic is consistently enhanced by the soundtrack with which they are adroitly harmonized throughout the adventure. Composed by Hitoshi Sakimoto, the musical score was performed by a full orchestra in Sydney, Australia, selected not only because of its inherent talent but also due to its youthful membership and resulting familiarity with the medium of anime. Oizaki himself attaches great importance to the acoustic aspect of the show, maintaining that alongside the "characters," the "art," the "cels" and the "backgrounds," his team regarded the "music" as "the biggest thing." Sakimoto's work on *Romeo x Juliet* has helped the director fully appreciate "just how powerful music can be" in completing an anime's aesthetic identity: "I don't think," he honestly remarks, "I've ever felt that so keenly as on this project."

Furthermore, the show is abetted throughout by the wizardry of Daiki Harada's character designs. Oizaki insisted on having Harada in charge of this particular facet of the anime's production insofar as he wished to foreground the "human drama" and felt that in order to achieve this aim, he "needed someone who ... could breathe life into his drawings." Harada is indeed capable of yielding "characters that seem ready to leap off the page," making it possible to "practically feel the warmth of their skin" and to appreciate at each turn of the drama the "richness of facial expressions" which the pencil has bestowed on them (Oizaki). Harada and his associates draw characters that genuinely reflect the dramatis personae's mentalities, down to the minutest virtue or eccentricity. At the same time, the design mirrors the actors' moral and psychological nuances in such a way that not even the most marginal (and potentially formulaic) members of the troupe come across as monolithic — as either undilutedly somber or simplistically hearty. This penchant for capturing a personality's inner shades is graphically paralleled by the adoption of chromatic palettes that avoid blatant contrasts and play instead with myriad gradations and modulations. Even the visual tension, used throughout the series as a symbolic leitmotif, between the Montagues' blue and the Capulets' red is not posited as a stark binary opposition, for the color-coding strategy consistently allows for elegantly varied intensities and shadings. Unadventurous though this may sound, it is the disarmingly clean and simple quality of Gonzo's style that makes it most memorable in this instance. The *Romeo x*

Juliet Destiny of Love Visual Fan Book, released by Gonzo itself in 2008, is especially useful in showcasing the anime's artwork with both robustness and warmth.

The most spectacular homage to supernatural motifs is regaled by the finale, where the theme of destiny so central to Shakespeare's play gains fresh resonance within a dramatic context of heightened mythical significance. Unfolding at a flawless pace, the climax follows the revelation that Romeo and Juliet alone can save the world by not only putting an end to a heinous regime but also healing an entire habitat ruptured by that tyranny's unfathomable evil. Juliet is well aware that in order to fulfill her duty, she must prioritize communal wellbeing to private satisfaction and is hence resolved to opt for self-immolation. Choosing to honor the ancient covenant that ties House Capulet to the Great Tree, Juliet selflessly relinquishes her personal dreams for the sake of the city she cherishes and of its brutally persecuted people. Romeo, for his part, is unwilling to accept his beloved's decision with no attempt at resistance. This emotive conflict imparts the finale with unique dramatic tension, spurring the action toward a resolution that does not feel utterly unavoidable until the very last moment — even though, with hindsight, its ineluctability can be seen to be embedded in the saga's fabric as a precondition of both its coherence and its ethical stance. The battle with the magical plant ensuing from the Juliet's decision and Romeo's resulting antagonism features many moments of intense action. At one point, it even witnesses the tantalizing sight of the star-crossed lovers themselves crossing blades as they did early in the series with Juliet disguised as the Red Whirlwind and Romeo as her savior. This time around, alas, the duel is conducted in earnest and not as a strategic masquerade.

Finally, Juliet must allow Escalus to live on inside her, metaphorically speaking, to prevent the Neo-Verona continent from crashing onto the planet below and allow it instead to land safely onto peaceful waters. A new world is thus engendered where Romeo and Juliet themselves — were one to opt for the rosiest of interpretations — might live on in some guise, and their love have a chance to flourish at long last. Hence, the Bard's "star-crossed lovers," prey to a "death-marked" passion, ultimately assert themselves not only as legendary personifications of feelings forbidden by prejudice and injustice but also, on a more pointedly cosmic plane, as agents of purification and renewal. Imbued with refined magic of the first water, Romeo and Juliet's undying devotion to each other thus translates into a life-enhancing elixir guaranteeing the survival of both human society and the natural environment. The force of love is triumphantly enshrined as a power whose influence extends well beyond the boundaries of private gratification with transformative effects of incontrovertibly magical immensity. The concept of purification axial to Shinto-based shamanic practices is here tangentially invoked in a very original metaphorical fashion.

Romeo x Juliet's climactic scenes bring to mind another major production issuing from Gonzo's masterful hands: namely, *Origin: Spirits of the Past* (movie; dir. Keiichi Sugiyama, 2006). The world in which this retrofuturistic adventure is set, "Neutral City," has haphazardly emerged from a major catastrophe triggered by the eruption of the "Forest-Beast" from a lunar forest and its descent onto the Earth in the form of a dragonesque ensemble of tangled creepers, vines, roots, lianas and tendrils, resulting in the destruction of the planet's atmosphere and the scorching of its surface to the ground. The human settlement reconstructed from the debris is dominated by the lowering shadow of the seemingly omnipotent "Forest" that has spread throughout the habitat and retains tyrannical control over the water supply under the aegis of its leaf-shrouded guardians, the "Druids." The relationship between humans and trees is so elementally symbiotic that protracted contact between the two parties is bound to result in radical metamorphoses of veritably magical proportions. This is patently borne out by the fate met by the protagonist, Agito. In order to prevent the unleashing of technological weapons intended to return the Earth to its pristine state and most likely to inflict horrendous damage on its current people in the process, the boy resolves to merge with the Forest and thus harmonize humanity's priorities with those of the surging mass of trees that dominates his ecosystem. Agito is guided by the conviction, inspired by Buddhist and Shintoist principles, that all life forms are inextricably intertwined. In surrendering his human nature, the hero follows in his father Agashi's footsteps, having endeavored to emulate his old man's actions since childhood. Agashi was the principal architect behind Neutral City's construction and has interacted so intimately with the Forest as to have morphed into a man-tree hybrid. (His physiognomy brings to mind the "Ents" from J. R. R. Tolkien's *The Lord of the Rings*.)

On moral grounds, the closest parallel between *Origin: Spirits of the Past* and *Romeo x Juliet* resides with their shared climactic assertion of selfless dedication to the general good. Where *Romeo x Juliet* is specifically concerned, this is also the area in which Oizaki's anime proclaims its distinctiveness from the original play with twinkling clarity. Shakespeare's dénouement lays emphasis on the story's *private* dimension. It does propose that the protagonists' tragic deaths are instrumental in triggering the rival houses' reconciliation but the sheer speed of this conversion makes it appear uncordially formulaic — almost a sarcastic afterthought on the playwright's part, in fact. The climax of the original play is made wrenchingly compelling by a chain of events that mock human self-determination so blatantly as to suggest that the workings of fate are not only arbitrary but wastefully so. A dark irony is thus inoculated into practically each and every line of Shakespeare's text as Romeo and Juliet advance toward deaths that cannot fail to come across, in the final and most dispassionate analysis, as anything other than meaningless. Oizaki's show, by contrast, foregrounds the *public* implications of Romeo and Juliet's sacrifice. It does so by integrating Shakespeare's bleak exposure of the capriciousness of fate with a strong sense of purpose issuing from its protagonists' dedication to the task of bringing a better world into existence for everyone's sake. The melancholy "woe" characteristic of the parent ending is retained but simultaneously counterbalanced by an uplifting mood of heroic commitment. While some audiences might view Oizaki's dramatic reorientation as so drastic a departure from the original play as to verge on infidelity or even an act of betrayal, others will warmly welcome it as a proclamation of anime's power to invigorate the sources whence it draws inspiration through unique energies of its own. Few viewers, in any case, could go so far as to deny the director's ability to generate refreshingly new worlds from an existing body of figurative stratifications so deeply enshrined in tradition as to have risen to the status of a myth in its own right.

The magic of *Romeo x Juliet,* allowed free rein in the show's climax, is most pithily encapsulated by one of William's gnomic remarks: "Reality often transcends fiction. And yet, people need stories and romance and heroism to navigate reality." This is the essential reason, arguably, for which people of all generations and of disparate geographical, cultural and social provenance come to be enthralled not only by an overtly magical anime like *Romeo x Juliet* but also, on a larger scale, by the art of animation at large: a discourse wherein even the tedium and drudgery of everyday life can gain spellbinding pathos — as they indeed often do in Shakespeare's own opus. It is at this exquisitely refined level of its magic that the art of animation succeeds in imbuing the potentially fathomless cauldron that accommodates the alchemical fusion of myriad narrative processes, psychological archetypes, character functions, metaphorical structures and cultural identities emanating therefrom — namely, the multifarious forces that gradually contribute to the constitution, in an accretional fashion reminiscent of the way in which a coral reef comes into being, of a pervasive collective imaginary.

> Our revels now are ended. These our actors,
> As I foretold you, were all spirits and
> Are melted into air, into thin air:
> And, like the baseless fabric of this vision,
> The cloud-capp'd towers, the gorgeous palaces,

The solemn temples, the great globe itself,
Yea, all which it inherit, shall dissolve
And, like this insubstantial pageant faded,
Leave not a rack behind. We are such stuff
As dreams are made on, and our little life
Is rounded with a sleep.
　— *The Tempest*, Act IV, Scene i

Filmography

Primary Titles

Aria the Animation (2005)

ORIGINAL TITLE: *Aria*. STATUS: TV series (13 episodes). EPISODE LENGTH: 25 minutes. DIRECTOR: Junichi Sato. ORIGINAL CREATOR: Kozue Amano. SERIES COMPOSITION: Sato. SCENARIO: Ayuna Fujisaki, Reiko Yoshida. MUSIC: Choro Club, Takeshi Senoo. CHARACTER DESIGNER: Makoto Koga. ART DIRECTOR: Junichiro Nishikawa. CHIEF ANIMATION DIRECTOR: Koga. ANIMATION DIRECTORS: Etsuko Sumimoto, Hiroshi Kazui, Hiroyuki Yanase, Koga, Masatsugu Arakawa, Masayuki Onchi, Mikio Fujiwara, Tadahito Matsubayashi, Takayuki Hanyuu, Takeshi Kusaka, Takuji Yoshimoto, Tomohisa Shimoyama, Toshiyuki Fujisawa, Yukiko Miyamoto, Yuuji Kondou. PRODUCERS: Shigeru Tateishi, Tetsuo Uchida, Yasutaka Hyuuga. EDITOR: Shigeru Nishiyama. COLOR DESIGNER: Yoshimi Kawakami. ANIMATION PRODUCTION: Hal Film Maker.

Aria the Natural (2006)

ORIGINAL TITLE: *Aria 2*. STATUS: TV series (26 episodes). EPISODE LENGTH: 24 minutes. DIRECTOR: Junichi Sato. ORIGINAL CREATOR: Kozue Amano. SERIES COMPOSITION: Sato. SCREENPLAY: Ayuna Fujisaki, Kazunobu Fusegi, Kenichi Takeshita, Mari Okada, Reiko Yoshida, Tatsuhiko Urahata, Yoshimasa Hiraike. MUSIC: Choro Club, Takeshi Senoo.

CHARACTER DESIGNER: Makoto Koga. ART DIRECTOR: Hiroshi Yoshikawa. CHIEF ANIMATION DIRECTOR: Tetsuya Kumagai. ART SETTING: Junichiro Nishikawa. DESIGN WORK: Hiroyuki Kasugai, Thomas Romain. EDITOR: Shigeru Nishiyama. COLOR SETTING: Miyuki Kibata. ANIMATION PRODUCTION: Hal Film Maker. PRODUCTION: ARIA Company.

Aria the Origination (2008)

ORIGINAL TITLE: *Aria 3*. STATUS: TV series (13 episodes). EPISODE LENGTH: 25 minutes. DIRECTOR: Junichi Sato. ORIGINAL CREATOR: Kozue Amano. SERIES COMPOSITION: Sato. SCREENPLAY: Ayuna Fujisaki, Reiko Yoshida, Tatsuhiko Urahata. MUSIC: Choro Club, Takeshi Senoo. CHARACTER DESIGNER: Makoto Koga. ART DIRECTOR: Kenichi Tajiri. CHIEF ANIMATION DIRECTOR: Masayuki Onchi. EDITOR: Kentarou Tsubone. COLOR DESIGNER: Yoshimi Kawakami. ANIMATION PRODUCTION: Hal Film Maker.

Aria the OVA — Arietta (2007)

ORIGINAL TITLE: *Aria OVA*. STATUS: OVA (1 episode). LENGTH: 30 minutes. DIRECTOR: Junichi Sato. ORIGINAL CREATOR: Kozue Amano. SCREENPLAY: Sato. MUSIC: Choro Club, Takeshi Senoo. CHARACTER DESIGNER: Makoto Koga. ART DIRECTOR: Hiroshi Yoshikawa. ANIMATION DIRECTOR: Hiroyuki Kaidou. DESIGN WORK: Hiroyuki Kasugai. EDITOR: Kentarou Tsubone. COLOR DE-

SIGNER: Yoshimi Kawakami. ANIMATION PRODUCTION: Hal Film Maker.

Darker Than Black (2007)

ORIGINAL TITLE: *Kuro no Keiyakusha.* STATUS: TV series (26 episodes). EPISODE LENGTH: 24 minutes. DIRECTOR: Tensai Okamura. ORIGINAL CREATOR: Okamura. SERIES COMPOSITION: Shoutarou Suga, Okamura. SCREENPLAY: Kurasumi Sunayama, Shinsuke Onishi, Suga; Okamura; Yuuichi Nomura. MUSIC: Yoko Anno. ORIGINAL CHARACTER DESIGNER: Yuji Iwahara. CHARACTER DESIGNER: Takahiro Komori. ART DIRECTOR: Takashi Aoi. CHIEF ANIMATION DIRECTOR: Takahiro Komori. PRODUCERS: Ryo Oyama, Yoshihiro Oyabu. SOUND DIRECTOR: Kazuhiro Wakabayashi. SOUND EFFECTS: Shizuo Kurahashi. COLOR DESIGNER: Nobuko Mizuta. ANIMATION PRODUCTION: BONES. PRODUCTION: Aniplex, DTB Production Committee. SOUND EFFECTS PRODUCTION: SOUNDBOX.

Earl and Fairy (2008)

ORIGINAL TITLE: STATUS: TV series (12 episodes). EPISODE LENGTH: 24 minutes. DIRECTOR: Kouichirou Sohtome. ORIGINAL CREATOR: Mizue Tani. SERIES COMPOSITION: Noriko Nagao. SCREENPLAY: Nagao. MUSIC: Takehiko Gokita. ORIGINAL CHARACTER DESIGNER: Asako Takaboshi. CHARACTER DESIGNER: Maki Fujii. ART DIRECTORS: Mitsuharu Miyamae, Yoichi Yajima. ANIMATION DIRECTORS: Miyamae, Fujii, Takafumi Shiokawa. PRODUCERS: Asuka Yamazaki, Masafumi Takatori, Rika Sasaki. BACKGROUND ART: Masao Ichitani, Takayuki Kotani. EDITOR: Hideaki Murai. SOUND EFFECTS: Noriko Izumo. SPECIAL EFFECTS: Naomi Kaneko. COLOR DESIGNER: Rika Nishio. ANIMATION PRO-

DUCTION: Artland. SOUND PRODUCTION: Dax Production.

The Familiar of Zero (2006)

ORIGINAL TITLE: *Zero no Tsukaima.* STATUS: TV series (13 episodes). EPISODE LENGTH: 24 minutes. DIRECTOR: Yoshiaki Iwasaki. ORIGINAL CREATOR: Noboru Yamaguchi. SERIES COMPOSITION: Takao Yoshioka. SCREENPLAY: Takao Yoshioka. MUSIC: Shinkichi Mitsumune. ORIGINAL CHARACTER DESIGNER: Eiji Usatsuka. CHARACTER DESIGNER: Masahiro Fujii. ART DIRECTOR: Yoshinori Hirose. CHIEF ANIMATION DIRECTOR: Masahiro Fujii. EDITOR: Masahiro Goto. SOUND DIRECTOR: Tsuyoshi Takahashi. COLOR DESIGNER: Kyousuke Ishikawa. ANIMATION PRODUCTION: J.C. Staff. SOUND EFFECTS PRODUCTION: GENCO, Zero no Tsukaima Production Committee.

The Familiar of Zero 2: The Knight of the Twin Moons (2007)

ORIGINAL TITLE: *Zero no Tsukaima: Futatsuki no Kishi.* STATUS: TV series (12 episodes). EPISODE LENGTH: 24 minutes. DIRECTOR: Yuu Kou. ORIGINAL CREATOR: Noboru Yamaguchi. SERIES COMPOSITION: Yuji Kawahara. MUSIC: Shinkichi Mitsumune. ORIGINAL CHARACTER DESIGNER: Eiji Usatsuka. CHARACTER DESIGNER: Masahiro Fujii. ART DIRECTOR: Yoshinori Hirose. CHIEF ANIMATION DIRECTOR: Fujii. CHIEF EDITOR: Masahiro Goto. SOUND DIRECTOR: Tsuyoshi Takahashi. COLOR KEY: Kyousuke Ishikawa. ANIMATION PRODUCTION: J. C. Staff. PRODUCTION: GENCO, Media Factory, Shochiku Co. Ltd., Zero no Tsukaima Production Committee.

The Familiar of Zero 3: The Princess's Rondo (2008)

ORIGINAL TITLE: *Zero no Tsukaima: Princess no Rondo*. STATUS: TV series (12 episodes). EPISODE LENGTH: 24 minutes. DIRECTOR: Yuu Kou. ORIGINAL CREATOR: Noboru Yamaguchi. SERIES COMPOSITION: Nahoko Hasegawa. SCREENPLAY: Hasegawa. MUSIC: Shinkichi Mitsumune. ORIGINAL CHARACTER DESIGNER: Eiji Usatsuka. CHARACTER DESIGNER: Masahiro Fujii. CHIEF ANIMATION DIRECTOR: Fujii. ANIMATION PRODUCTION: J. C. Staff.

Ghost Hound (2007–2008)

ORIGINAL TITLE: *Shinreigari*. STATUS: TV series (22 episodes). EPISODE LENGTH: 25 minutes. DIRECTOR: Ryutaro Nakamura. ORIGINAL CREATOR: Masamune Shirow. SERIES COMPOSITION: Chiaki J. Konaka. SCREENPLAY: Konaka. MUSIC: TENG. CHARACTER DESIGNER: Mariko Oka. ART DIRECTOR: Hiromasa Ogura. CHIEF ANIMATION DIRECTOR: Oka. 3D DIRECTOR: Kenji Kobayashi. PRODUCERS: Daisuke Katagiri, Masahiro Yonezawa, Tetsuya Kinoshita. EDITOR: Taeko Hamauzu. SOUND DIRECTOR: Yota Tsuruoka. SPECIAL EFFECTS: Masahiro Muragami. COLOR DESIGNER: Hitomi Sano. ANIMATION PRODUCTION: Production I.G. PRODUCTION: Pony Canyon, Production I.G, Showgate, WOWOW. SOUND PRODUCTION: Rakuonsha.

Ghost Hunt (2006–2007)

ORIGINAL TITLE: *Ghost Hunt*. STATUS: TV series (25 episodes). EPISODE LENGTH: 25 minutes. DIRECTOR: Rei Mano. ORIGINAL MANGA: Shiho Inada. ORIGINAL NOVEL: Fuyumi Ono. SERIES COMPOSITION: Tsutomu Kamishiro. SCREENPLAY: Reiko Yoshida, Rika Nakase. MUSIC: Toshio Masuda. CHARACTER DESIGNER: Satoshi Iwataki. ART DIRECTOR: Mie Kasai. ANIMATION DIRECTORS: Ayako Tauchi, Kouji Ogawa, Minami Tsuruakari, Minoru Watanabe, Sachiko Kotani, Shiro Shibata, Tatsuya Urano, Tetsuya Kawagami, Yoshiaki Katayama, Yuki Imoto, Yumi Nakayama. CG DESIGNER: Yoshihide Mukai. ANIMATION PRODUCER: Yuji Matsukura. EDITOR: Kazuhiko Seki. SOUND DIRECTOR: Yasunori Ebina. COLOR DESIGNER: Tomomi Andou. ANIMATION PRODUCTION: J. C. Staff. PRODUCTION: avex entertainment, Marvelous Entertainment, TV Tokyo. SOUND PRODUCTION: Delphi Sound.

The Girl Who Leapt Through Time (2006)

ORIGINAL TITLE: *Toki o Kakeru Shoujo*. STATUS: movie. LENGTH: 98 minutes. DIRECTOR: Mamoru Hosoda. ORIGINAL CREATOR: Yasutaka Tsutsui. SCREENPLAY: Satoko Okudera. MUSIC: Kiyoshi Yoshida. CHARACTER DESIGNER: Yoshiyuki Sadamoto. ART DIRECTOR: Nizo Yamamoto. ANIMATION DIRECTORS: Chikashi Kubota, Hiroyuki Aoyama, Masashi Ishihama. PRODUCERS: Jungo Maruta, Shinichiro Inoue. EDITOR: Shigeru Nishiyama. SOUND EFFECTS: Shizuo Kurahashi. SPECIAL EFFECTS: Ayumi Arahata, Keiko Itogawa, Kumiko Taniguchi. COLOR CHECK: Aki Yoshida, Fumie Hayashi, Fumiko Tanaka, Masako Torigata, Yoshinori Horikawa, Youko Suzuki. ANIMATION PRODUCTION: Madhouse Studios. PRODUCTION: Kadokawa Shoten, The Girl Who Leapt Through Time Production Committee. SOUND EFFECTS PRODUCTION: Sound Box. SPECIAL EFFECTS PRODUCTION: Team Taniguchi. CG PRODUCTION: Asahi Production, Spooky Graphic.

Hell Girl (2005–2006)

ORIGINAL TITLE: *Jigoku Shoujo.* STATUS: TV series (26 episodes). EPISODE LENGTH: 25 minutes. DIRECTOR: Takahiro Ohmori. SERIES COMPOSITION: Kenichi Kanemaki. SCREENPLAY: Kanemaki, Maki Hiro, Masashi Suzuki, Natsuko Takahashi, Noburu Takagi, Satoru Nishizono, Yoshifumi Fukushima. MUSIC: Hiromi Mizutani, Yasuharu Takanashi. CHARACTER DESIGNER: Mariko Oka. ART DIRECTOR: Yoshinori Hishinuma. CHIEF ANIMATION DIRECTOR: Masahiro Aizawa. PRODUCERS: Ai Abe, Norihiro Hayashida. COLOR DESIGNERS: Masato Sasaki, Shinji Matsumoto. ANIMATION PRODUCTION: Studio DEEN. PRODUCTION: Aniplex, SKY Perfect Well Think Co., Ltd. SOUND PRODUCTION: Darks Production. SUPERVISION: Takahiro Ohmori.

Hell Girl Second Cage (2006–2007)

ORIGINAL TITLE: *Jigoku Shoujo Futakomori.* STATUS: TV series (26 episodes). EPISODE LENGTH: 30 minutes. DIRECTOR: Takahiro Ohmori. ORIGINAL SCRIPT: Hiroshi Watanabe. SERIES COMPOSITION: Kenichi Kanemaki. SCREENPLAY: Hiroyuki Kawasaki, Kanemaki, Maki Hiro, Masashi Suzuki, Natsuko Takahashi, Noboru Takagi. MUSIC: Hiromi Mizutani, Yasuharu Takanashi. CHARACTER DESIGNER: Mariko Oka. ART DIRECTORS: Nariyuki Ogi, Yoshinori Hishinuma. ANIMATION DIRECTORS: Ayako Suzuki, Hiromitsu Hagiwara, Kazuo Noguchi, Kazuyuki Igai, Oka, Takehiro Nakayama, Tomomi Ishikawa, Youichi Ishikawa, Yukiko Akiyama PRODUCERS: Ai Abe, Norihiro Hayashida. EDITOR: Masahiro Matsumura. SOUND DIRECTOR: Minoru Yamada. COLOR SETTING: Hiromi Kato. ANIMATION PRODUCTION: Studio DEEN. PRODUCTION:

Aniplex, Wellthink. SOUND PRODUCTION: Darks Production.

Hell Girl: Cauldron of Three (2008)

ORIGINAL TITLE: *Jigoku Shoujo Mitsuganae.* STATUS: TV series (26 episodes). EPISODE LENGTH: 24 minutes. DIRECTOR: Kenichi Kanemaki. ORIGINAL CONCEPT: Hiroshi Watanabe. SERIES COMPOSITION: Kanemaki. MUSIC: Hiromi Mizutani, Kenji Fujisawa, Yasuharu Takanashi. CHARACTER DESIGNER: Mariko Oka. ART SUPERVISOR: Nariyuki Ogi. ANIMATION DIRECTORS: Mariko Oka, Yukiko Akiyama. EDITOR: Masahiro Matsumura. COLOR DESIGNER: Shinji Matsumoto. ANIMATION PRODUCTION: Studio DEEN. PRODUCTION: Aniplex.

Kagihime (2006)

ORIGINAL TITLE: *Kagihime Monogatari Eikyuu Alice Rondo* (a.k.a. *Kagihime Monogatari — Eikyuu Alice Rinbukyoku*). STATUS: TV series (13 episodes). EPISODE LENGTH: 24 minutes. DIRECTOR: Nagisa Miyazaki, ORIGINAL CREATOR: Kaishaku. SERIES COMPOSITION: Mamiko Ikeda. SCENARIO: Ikeda. MUSIC: Hikaru Nanase. ART DIRECTOR: Shigeru Morimoto. ANIMATION DIRECTORS: Hiroko Kuryube; Sawako Yamamoto. PRODUCERS: Kousaku Sakamoto, Saburo Omiya, Takashi Nakanishi. EDITOR: Jun Takuma. SOUND DIRECTOR: Yasunori Ebina. COLOR KEY: Yoshimi Kawakami. ANIMATION PRODUCTION: Picture Magic, Trinet Entertainment.

Magical Shopping Arcade Abenobashi (2002)

ORIGINAL TITLE: *Abenobashi Mahou Shotengai.* STATUS: TV series (13 episodes). EPISODE LENGTH: 24 minutes. DIRECTOR: Hiroyuki Yamaga. SCREENPLAY: Yamaga, Jukki Hanada, Satoru Akahori. PRODUCERS: Hiroyuki Yamaga, Masafumi Fukui, Taiji Suinou, Toshimichi Ootsuki. ART DIRECTOR: Hiroshi Kato. ANIMATION DIRECTORS: Fumie Mutoi, Hideaki Anno, Hiroshi Kato, Hiroshi Shimizu, Hiroyuki Imaishi, Hiroyuki Ochi, Kim Gi-Du, Masaaki Sakurai, Noriyuki Fukuda, Ryu Kase, Shinji Takeuchi, Tadashi Hiramatsu. CHARACTER DESIGNERS: Kazuhiro Takamura, Kenji Tsuruta, Sadafumi Hiramatsu, Tadashi Hiramatsu. MECHANICAL DESIGNER: Takeshi Takakura. SOUND DIRECTOR: Kazuya Tanaka. ANIMATION PRODUCTION: Gainax, Madhouse Studios. PRODUCTION: *Abenobashi* Project, Dentsu Inc., Gainax, Imagica, Starchild Records. MUSIC: Shiro Sagisu.

Magikano (2006)

ORIGINAL TITLE: *Magikano*. STATUS: TV series (13 episodes). EPISODE LENGTH: 30 minutes. DIRECTOR: Seiji Kishi. ORIGINAL MANGA: Takeaki Momose. SERIES COMPOSITION: Hideki Mitsui. SCREENPLAY: Mitsui. MUSIC: Katsuyuki Harada. CHARACTER DESIGNER: Takashi Kobayashi. ART DIRECTOR: Masakazu Miyake. CHIEF ANIMATION DIRECTOR: Kobayashi. EDITOR: Takashi Sakurai. SOUND DIRECTOR: Satoki Iida. ANIMATION PRODUCTION: Tokyo Kids. PRODUCTION: Magikano Production Committee.

Mai-HiME (2004–2005)

ORIGINAL TITLE: *Mai-HiME*. STATUS: TV series (26 episodes). EPISODE LENGTH: 25 minutes. DIRECTOR: Masakazu Obara. ORIGINAL CONCEPT: Hajime Yatate. SERIES COMPOSITION: Hiroyuki Yoshino. SCREENPLAY: Hiroyuki Yoshino, Noboru Kimura. MUSIC: Yuki Kajiura. CHARACTER DESIGNER: Hirokazu Hisayuki. CREATURE DESIGNERS: Junichi Akutsu, Kazutaka Miyatake. ART DIRECTOR: Shinji Takasuka. ANIMATION DIRECTORS: Hirokazu Hisayuki, Hiroshi Takeuchi, Kazushi Takano, Keizou Ichikawa, Ken Ootsuka, Kenichi Takase, Kohei Yoneyama, Masahiko Kaneda, Masami Nagata, Masayoshi Tanaka, Minoru Mihara, Naoki Aisaka, Satoshi Ishino, Satoshi Shigeta, Shuuji Sakamoto, Takuro Shinbo, Tomohiro Kawahara, Tomoshige Inayoshi. PRODUCERS: Hisanori Kunisaki, Naotake Furusato. EDITOR: Kazuhiko Seki. SOUND DIRECTOR: Masafumi Mima. SOUND EFFECTS: Kenji Koyama. COLOR COORDINATION: Sayoko Yokoyama. ANIMATION PRODUCTION: Sunrise. PRODUCTION: Sunrise. SOUND EFFECTS PRODUCTION: Techno Sound. MUSIC PRODUCTION: Lantis, TV Tokyo Music.

Mai-Otome (2005–2006)

ORIGINAL TITLE: *Mai-Otome*. STATUS: TV series (26 episodes). EPISODE LENGTH: 30 minutes. DIRECTOR: Masakazu Obara. ORIGINAL CONCEPT: Hajime Yatate. SERIES COMPOSITION: Hiroyuki Yoshino. SCREENPLAY: Yoshino, Kazushi Takano. MUSIC: Yuki Kajiura. CHARACTER DESIGNER: Hirokazu Hisayuki. ART DIRECTOR: Shinji Takasuka. PRODUCERS: Hisanori Kunisaki, Naotake Furusato. EDITOR: Kazuhiko Seki. SOUND DIRECTOR: Masafumi Mima. SOUND EFFECTS: Kenji Koyama. SPECIAL EFFECTS: Toshio Hasegawa. COLOR COORDINATION: Sayoko Yokoyama. ANIMATION PRODUCTION: Sunrise. PRODUCTION: Sunrise. SOUND EFFECTS PRODUCTION: SOUNDBOX. MUSIC PRODUCTION: Lantis.

Mononoke (2007)

ORIGINAL TITLE: *Mononoke*. STATUS: TV series (12 episodes). EPISODE LENGTH: 23 minutes. DIRECTOR: Kenji Nakamura.

SCREENPLAY: Chiaki J. Konaka, Ikuko Takahashi, Manabu Ishikawa, Michiko Yokote. MUSIC: Yasuharu Takanashi. CHARACTER DESIGNER: Takashi Hashimoto. ART DIRECTORS: Takashi Kurahashi, Yumi Hosaka. CHIEF ANIMATION DIRECTOR: Takashi Hashimoto. ANIMATION PRODUCTION: Toei Animation.

Mushi-Shi (2005)

ORIGINAL TITLE: *Mushi-Shi*. STATUS: TV series (26 episodes). EPISODE LENGTH: 25 minutes. DIRECTOR: Hiroshi Nagahama. ORIGINAL MANGA: Yuki Urushibara. SERIES COMPOSITION: Hiroshi Nagahama. SCREENPLAY: Aki Itami, Kinuko Kuwabata, Yuka Yamada. MUSIC: Toshio Masuda. ORIGINAL CHARACTER DESIGNER: Yoshihiko Umakoshi. ART DIRECTOR: Takeshi Waki. CHIEF ANIMATION DIRECTOR: Yoshihiko Umakoshi. PRODUCERS: Aya Kawamura, Hiroyuki Ooizumi, Shin Hieda, Yoshiaki Tamura. EDITORS: Masahiro Matsumura, Naoki Watanabe. SOUND DIRECTOR: Kazuya Tanaka. SOUND EFFECTS: Noriko Izumo, Yuki Okuda. SPECIAL EFFECTS: Azusa Sasaki, Kuniharu Okano, Takeshi Hirooka, Tomomi Ishihara, Tomoyuki Shimizu. COLOR DESIGNERS: Keiko Yamashita, Kuniharu Okano, Rika Nishio, Tomoko Yamazaki. ANIMATION PRODUCTION: Artland. PRODUCTION: Marvelous Entertainment, Mushishi Production Committee. SOUND PRODUCTION: Delphi Sound.

Natsume Yuujinchou (2008)

ORIGINAL TITLE: *Natsume Yuujinchou*. STATUS: TV series (13 episodes). EPISODE LENGTH: 30 minutes. DIRECTOR: Takahiro Ohmori. ORIGINAL CREATOR: Yuki Midorikawa. SERIES COMPOSITION: Kenichi Kanemaki. MUSIC: Makoto Yoshimori. CHARACTER DESIGNER: Akira Takata. MONSTER DESIGNER: Tatsuo Yamada. ART DIRECTOR: Yukihiro Shibutani. CHIEF ANIMATION DIRECTORS: Akira Takata, Tatsuo Yamada. PRODUCER: Shosuke Miyake. EDITOR: Kazuhiko Seki. SOUND DIRECTOR: Ohmori. SOUND EFFECTS: Sho Urahata. COLOR SETTING: Ayako Saito, Yufuko Fukuda, Yumi Miyawaki. ANIMATION PRODUCTION: Brains Base. PRODUCTION: NAS. SOUND EFFECTS PRODUCTION: Darks Production. SPECIAL EFFECTS PRODUCTION: Ray Art.

Negima! (2005)

ORIGINAL TITLE: *Mahou Sensei Negima!* STATUS: TV series (26 episodes). EPISODE LENGTH: 30 minutes. DIRECTOR: Nagisa Miyazaki. ORIGINAL MANGA: Ken Akamatsu. SERIES COMPOSITION: Ichiro Okouchi. SCREENPLAY: Okouchi. MUSIC: Shinkichi Mitsumune. CHARACTER DESIGNER: Hatsue Kato. ART DIRECTOR: Yoshimi Umino. ANIMATION DIRECTOR: Hatsue Kato. ART DESIGNER: Junko Nagasawa. PROP DESIGNER: Tadashi Sakazaki. PRODUCERS: Shinichi Ikeda, Takatoshi Chino. EDITOR: Tomoki Nagasaka. SOUND DIRECTOR: Yota Tsuruoka. COLOR DESIGNER: Miyoko Kobayashi. ANIMATION PRODUCTION: Xebec. PRODUCTION: Kanto Magic Society, Xebec. MUSIC PRODUCTION: Starchild Records.

Negima!? (2006–2007)

ORIGINAL TITLE: *Negima!?* STATUS: TV series (26 episodes). EPISODE LENGTH: 25 minutes. DIRECTOR: Akiyuki Shinbou. ORIGINAL CREATOR: Ken Akamatsu. SERIES COMPOSITION: Kenichi Kanemaki. MUSIC: Kei Haneoka. CHARACTER DESIGNER: Kazuhiro Ota. ART DIRECTOR: Megumi Kato. CHIEF ANIMATION DIRECTOR: Minoru Mihara. PRODUCERS:

Fukashi Azuma, Gou Nakanishi, Shinichi Ikeda. EDITOR: Kazuhiko Seki. SOUND DIRECTOR: Yota Tsuruoka. VISUAL EFFECTS: Motoi Sakai. COLOR SETTING: Izumi Takizawa. COLOUR DESIGNERS: Hiroshi Hibino, Izumi Takizawa. ANIMATION PRODUCTION: GANSIS, SHAFT. PRODUCTION: Kanto Magic Society, SHAFT, TV Tokyo. Sound Production. MUSIC PRODUCTION: Starchild Records.

Negima!— Spring (2006)

ORIGINAL TITLE: *Mahou Sensei Negima! OVA Haru.* STATUS: OVA (1 episode). EPISODE LENGTH: 25 minutes. DIRECTOR: Akiyuki Shinbou. ORIGINAL CREATOR: Ken Akamatsu. SCREENPLAY: Kenichi Kanemaki. MUSIC: Kei Haneoka. CHARACTER DESIGNER: Kazuhiro Ota. ART DIRECTOR: Hiroshi Kato. PRODUCER: Gou Nakanishi. EDITOR: Kazuhiko Seki. SOUND DIRECTOR: Yota Tsuruoka. SOUND EFFECTS: Minoru Yamada. VISUAL EFFECTS: Motoi Sakai. COLOR DESIGNER: Izumi Takizawa. ANIMATION PRODUCTION: GANSIS, SHAFT. PRODUCTION: Kanto Magic Society. SOUND PRODUCTION: Rakuonsha. MUSIC PRODUCTION: Starchild Records.

Negima!— Summer (2006)

ORIGINAL TITLE: *Mahou Sensei Negima! OVA Natsu.* STATUS: OVA (1 episode). EPISODE LENGTH: 25 minutes. DIRECTOR: Akiyuki Shinbou. ORIGINAL CREATOR: Ken Akamatsu. SCREENPLAY: Katsuhiro Takayama. MUSIC: Kei Haneoka. CHARACTER DESIGNER: Kazuhiro Ota. ART DIRECTOR: Megumi Kato. CHIEF ANIMATION DIRECTOR: Ota. PRODUCER: Gou Nakanishi. EDITOR: Kazuhiko Seki. SOUND DIRECTOR: Yota Tsuruoka. SOUND EFFECTS: Minoru Yamada. VISUAL EFFECTS: Motoi Sakai. COLOR DESIGNER: Izumi Takizawa.

COLOR DIRECTOR: Hiroshi Hibino. ANIMATION PRODUCTION: GANSIS, SHAFT. PRODUCTION: Kanto Magic Society. MUSIC PRODUCTION: Starchild Records.

Oh My Goddess! (1993)

ORIGINAL TITLE: *Aa! Megamisama!* STATUS: OVA series (5 episodes). EPISODE LENGTH: 30 minutes. DIRECTOR: Hiroaki Gouda. ORIGINAL MANGA: Kosuke Fujishima. SCREENPLAY: Kunihiko Kondo, Nahoko Hasegawa. MUSIC: Takeshi Yasuda. CHARACTER DESIGNERS: Hidenori Matsubara, Hiroshi Kato, Osamu Tsuruyama. ART DIRECTOR: Kato. ANIMATION DIRECTORS: Hidenori Matsubara, Noriyuki Matsutake. PRODUCERS: Hiroo Takimoto, Masao Shindou, Takaro Asaga, Toru Miura, Yoshimasa Mizuo. EDITORS: Shigeyuki Yamamori, Toshio Henmi. SOUND EFFECTS: Junichi Sasaki. PRODUCTION: AIC, Kodansha, KSS, TBS.

Ponyo on the Cliff by the Sea (2008)

ORIGINAL TITLE: *Gake no Ue no Ponyo.* STATUS: movie. LENGTH: 101 minutes. DIRECTOR: Hayao Miyazaki. ORIGINAL CREATOR: Miyazaki. SCREENPLAY: Miyazaki. MUSIC: Joe Hisaishi. ART DIRECTOR: Noboru Yoshida. ANIMATION DIRECTOR: Katsuya Kondo. PRODUCER: Toshio Suzuki. EDITOR: Takeshi Seyama. SOUND DIRECTOR: Eriko Kimura. SOUND EFFECTS: Koji Kasamatsu. COLOR DESIGNER: Michiyo Yasuda. ANIMATION PRODUCTION: Studio Ghibli. PRODUCTION: Ponyo on the Cliff Production Committee.

Rental Magica (2007–2008)

ORIGINAL TITLE: *Rental Magica.* STATUS: TV series (24 episodes). EPISODE

LENGTH: 30 minutes. DIRECTOR: Itsuro Kawasaki. ORIGINAL CREATOR: Makoto Sanda. SERIES COMPOSITION: Sanda, Mamiko Ikeda. MUSIC: Jun Ichikawa, Takahito Eguchi. ORIGINAL CHARACTER DESIGNER: pako. CHARACTER DESIGNER: Minako Shiba. CREATURE DESIGNER: Hideki Hashimoto. ART DIRECTOR: Masaru Ohta. EDITOR: Daisuke Hiraki. SOUND DIRECTOR: Yoshikazu Iwanami. COLOR DESIGNER: Hiromi Iwaida. ANIMATION PRODUCTION: ZEXCS. MUSIC PRODUCTION: Victor Entertainment.

Romeo x Juliet (2007)

ORIGINAL TITLE: *Romio to Jurietto*. STATUS: TV series (24 episodes). EPISODE LENGTH: 30 minutes. DIRECTOR: Fumitoshi Oizaki. ORIGINAL CREATOR: William Shakespeare. SERIES COMPOSITION: Reiko Yoshida. SCREENPLAY: Kurasumi Sunayama, Miharu Hirami, Natsuko Takahashi, Reiko Yoshida. MUSIC: Hitoshi Sakimoto. CHARACTER DESIGNER: Daiki Harada. ART DIRECTOR: Masami Saito. PRODUCER: Touyou Ikeda. EDITOR: Seiji Hirose. SOUND DIRECTOR: Tomohiro Yoshida. COLOR DESIGNER: Toshie Suzuki. ANIMATION PRODUCTION: Gonzo. BACKGROUNDS PRODUCTION: Cosmos Arts, Ogura Kobo, Tezuka Productions. PRODUCTION: CBC, G.D.H., Gonzo, SKY Perfect Well Think Co., Ltd. SOUND PRODUCTION: Rakuonsha.

Rozen Maiden (2004)

ORIGINAL TITLE: *Rozen Maiden*. STATUS: TV series (12 episodes). EPISODE LENGTH: 24 minutes. DIRECTOR: Kou Matsuo. ORIGINAL CREATOR: Peach-Pit. SERIES COMPOSITION: Jukki Hanada. SCREENPLAY: Hanada, Mari Okada, Tsuyoshi Tamai. MUSIC: Shinkichi Mitsumune. CHARACTER DESIGNER: Kumi Ishii. ART DIRECTOR: Chikako Shibata.

CHIEF ANIMATION DIRECTOR: Ishii. PRODUCERS: Hiroichi Kokago, Kozue Kana, Masaru Kitao, Shinichi Nakamura, Takashi Jinguuji. EDITOR: Mutsumi Takemiya. SOUND DIRECTOR: Yota Tsuruoka. COLOR COORDINATION: Madoka Katsunuma. ANIMATION PRODUCTION: Nomad. PRODUCTION: Memory Tech, Novic, Pony Canyon, Rozen Maiden Production Committee. MUSIC PRODUCTION: Mellow Head.

Rozen Maiden: Träumend (2005–2006)

ORIGINAL TITLE: *Rozen Maiden: Toroimento*. STATUS: TV series (12 episodes). EPISODE LENGTH: 25 minutes. DIRECTOR: Kou Matsuo. ORIGINAL CREATOR: Peach-Pit. SERIES COMPOSITION: Jukki Hanada. SCREENPLAY: Hanada, Mari Okada, Tsuyoshi Tamai. MUSIC: Shinkichi Mitsumune. CHARACTER DESIGNER: Kumi Ishii. ART DIRECTOR: Chikako Shibata. ANIMATION DIRECTORS: Ishii, Masafumi Tamura, Masaki Yamada, Naoki Yamauchi, Norika Togawa, Satonobu Kikuchi. PRODUCERS: Hiroichi Kokago, Kozue Kana, Masaru Kitao, Shinichi Nakamura, Takashi Jinguuji. EDITOR: Mutsumi Takemiya. SOUND DIRECTOR: Yota Tsuruoka. COLOR DESIGNERS: Eiko Inoue, Kiyomi Yamazaki, Madoka Katsunuma. Madoka Katsunuma. ANIMATION PRODUCTION: Nomad. PRODUCTION: Rozen Maiden Production Committee, TBS. SOUND PRODUCTION: Rakuonsha.

Shounen Onmyouji (2006–2007)

ORIGINAL TITLE: *Shounen Onmyouji*. STATUS: TV series (26 episodes). EPISODE LENGTH: 24 minutes. DIRECTOR: Kunihiro Mori. ORIGINAL NOVEL: Mitsuru Yuuki. SERIES COMPOSITION: Miya

Asakawa. SCREENPLAY: Miya Asakawa. MUSIC: Kou Nakagawa. ORIGINAL CHARACTER DESIGNERS: Sakura Asagi, Sakura Asaki. CHARACTER DESIGNER: Shinobu Tagashira. ART DIRECTOR: Toshihisa Koyama. CHIEF ANIMATION DIRECTOR: Kumiko Horikoshi. SOUND DIRECTOR: Satoshi Motoyama. SOUND EFFECTS: Emi Takanashi. SPECIAL EFFECTS: Shouichi Uehara. ANIMATION PRODUCTION: Studio DEEN. SOUND PRODUCTION: Omnibus Promotion. MUSIC PRODUCTION: Frontier Works, Marine Entertainment.

Sola (2007)

ORIGINAL TITLE: *Sola*. STATUS: TV series (15 episodes). EPISODE LENGTH: 24 minutes. DIRECTOR: Tomoki Kobayashi. ORIGINAL CREATOR: Naoki Hisaya. SERIES COMPOSITION: Jukki Hanada. SCREENPLAY: Hanada, Kenji Sugihara, Makoto Uezu, Hisaya. MUSIC: Hitoshi Fujima. ORIGINAL CHARACTER DESIGNER: Naru Nanao. CHARACTER DESIGNER: Makoto Koga. ART DIRECTOR: Yoshinori Hirose. CHIEF ANIMATION DIRECTOR: Koga. EDITOR: Kengo Shigemura. SOUND DIRECTOR: Jin Aketagawa. COLOR DESIGNER: Hiroko Umezaki. ANIMATION PRODUCTION: Nomad. SOUND PRODUCTION: Magic Capsule. MUSIC PRODUCTION: Lantis.

xxxHolic (2006)

ORIGINAL TITLE: *xxxHolic*. STATUS: TV series (24 episodes). EPISODE LENGTH: 25 minutes. DIRECTOR: Tsutomu Mizushima. ORIGINAL CREATOR: CLAMP. SERIES COMPOSITION: Ageha Ohkawa, Michiko Yokote. SCREENPLAY: Ageha Ohkawa, Michiko Yokote, Miharu Hirami, Tsutomu Mizushima, Yoshiki Sakurai. MUSIC: S.E.N.S. CHARACTER DESIGNER: Kazuchika Kise. PROP DESIGNER: Minoru Ueda. ART DIRECTOR:

Hiromasa Ogura. ANIMATION DIRECTORS: Fumiko Urawa, Hiroyo Izumi, Junichiro Taniguchi, Kaoru Agatsuma, Kenichi Ishimaru, Masayuki Nomoto, Minoru Ueda, Ryouko Nakano, Shinsuke Terasawa, Tomoyuki Matsumoto. PRODUCERS: Ikuko Shikano, Katsuji Morishita, Naohiro Futono, Naomi Sudou, Takuya Matsushita, Toyoaki Iwasaki, Yoshihisa Nakayama. EDITOR: Taeko Hamauzu. SOUND DIRECTOR: Kazuhiro Wakabayashi. SOUND EFFECTS: Michihiro Ito. SPECIAL EFFECTS: Masahiro Murakami. COLOR SETTING: Izumi Hirose, Mina Noguchi. ANIMATION PRODUCTION: Production I.G. PRODUCTION: Ayakashi Research Society.

xxxHolic: Kei (2008)

ORIGINAL TITLE: *xxxHolic: Kei*. STATUS: TV series (13 episodes). EPISODE LENGTH: 24 minutes. DIRECTOR: Tsutomu Mizushima. ORIGINAL CREATOR: CLAMP. SERIES COMPOSITION: Ageha Ohkawa, Michiko Yokote. MUSIC: S.E.N.S. CHARACTER DESIGNER: Kazuchika Kise. PROP DESIGNER: Minoru Ueda. ART DIRECTOR: Hiromasa Ogura. ANIMATION DIRECTORS: Hiroyo Izumi, Junichiro Taniguchi, Kazuya Kise, Minoru Ueda, Ryouko Nakano, Sachiko Kotani, Satoshi Hata, Shinsuke Terasawa, Yumiko Hara. PRODUCERS: Junichiro Tanaka, Kozue Kaneniwa, Nahomi Sudo, Takuya Matsushita, Tomoyuki Sagawa. SOUND DIRECTOR: Kazuhiro Wakabayashi. SOUND EFFECTS: Michihiro Ito. SPECIAL EFFECTS: Masahiro Muragami. COLOR SETTING: Chie Tanimoto, Daisuke Yamazaki, Hatsumi Okada, Izumi Hirose, Kumiko Akahori. ANIMATION PRODUCTION: Production I.G. PRODUCTION: BMG Japan, KIDS STATION, Kodansha, Production I.G. SOUND PRODUCTION: Phoenicia.

xxxHolic the Movie: A Midsummer Night's Dream (2005)

ORIGINAL TITLE: *Gekijouban xxxHOLiC Manatsu no Yoru no Yume.* STATUS: movie. LENGTH: 60 minutes. DIRECTOR: Tsutomu Mizushima. ORIGINAL CREATOR: CLAMP. SCREENPLAY: Jun'ichi Fujisaku, Yoshiki Sakurai. MUSIC: Tsuneyoshi Saito. CHARACTER DESIGNER: Kazuchika Kise. PROP DESIGNER: Minoru Ueda. ART DIRECTOR: Shuichi Hirata. ANIMATION DIRECTOR: Kise. PRODUCERS: Ikuko Shikano, Junji Seki, Natsumi Shirahama, Tetsuya Watanabe, Toru Kawaguchi, Toshiaki Doushita, Yoshihiro Iwasaki. EDITOR: Taeko Hamauzu. COLOR DESIGNER: Sayuri Yoshida. ANIMATION PRODUCTION: Production I.G. PRODUCTION: Dentsu Inc., Kodansha, MOVIC, Nippan, Production I.G, Pyrotechnist, Shochiku, Co. Ltd. SOUND PRODUCTION: Pony Canyon.

xxxHolic: Shunmuki (2009)

ORIGINAL TITLE: STATUS: OVA series (2 episodes). EPISODE LENGTH: 27 minutes. DIRECTOR: Tsutomu Mizushima. ORIGINAL CREATOR: CLAMP. SCREENPLAY: Nanase Ohkawa. CHARACTER DESIGNER: Kazuchika Kise. PROP DESIGNER: Minoru Ueda. ART DIRECTOR: Hiromasa Ogura. EDITOR: Junichi Uematsu. SOUND DIRECTOR: Kazuhiro Wakabayashi. COLOR SETTING: Mayumi Satou. ANIMATION PRODUCTION: Production I.G.

Yume Tsukai (2006)

ORIGINAL TITLE: *Yume Tsukai.* STATUS: TV series (12 episodes). EPISODE LENGTH: 30 minutes. DIRECTOR: Kazuo Yamazaki. ORIGINAL CREATOR: Riichi Ueshiba. SERIES COMPOSITION: Yasuko Kobayashi. MUSIC: Tamiya Terashima. CHARACTER DESIGNER: Shuichi Shimamura. MECHANICAL DESIGNER: Shinya Terashima. ART DIRECTOR: Chikara Nishikura. CHIEF ANIMATION DIRECTORS: Akemi Kobayashi, Noriyuki Fukuda. SOUND DIRECTOR: Kazuo Tanaka. COLOR SETTING: Harue Ono. ANIMATION PRODUCTION: Madhouse Studios PRODUCTION: Pony Canyon. SOUND PRODUCTION: Darks Production. MUSIC PRODUCTION: Happinet Pictures.

Zoku Natsume Yuujinchou (2009)

ORIGINAL TITLE: *Zoku Natsume Yuujinchou* STATUS: TV series (13 episodes). EPISODE LENGTH: 24 minutes. DIRECTOR: Takahiro Ohmori. ORIGINAL CREATOR: Yuki Midorikawa. SERIES COMPOSITION: Kenichi Kanemaki. CHARACTER DESIGNER: Akira Takata. MONSTER DESIGNER: Tatsuo Yamada. PRODUCTION: Brains Base.

Ancillary Titles

Cardcaptor Sakura (TV series; dir. Morio, Asaka, 1998–2000)

D. C.—Da Capo—(TV series; dir. Nagisa Miyazaki, 2003)

D. C. S. S.—Da Capo Second Season—(TV series; dir. Munenori Nawa, 2005)

Death Note (TV series; dir. Tetsurou Araki, 2006–2007)

Dolls (movie; dir. Takeshi Kitano, 2002)

Escaflowne: The Movie (movie; dir. Kazuki Akane, 2000)

Fate/stay Night (TV series; dir. Yuji Yamaguchi, 2006)

Fullmetal Alchemist (TV series; dir. Seiji Mizushima, 2003–2004)

Fushigi Yuugi (a.k.a. *Mysterious Play*; TV series; dir. Hajime Kamegaki, 1995–1996)

Touka Gettan (TV series; dir. Yuji Yamaguchi, 2007)

The Tower of Druaga — The Aegis of Uruk (TV series; dir. Koichi Chigira, 2008)

The Tower of Druaga — The Sword of Uruk (TV series; dir. Koichi Chigira, 2009)

Tsubasa: RESERVoir CHRoNiCLE (TV series; dir. Koichi Mashimo, 2005–2006)

Vision of Escaflowne (TV series; dirs. Kazuki Akane and Shouji Kawamori, 1996)

When Cicadas Cry (a.k.a. *When They Cry — Higurashi*) TV series; dir. Chiaki Kon, 2006)

When Cicadas Cry — Solutions (TV series; dir. Chiaki Kon, 2007)

Yami to Boushi to Hon no Tabibito (a.k.a. *Darkness, Hat and Book Traveler*; TV series; dir. Yuji Yamaguchi, 2003)

Yume (movie; dir. Akira Kurosawa, 1992)

Zegapain (TV series; dir. Masami Shimoda, 2006)

Zombie Loan (TV series; dir. Akira Nishimori, 2007)

Chapter Notes

Chapter 1

1. Shinto beliefs are integral to the world views projected by two of the most cherished *mecha*-oriented anime sagas ever produced, namely, *Neon Genesis Evangelion* (TV series; dir. Hideaki Anno, 1995–1996) and *RahXephon* (TV series; dir. Yutaka Izubuchi, 2002).

Chapter 2

1. The sensationally popular team of *manga ka* behind both *Tsubasa: RESERVoir CHRoNiCLE* and *xxxHolic*, CLAMP, has a reputation for incorporating characters from their prior productions into their new titles, always ensuring that the recycled personae gain fresh personalities and roles with each crossover. *Tsubasa* also shares the characters of Sakura, Syaoran, Princess Tomoyo, Touya and Yukito with *Cardcaptor Sakura*, and the characters of Mokona and Princess Emeraude with *Magic Knight Rayearth*, which are here discussed in Chapter 5 and Chapter 6 respectively.

Chapter 3

1. Lewis Carroll's writings — particularly *Through the Looking-Glass, and What Alice Found There* (1871) — are used as an important point of reference in the anime series *RahXephon* (TV series; dir. Yutaka Izubuchi, 2002) and even more prominently in the movie version of the saga supplied by *RahXephon: Pluralitas Concentio* (dirs. Yutaka Izubuchi and Tomoki Kyoda, 2003). The female lead, Haruka, comments thus on Alice's adventures in the world beyond the mirror in the film's finale: "It doesn't matter what world was real because she was left with memories, wonderful memories of her experiences in the looking-glass world and those were real to her."

Chapter 4

1. A notable Western correlative of this motif can be found in Angela Carter's magical realist novel *The Magic Toyshop* (1967), where the titular location is enthroned as a protagonist in its own right.

Chapter 5

1. Please note that *Princess Mononoke* is here briefly alluded to in Chapter 2. *Spirited Away* and *Howl's Moving Castle* are discussed in Chapter 3 and Chapter 2 respectively).

2. As an aesthetic concept, the term "grotesque" originates in the Italian *grotta/grotto*: a cave-like location, commonly favored by Renaissance patrons in the design of their grounds and parks, distinguished by the lavish employment of bizarre ornamentation — most notably, sculptures and medallions representing extravagant hybrids of human, animal and vegetable forms in distorted and caricatured fashions.

3. Norse mythology is also brought into play to great dramatic effect in the TV series *The Mythical Detective Loki Ragnarok* (dir. Hiroshi Watanabe, 2003), where the protean Norse deity Loki is trapped inside a child's body and exiled to Earth.

Chapter 6

1. Please note that the Tarot deck is also graphically central to the popular CLAMP manga *X/1999*, where each volume is

adorned with a card symbolically relevant to one of the characters.

2. *"Hikikomori"* (ひきこもり or 引き籠もり) is the Japanese word used to designate "the phenomenon of reclusive individuals who have chosen to withdraw from social life, often seeking extreme degrees of isolation and confinement because of various personal and social factors in their lives. ... Although there are occasions where the *hikikomori* may venture outdoors, usually at night to buy food, the Japanese Ministry of Health, Labour and Welfare defines *hikikomori* as individuals who refuse to leave their parents' house, and isolate themselves from society in their homes for a period exceeding six months. ... Often *hikikomori* start out as school refusals, or *toukoukyohi* (登校拒否) in Japanese" (*Wikipedia, the free encyclopedia —Hikikomori*).

Bibliography

Ashkenazi, M. 2003. *Handbook of Japanese Mythology*. Oxford: Oxford University Press.

Avella, N. 2004. *Graphic Japan: From Woodblock and Zen to Manga and Kawaii*. Hove, East Sussex, England: RotoVision.

Bailey, M. D. 2006. "The Meanings of Magic." *Magic, Ritual, and Witchcraft*. Summer. Philadelphia: University of Pennsylvania Press. http://magic.penn press.org/PennPress/journals/magic/sam pleArt2.pdf.

Bashou, M. 1994. *Anthology of Japanese Literature*, ed. D. Keene. New York: Grove.

Berger, J. 1972. *Ways of Seeing*. London: British Broadcasting Corporation and Penguin.

Besen, E. 2003. "Analogy and Animation: A Special Relationship Part 2 — Think Like an Animator, Walk Like a Duck." *Animation World Magazine*. http://mag.awn. com/index.php?ltype=Columns&column =AnalogyAni&article_no=1918.

Bettelheim, B. "Bruno Bettelheim Quotes." *ThinkExist*. http://thinkexist.com/quotes/ bruno_bettelheim/.

Bianchi, E. 1000. "Dalla parte del mare." *Meridiani* XXII.75. Milan, Italy: Editoriale Domus.

Blanchot, M. 1882. "The Two Versions of the Imaginary." In *The Space of Literature*. Trans. A. Smock. Lincoln: Nebraska University Press.

Blatty, W. P. 1999. "Elsewhere." In *999*, edited by A. Sarrantonio. London: Hodder & Stoughton.

Bloom, C. 1998. *Gothic Horror*, ed. C. Bloom. London: Macmillan.

Campbell, J. 1988. *The Power of Myth*. New York: Doubleday.

Campbell, R. 2000. "Welcome to My Haunted Domain." *British Fantasy Society*. http://www.herebedragons.co.uk/camp- bell/main.htm.

Carter, A. 1967. *The Magic Toyshop*. London: Virago.

Coben, H. 2009. *Long Lost*. London: Orion.

Corliss, R. 2008. "*Ponyo*: More Ani-Magic from Miyazaki." *Time*. http://www.time. com/time/arts/article/0,8599,1838053, 00.html.

Covino, W. A. 1994. *Magic, Rhetoric and Literacy: An Eccentric History of the Composing Imagination*. Albany: State University of New York Press.

Dawson, C. 1901. "Japan and Its Colour Prints." In *The Process Yearbook*. Bradford, England: Percy, Lund & Humphries.

Dryden, J. 1962. "Of Heroic Plays: An Essay." In *Of Dramatic Poesy and Other Critical Essay*, ed. G. Watson. London: Dent.

During, S. 2002. *Modern Enchantments—The Cultural Power of Secular Magic*. Cambridge, MA, and London: Harvard University Press.

Durkheim, É. 2001. [1912.] *The Elementary Forms of Religion*. Trans. C. Cosman. Oxford: Oxford University Press.

Ebert, R. 2004. "Interview." *Grave of the Fireflies* Double Disc Special Edition, Disc Two. Optimum Releasing.

Einstein, A. 1949. *The World As I See It*. New York: Philosophical Library.

Eisenbraun, C. "Butterflys." *The Symbols One Word at a Time*. http://www.scootermy- daisyheads.com/fine_art/symbol_dic tionary/butterfly.html.

"Female Roles in the Fairy Tales of Charles Perrault." http://iabramson.web.wesley an.edu/perrault.htm.

Flusser, V. 1992. "Key Words," ed. A. Müller- Pohle and B. Neubauer. http://www.equi valence.com/labor/lab_vf_glo_e.shtml.

Flusser, V. 2000. *Towards a Philosophy of Photography*. London: Reaktion.

Foucault, M. 1986. "Of Other Spaces." *Diacritics* 16, no. 1, Spring: 22–7.

Foucault, M. 1994. [1973.] *The Order of Things*. New York: Vintage.

Frazer, J. G. 1992. [1913–20.] *The Golden Bough: A Study in Magic and Religion*. Third Ed. New York: Macmillan. Electronic edition: *Bartleby.com*. 2000. http://www.bartleby.com/196/.

Genocchio, B. 1995. "Discourse, Discontinuity, Difference: The Question of 'Other' Spaces." In *Postmodern Cities and Spaces*, ed. S. Watson and K. Gibson. Oxford: Blackwell.

Gibson, W. 1995. *Mona Lisa Overdrive*. London: Penguin.

Gibson, W. 1997. *Idoru*. London: HarperCollins.

von Goethe, J. W. 1948–1960. "*Maximen und Reflexionen.*" In *Werke: Hamburger Ausgabe*, ed. E. Trunz. Hamburg: Christian Wegner.

Gombrich, E. H. 2006. *The Story of Art*. Sixteenth Ed. London: Phaidon.

Goy, R. 1998. *Venice: The City and its Architecture*. London: Phaidon.

Gritten, D. 2008. "Venice Film Festival: Hayao Miyazaki's *Ponyo on the Cliff by the Sea.*" *Telegraph.co.uk*. http://www.telegraph.co.uk/culture/film/3559471/Venice-Film-Festival-Hayao-Miyazakis-Ponyo-on-the-Cliff-by-the-Sea.html.

Halligan, F. 2008. "*Ponyo on the Cliff by the Sea (Gake no Ue no Ponyo).*" *Screen Daily*. http://www.screendaily.com/ponyo-on-the-cliff-by-the-sea-gake-no-ue-no-ponyo/4040414.article.

"Hayao Miyazaki's *Ponyo* Review." *Twitch*. http://twitchfilm.net/site/view/hayao-miyazakis-ponyo-review/.

Ho, M. "Tarot and the Eye of Escaflowne." *University of Chicago Japanese Animation Society*. http://ucjas.pbworks.com/Tarot-and-the-Eye-of-Escaflowne.

Høgset, S. 2004. "*Rozen Maiden* Review." *T.H.E.M. Anime Reviews*. http://www.themanime.org/viewreview.php?id=900.

Hume, N. G. 1995. *Japanese Aesthetics and Culture: A Reader*. Albany: State University of New York Press.

Huxley, A. 1977. [1956.] *Heaven and Hell*. London: Grafton.

Ide, W. 2008. "*Ponyo on the Cliff by the Sea.*" *Times Online*. http://entertainment.timesonline.co.uk/tol/arts_and_entertainment/film/film_reviews/article4653020.ece.

Ikkyuu, S. 2000. *Crow with No Mouth: Ikkyuu, Fifteenth Century Zen Master*. Trans. S. Berg. Port Townsend, WA: Copper Canyon.

Joyce, J. 1957. *Letters*. New York: Viking.

Juniper, A. 2003. *Wabi Sabi—The Japanese Art of Impermanence*. Tokyo, Rutland, and Singapore: Tuttle.

Kanoh, A. 2005. "War of the Worlds." *Newtype USA*, vol. 04, no. 09.

Kawai, H. 1995. *Dreams, Myths and Fairy Tales in Japan*. Einsiedeln, Switzerland: Daimon.

Keown, D. 2004. "Hell." *A Dictionary of Buddhism*. Oxford: Oxford University Press. *Encyclopedia.com*. 27 May 2009. http://www.encyclopedia.com.

Kready, L. 1916. *A Study of Fairy Tales*. Boston: Houghton Mifflin. http://www.sacred-texts.com/etc/sft/sft01.htm.

Lacan, J. 1977. *Écrits: A Selection*. Trans. A. Sheridan. New York: W. W. Norton.

Lao, M. 1999. *Sirens: Symbols of Seduction*. Trans. J. Oliphant. Rochester, VT: Park Street.

Larsen, J. L. 2001. "The Inspiration of Japanese Design." *Traditional Japanese Design: Five Tastes*. New York: Japan Society.

Leach, E. 1972. "Anthropological Aspects of Language: Animal Categories and Verbal Abuse." In *Mythology: Selected Readings*, ed. P. Maranda. Harmondsworth: Penguin.

Lefebvre, H. 1991. [1974.] *The Production of Space*. Oxford: Blackwell.

Lessing, G. E. 1984. [1766.] *Laocoön; or, The Limits of Painting and Poetry*. Trans. E. A. McCormick. Baltimore, MD: Johns Hopkins University Press.

de Lint, C. 2003. "Ghosts of Wind and Shadow." In *Dreams Underfoot: A Newford Collection*. New York: Orb.

Lonsdale, S. 2008. *Japanese Style*. London: Carlton.

Lowell, P. 2005. [1894.] *Occult Japan or The Way of the Gods*. Boston: Elibron Classics.

Lowenthal, D. 1961. "Geography, Experience and Imagination: Towards a Geographical Epistemology." *Annals of the Association of American Geographers* 51.

Mackenzie, S. 1999. "Fear, Be My Friend." *The Guardian Weekend*. 23 October.

"Magically Binding Contract." *TV Tropes*.

http://tvtropes.org/pmwiki/pmwiki.php/Main/MagicallyBindingContract.

Mauss, M. 2002. [1972.] *A General Theory of Magic*. Trans. R. Brain. London and New York: Routledge.

McCole, J. 1993. *Walter Benjamin and the Antinomies of Tradition*. Ithaca, NY: Cornell University Press.

McGinn, C. 2004. *Mindsight—Image, Dream, Meaning*. Cambridge, MA, and London: Harvard University Press.

McKiernan, D. L. 1999. "Darkness." In *999*, ed. A. Sarrantonio. London: Hodder & Stoughton.

Murakami, H. 2007. *Blind Willow, Sleeping Woman*. Trans. P. Gabriel and J. Rubin. London: Vintage.

Nietzsche, F. W. 1989. [1886.] *Beyond Good and Evil*. Trans. W. Kaufmann. New York: Random House.

Oizaki, F. 2009. "Interview." *Romeo x Juliet: Romeo Collection*. FUNimation.

"*Onmyoudou*." *Onmyoudou Awakening*. http://hushicho.captainn.net/onmy/onmy intro.htm.

Ortega y Gasset, J. "José Ortega y Gasset Quotes." *ThinkExist*. http://thinkexist. com/quotation/the_metaphor_is_per haps_one_of_man-s_most/212126.html.

Phillpotts, E. "Eden Phillpotts Quotes." http://thinkexist.com/quotes/eden_phillpotts/.

Pile, S. 1996. *The Body and the City: Psychoanalysis, Space and Subjectivity*. London: Routledge.

Pliny the Elder. 1963. *Natural History*. W. H. S. Jones. Cambridge, MA, and London: Harvard University Press.

Pulver, A. 2008. "*Ponyo on the Cliff by the Sea*." *The Guardian*. 4 September. http://www.guardian.co.uk/film/2008/sep/03/ve nicefilmfestival.

Radcliffe, J. 2001. "Alchemy and Daoism." http://homepages.ihug.com.au/~pano pus/jeannie/alchemy%20&%20daoism.ht ml.

Reeve, J. 2006. *Japanese Art in Detail*. London: British Museum.

Richie, D. 2007. *A Tractate on Japanese Aesthetics*. Berkeley, CA: Stone Bridge.

Rilke, R. M. 1996. "Letter to Witold von Hulewicz." In *Selected Letters 1902–1926*. Trans. R. F. C. Hull. Cited in *The Inner Eye* by M. Warner. London: National Touring Exhibitions/South Bank Centre.

Robinson, T. 2007. "Reviews: Anime—*Mushi-Shi*." *Sci Fi Weekly*. http://www.scifi.com/sfw/anime/sfw16773.html.

Rogers, M. "Witch." *Anime-Myth.com*. http://www.anime-myth.com/witch.html.

Rollins, J. 2006. *Map of Bones*. London: Orion.

Ross, C., and C. Carpenter. "*Card Captor Sakura*." *T.H.E.M. Anime Reviews*. http://www.themanime.org/viewreview.php?id=9 2.

"Rozen Maiden Field of N." *Crunchyroll*. http://www.crunchyroll.com/group/Rozen _Maiden_Field_of_N.

Ryle, G. 1949. *The Concept of Mind*. Harmondsworth: Penguin.

de Saint-Exupéry, A. 1991. [1943.] *The Little Prince*. London: Egmont.

Schlegel, F. 1968. [1800.] *Dialogue on Poetry and Literary Aphorisms*. Trans. E. Behler and R. Struc. University Park: Pennsylvania State University Press.

Seifert, L. C. 1996. *Fairy Tales, Sexuality, and Gender in France 1690–1715*. New York: Cambridge University Press.

Seligmann, K. 1997. [1948.] *The History of Magic: A Catalogue of Sorcery, Witchcraft, and the Occult*. New York: Quality Paperback Book Club.

"The Shinto Tradition." *Street Magic*. http://www.shadowrun4.com/resources/down loads/catalyst_streetmagic_preview2.pdf.

shoujoboy. 2008. "*Sola* Review." *Minitokyo*. http://reviews.minitokyo.net/1367/sola.

Smith, J. 2002. "Rune Magic." *The Runic Journey*. http://www.tarahill.com/runes/runemagi.html.

Soja, E. 1995. "Heterotopologies: A Remembrance of Other Spaces in the Citadel-LA." In *Postmodern Cities and Spaces*, ed. S. Watson and K. Gibson. Oxford: Blackwell.

Stanley-Baker, J. 2000. *Japanese Art*. London and New York: Thames & Hudson.

Stern, E. 2002. "A Touch of Medieval: Narrative, Magic and Computer Technology in Massively Multiplayer Computer Role-Playing Games." http://www.digra.org/dl/db/05164.03193.pdf.

Stivers, R. 2001. *Technology as Magic: The Triumph of the Irrational*. London and New York: Continuum.

Suzuki, S. "Shunryu Suzuki Quotes." *ThinkExist*. http://thinkexist.com/quotes/shun ryu_suzuki/.

Tanizaki, J. 2001. [1933.] *In Praise of Shadows*. Trans. T. J. Harper and E. G. Seidensticker. London: Vintage.

Tiu, D. "*xxxHolic Kei*." *T.H.E.M. Anime Reviews*. http://www.themanime.org/viewreview.php?id=1108.

Todorov, T. 1973. *The Fantastic: A Structural Approach to a Literary Genre*. Trans. R. Howard. Cleveland, OH: Case Western Reserve University Press.

Tuan, Y. 2008. [1977.] *Space and Place: The Perspective of Experience*. Minneapolis: University of Minnesota Press.

Tuan, Y. 2004. *Place, Art, and Self*. Santa Fe, NM, and Stanton, VA: Center for American Arts and Columbia College, Chicago.

Tylor, E. B. [1871.] *Primitive Culture*. London: J. Murray.

VivisQueen. 2008. "*Natsume Yuujincou* Review." *Anime-Planet*. http://www.anime-planet.com/reviews/a536.html.

Warner, M. 2000. *No Go the Bogeyman*. London: Vintage.

Warner, M. 2006. *Phantasmagoria*. Oxford: Oxford University Press.

Wikipedia. Hikikomori. http://en.wikipedia.org/wiki/Hikikomori.

______. *Karakuri ningyou*. http://en.wikipedia.org/wiki/Karakuri_ningyM.

______. *Rental Magica*. http://en.wikipedia.org/wiki/Rental_Magica.

Williams, Raymond. 1993. "Advertising: The Magic System." In *The Cultural Studies Reader*, ed. S. During. London: Routledge.

Williams, Richard. 2001. *The Animator's Survival Kit*. London and New York: Faber & Faber.

Winterson, J. 1989. *The Passion*. London: Vintage.

Wittgenstein, L. 1981. *Zettel*. Trans. G. E. M. Anscombe. 2nd Ed. Oxford: Basil Blackwell.

Wordsworth, W. 1994. *The Collected Poems*. Ware, Hertfordshire: Wordsworth Editions.

Wright, J. K. 1947. "Terrae Incognitae: The Place of the Imagination in Geography." *Annals of the Association of American Geographers* 37 (1).

xenocrisis0153. 2006. "*Magikano*." *Anime Source* http://www.anime-source.com/banzai/modules.php?name=Content&pa=showpage&pid=953.

"*xxxHolic*, Season One Review." *The Anime Blog*. http://www.theanimeblog.com/anime/anime-reviews-anime-2/xxxholic-season-one/.

Zipes, J. 1991. *Fairy Tales and the Art of Subversion*. New York: Routledge.

zzeroparticle. 2008. "*Ghost Hound*." *The Nihon Review*. http://www.nihonreview.com/anime/ghost-hound/.

Index

www.ingramcontent.com/pod-product-compliance
Ingram Content Group UK Ltd.
Pitfield, Milton Keynes, MK11 3LW, UK
UKHW041355190726
13851UKWH00014B/117